Unequal Partners

A Primer on Globalization

WILLIAM K. TABB

THE NEW PRESS

NEW YORK

Published in the United States by The New Press, New York, 2002
Distributed by W. W. Norton & Company, Inc., New York

LIBRARY OF CONGRESS CATALOGING-IN-PUBLICATION DATA

Tabb, William K.
    Unequal partners : a primer on globalization / William K. Tabb.
        p.   cm.
    Includes bibliographical references.
    ISBN 1-56584-722-9 (pbk.)
    1. International economic relations.   2. Regional economic disparities.
3. International business enterprises—Moral and ethical aspects.   4. Globalization—
Economic aspects.   5. Globalization—Social aspects.   6. Globalization—
Environmental aspects.   7. Globalization—Moral and ethical aspects.

HF1359 .T3323 2002
337—dc21

                                                                    2001052209

The New Press was established in 1990 as a not-for-profit alternative to the large,
commercial publishing houses currently dominating the book publishing industry.
The New Press operates in the public interest rather than for private gain,
and is committed to publishing, in innovative ways, works of educational, cultural, and
community value that are often deemed insufficiently profitable.

The New Press
450 West 41st Street, 6th floor
New York, NY 10036

www.thenewpress.com

Printed in the United States of America

2   4   6   8   10   9   7   5   3   1

Contents

Unequal Partners

I

Corporate Globalization and the Global Justice Movement

At the start of the twenty-first century the inadequacy of the nation-state as the sovereign unit of political organization and economic regulation is increasingly clear. The question remains, however, whether this is because governments are unable or unwilling to take the steps necessary to more effectively regulate transnational corporations and financial markets and come to terms with such problems as the spread of diseases, migration, and wars that threaten the stability and well-being of global society. Although many people around the world seek to escape from the forces of globalization by attempting to isolate themselves and their group based on ethnicity, religion, or nationality, identity politics poorly fits the needs of the time. Individual self-definition is destabilized when the nature of what is taken to be the relevant understanding of the world in which we live is in constant flux. While many individuals react by turning inward and seeking local communities of meaning, this reaction should not obscure what will be the question of the twenty-first century, namely, What form of global governance is there to be? The clash is between advocates of free-market neoliberalism who espouse deregulation of the political economy, open borders for increasingly mobile investment, trade, and money flows with minimal government intervention, and worldwide acceptance of Western-style democracy and those who privilege social justice and call for an alternative globalization from below, which regulates capital, respects local cultural preferences, and builds a shared international sense of how best to meet global societal needs.

The first vision is called *corporate globalization,* or globalization from above. It is encouraged by transnational capital and international finance and by politicians who stress the efficiency of markets in promoting more rapid growth. While many companies had of course long been active in exporting and investing in other countries before roughly the start of the 1970s, business was predominantly oriented to national markets. The era of globalization captures an awareness that at a certain point in the last third of the twentieth century large corporations became more single-mindedly transnational in focus, seeing their home country as only one among many profit centers and reorganizing their operations to coincide with this vision of a globalized world economy. The large transnational corporations (TNCs) used their considerable power to influence governments to accept rules favorable to their views of how trade and investment should be focused. Over the last decades of the twentieth century transnational corporations expanded their influence through the creation of new rules that restrict what governments can and cannot do in terms of interfering with globalized corporate interests.

The opposition to this expanding power of transnational corporations is more diffuse and made up of many coalitions. In general, the groups include those who on a visceral level feel their lives becoming more insecure and their future uncertain because of the nature of the changes in the global political economy. These are the organizations of global civil society that offer an alternative vision of globalization from below: environmentalists, labor rights activists, and advocates of the good global society that is inclusive and caring in its policies of distribution and regulation, organizations that would put people before profit and the precautionary principle in place of the risk society. They focus on the incidence of costs and benefits, actual and potential, of particular patterns of globalization.

The resistance to corporate globalization is very different from other waves of popular protest—which have targeted such issues as racial discrimination, colonialism, women's rights, unionization, peace movements, and other causes—in that it is a movement of many movements, a coalition of many coalitions, a coming together, as observers and participants have seen, of those opposed to the commodification of all social relations. As Maud Barlow of the Council of Canadians has said, it is not about trade, but transformation of public space and a validation of democratic self-determination and diversity. Despite the presence of a seeming expansion of commodity choices offered by a consumer society, corporate globalization disempowers citizens and imposes a uniformity in that persons exist only as individuals in the marketplace, and entitlements of citizenship and the legitimacy of society as a unit in which choices can collectively be made is denied.

Within this broad movement for an alternative globalization from below, differences of strategy, tactics, and sometimes purpose remain important. It is not necessarily a problem that different segments of what we will call the *Global Justice Movement* have different central issues, emphases, and orientations. So long as a general philosophical unity in the face of the corporate globalization model is maintained, the movement can be built, sustained, and made more effective as a political and social force. Already the international relations textbooks, which used to talk of two level games—negotiations between the domestic interest groups and the legislature on the one hand and the negotiators of different countries on the other—are being qualified with endless talk of civil society. *Civil society* (the space between state and family occupied by nongovernmental groups of all sorts) has been increasingly effective in making itself heard and influencing corporate and government policymaking and behavior.

The beginnings of the great drama that will shape the twenty-first century were evident even as the old century was winding down. In a rather amazing series of demonstrations that took place in Seattle, Washington, at the 1999 Ministerial Meetings of the World Trade Organization (WTO), more than sixty thousand people from around the world representing a wide array of groups and causes—including environmental activists, labor rights advocates, defenders of the rights of indigenous peoples, and others—protested what they saw as a loss of democratic control to an unelected and unaccountable shadow world-government. The WTO's rules had trumped national environmental regulations and denied that labor rights were any of its business. Its job was to promote and enforce free trade. The demonstrators called for a rejection of the WTO's concept of free trade and demanded, instead, fair trade. By that they meant that while corporations wanted to be able to compete free of any restrictions, it would be fairer to limit their freedoms where their actions would harm society. Fair trade involves protecting the environment from the effects of transnational corporate activities, protecting worker rights, and making sure that taxation is imposed on an equitable basis so that the greater mobility of capital does not allow tax avoidance, which deprives the public sector of needed resources. When asked, most citizens of the United States thought the demonstrators were right and that they had more credibility than the transnational corporations or the governments assembled to plan the world's future. It did the WTO officials no good to point out that their organization had been created by the governments of the world, that they were just bureaucrats, and that the WTO in any case was devoted to expanding the economic prospects of all people and nations.

While there have been equally impressive demonstrations in Africa, Asia, Europe, and Latin America, the fact that so many North Americans were willing to protest in Seattle (and again in the spring of 2001 in Quebec against those negotiating a Free Trade Area for the Americas, another governance proposal) awakened the people of the United States to the role of the global state economic governance institutions in structuring corporate globalization. In terms of the critical mass of the movement, the Seattle protest is regarded as the key milestone of this awakening.

Just to play it safe, the WTO decided its next meeting would be in Doha, the capital of the Persian Gulf state of Qatar, a country whose human rights record draws universal criticism but whose location and closed borders, it was said, would deter demonstrators from troubling their next gathering. The emir of Qatar had few competitors for the hostly duties, since it was clear that tens of thousands of people, representing a wide spectrum of global civil society, and possibly hundreds of thousands if there was any guarantee that they could be safe from police violence, would be there to protest were the meeting to be held in a more accessible location. When such meetings are held in democratic countries there has been a noticeable increase in attacks on basic democratic rights. Receiving less media attention than the demonstrations themselves have been the arbitrary beatings, the use of rubber bullets and tear gas on peaceful demonstrators, and the punishing of the violence of the few by curtailing the rights of the many to peacefully assemble and to exercise free speech.

In Quebec in the days leading up to the Summit of the Americas in April 2001, not only were United States citizens who were thought to be potential demonstrators prevented from entering Canada ("a privilege and not a right") because, as one official put it, "It is my job to protect the Canadian economy," but plain-clothes officers arrested young people in downtown Quebec for handing out pamphlets denouncing the summit security's violation of their civil rights! Officers threatened to arrest any group of people numbering more than two, in what seemed to many a bizarre interpretation of strictures against unlawful assembly.[1] Although Quebec's mayor, once such events were publicized, quickly said they were "mistakes," the increasing infringement of rights to peaceful assembly and free speech is a cause for concern. It is not that police have difficulty distinguishing between violent protesters and the overwhelming majority of peaceful ones, but that the large numbers of peaceful ones make opposition to corporate globalization graphically clear. After the terrorist attacks of September 11, 2001, the politics and logistics of peaceful protest became further complicated.

Hiding in Doha was not enough to protect the WTO from critics. The accumulated impacts of the decisions of the shadow global quasi-governments like the WTO and the decisions by transnational corporations that they support have led social movements to become increasingly active in mobilizing a wide array of the sectors of civil society. As Mary Kaldor notes, what was significant about Seattle was that it was the first time that "the political presence of a range of new actors was taken seriously, the first time those inside the talks did not ignore or just pay lip service to the role of those outside."[2] Such mass demonstrations generate debate about the very nature of globalization and its impact on the public quality of life. They have brought about a new stage in the public discussion of the world economy and the best rules under which it should operate. They have created more intense interest in the discussion of what kind of globalization is best, and of how international interconnectedness could be managed in ways different from the corporate version of management that is supported by the WTO, the International Monetary Fund (IMF), and the other global state economic governance institutions whose roles have grown dramatically in the last quarter of the twentieth century.

The protests challenge a theory and practice widely called *neoliberalism,* a term used to encompass the privatization of the public provision of goods and services—moving their provision from the public sector to the private—along with deregulating how private producers can behave, giving greater scope to the single-minded pursuit of profit and showing significantly less regard for the need to limit social costs or for redistributions based on nonmarket criteria. The aim of neoliberalism is to put into question all collective structures capable of obstructing the logic of the pure market.[3] Hence the attack on unions, which it is claimed conspire to raise wages and improve working conditions beyond what they would be in an efficient market, and the condemnation of governments that are said to waste our money. The neoliberalists attempt to atomize society and weaken collective identities and organized forms of market control, to in effect make real Margaret Thatcher's claim that there is no such thing as society, there are only individuals.

Until Seattle, globalization had been mostly synonymous with the neoliberal agenda. It accepted the inevitability of the economic pressures of the market that undermined national economic autonomy and control, especially the campaign by financial markets to push governments to balance national budgets, diminish social spending, cut public services, reduce public deficits, and deregulate markets. The vehicles for such global restructuring were the World Trade Organization, the International Monetary Fund, the World Bank, and a host of lesser organizations, all of which we collectively call *global state economic governance institutions.* These all function outside of the United Nations system and are run by a handful of the largest economies. Most notably, the influence of the United States has been predominant.

Global Justice Movement activists point out that there is no "World Social Organization" to promote global welfare policies by representing the interests of the victims of neoliberal policies. Nor is there much interest of the major economic powers in a world environmental organization to enforce environmental compliance. In setting up global governance corporate-style, only those agencies useful to the capitalist agenda are encouraged. What we have had is a very selective and one-sided (the business side) governance structure. That is why there were so many people in the streets of Seattle despite the force that was used against peaceful protesters and the way violent acts by the few were the occasion for police violence toward the many.

The Seattle protests were a major milestone in the journey of a burgeoning global civil society that has challenged not only the WTO but the IMF for its role as a collection agency for international financiers and for its imposition of harsh austerity on the poor of the world—people who were suffering and dying to pay a debt that was incurred by their rulers and was structured to benefit transnational capital. The IMF claimed it was there to help the poor. But again, the abolish-the-debt coalition did not see it that way. Peter Engardo (with Catherine Belton) writes: "It all adds up to a breakdown of what was known as the Washington Consensus, the world view pushed aggressively by the U.S. Treasury, the IMF, and the World Bank in the early 1990s. This dictum held that all countries should open their markets to trade, direct investment, and short-term capital as quickly as possible. The transition would be painful, but inevitably, prosperity would result." But, as he concludes, "In hindsight, it was a naive and self-interested view."[4] In a similar vein, Joseph Stiglitz, the former research director of the World Bank, said, "The IMF push for capital-market liberalization for all nations was driven by financial market ideology." He added that "they have conceded defeat, but only after the damage was done."[5]

The Washington Consensus was criticized not only because its policies didn't work in terms of the promised results, but because they did work for those who ultimately sponsored them, the international financiers and other speculators who made billions on the short-term capital flows that were so destabilizing to the vast majority of the people in most of the countries involved. It is now widely accepted that there is no automatic link between opening markets to international forces and growth, but there is a close connection between financial liberalization and financial crisis. Yet the reforms that are promised need to be looked at very carefully. They represent a tactical retreat at best. The self-interest of the powerful groups pushing such policies has hardly changed, nor has their influence diminished. Their legitimacy, however, has been widely questioned and their reputation severely damaged.

The Global Justice Movement has also targeted the World Economic Forum, the annual meeting of the global elite that takes place in Davos, Switzerland, a small and peaceful mountain village once known as the place where Thomas Mann wrote *The Magic Mountain*. Each year, Davos turns into a heavily fortified compound protected by the largest military mobilizations, in Swiss experience, since the Second World War, because demonstrators find the managers of the global political economy even there. In Zurich, disembarking protesters are met by police with water cannons and tear gas, actions that are condemned as a threat to political liberties in Switzerland by even its conservative newspapers. As an editorial in *The Financial Times* suggests, "The water cannon has become an uncomfortable symbol of the divide between global capitalism and its critics."[6] Given such unwanted attention, the World Economic Forum "turned into an unprecedented public expression of guilty conscience from the planet's most exclusive gathering of political and business leaders," one sympathetic commentator said.[7] But if either its guilt or, perhaps more accurately, the bad press corporate globalization was so widely receiving led to professions of lofty ideals, not much changes once they have all gone home. It is difficult to see how top executives can stay enthusiastically engaged once their attention is drawn back to making money, which is what they are paid to do—unless the movements stay after them wherever they go and give them no peace. At least that was the conclusion most activists drew from the no-action–lots-of-talk public relations efforts of the corporate leaders and their government allies. Subsequent gatherings such as the G-7 meetings in Geneva in the summer of 2001 reinforced such understandings.

One of the consequences of the political abdication of responsibility over who controls the globalization process is to increase the power of corporations and to diminish the role of government. Nancy Adler, a McGill University management professor, expects that in twenty years "society's leaders will not be elected politicians but members of the private sector. The onus will fall on CEOs to address issues that were once seen as matters of social policy but which will have become vital to the interests of thoroughly global corporations."[8] In her scenario it will be their decisions that will shape our lives even more completely than they do today. "In 2020, I would see a third of a CEO's time being spent on issues bigger than the company—world education, world health, world peace, the environment." But the CEO is chosen for his or her ability to maximize stock value, not their knowledge of such issues. They are not responsible to citizens for how the corporation approaches such issues and uses power to influence their outcome. If the CEOs have the power, what is the role of the elected officials? They would be reduced to lobbying CEOs on behalf of their constituencies. They would do so from the inferior supplicant position given the power relation between most governments vis-à-vis the giant transnational corporations. This is not all that far from where things are now.

The Global Justice Movement does not share Professor Adler's optimistic interpretation of a world dominated by ever more powerful corporations.

As the World Economic Forum was meeting in Davos in January 2001, the first World Social Forum is meeting in Porto Alegre, Brazil, as guests of the local and state governments there, which were under Brazilian Workers Party (PT) leadership. Porto Alegre itself offers a positive example of effective democratic decentralization of the sort the Global Justice Movement celebrates. It is governed by the PT, which from its birth in 1980 was a social movement political party that was formed in an alliance of human rights groups, church groups, peasants associations, revolutionary organizations, and trade unions. It was created as an instrument of struggle against what was then an authoritarian military regime and its corporate structures. The PT has successfully maintained its ties to a multitude of grassroots social movements and has created a highly decentralized internal structure responsive to these movements of civil society.[9] Porto Alegre offered the visiting social activists a glimpse of how grassroots democracy can work in a progressive state formation.

The Porto Alegre meeting itself can be seen as a key moment in the development of the Global Justice Movement. It was to begin the construction of a program for globalization from below, with the official slogan, Another World Is Possible. As necessary as a critique of corporate globalization was understood to be, the movement knew it also had an obligation to set forth an alternative vision, a vision of a better world. At Porto Alegre, Jean-Pierre Chevenement, who had recently resigned from the French cabinet in protest of his government's capitulation to particular corporate globalist demands, explained the opposition to "a world in which the domination of capital and of the financial markets works against democracy, and works against the need for long-term investments in health, in education, in culture."[10] The activists assembled (organizers expected two thousand participants, but instead more than ten thousand showed up, from 120 countries and representing more than a thousand groups) and took part in workshops and cultural celebrations that marked the resurgence of anti–free market activism. The purpose of that meeting, and indeed of this book, is to look at what is wrong with the corporate version of globalization, to make systemic connections among the various protests, and to suggest a holistic vision of an alternative campaign for globalization from below.

Hegemony and Globalization

Raymond Williams, the great English cultural historian, once described returning to Cambridge from the army after World War II and finding that those who had stayed and those who had gone just didn't speak the same language. He saw different immediate values or different kinds of valuation. Each group was speaking its native language "but its uses are significantly different, and especially when strong feelings or important ideas are in question."[11] Because the problem of definition was so inextricable, he decided it was useful to make a list of what he called "keywords," or words that seemed to come up most often and to matter most to the conversations he was having with his academic colleagues.

"Globalization" is surely one of the keywords of our era, although it was just coming into popular usage when Williams published his "list," in a book entitled *Keywords*. The term makes its appearance in the Oxford English Dictionary only in 1992, with a reference drawn from *The Spectator,* which declared that "globalization is, indeed, a staggering concept." And so it is.

Globalization seems to mean that everything in the world affects everything else—and a lot faster than it used to. The Internet, transnational corporations everywhere producing and selling, a handful of media companies controlling access (so there are five hundred channels and nothing on them), and the rule of international finance to the point where James Carville quips that rather than return after he dies as the president—so he could have power—he would come back as the bond market instead, because it tells *everybody* what to do. But neither the bond market nor globalization is a phenomenon beyond human control. When Richard Tompkins tells us that "globalization has a lot to answer for: Chicken McNuggets, the World Trade Organization, the rising cost of tear gas,"[12] he is also making a comment on the United States, our government's role in the world as the hegemonic power, and our responsibility as U.S. citizens for the actions taken in our name.

"Hegemony" is the second keyword of importance here. It is featured on Williams's listing, where it is used "to describe a policy expressing or aimed at political predominance." There is also a discussion of creating an alternative hegemony—"a new predominant practice and consciousness. Thus an emphasis on hegemony and the hegemonic has come to include cultural as well as political and economic factors."[13] Hegemony, we might say, is when something is so powerful that you need have no conscious awareness of it. To call attention to U.S. hegemony rather than to talk about international cooperation is to sound rather un-American. It is to point out what is both obvious and yet too often the absent center of discussion of the way the world works. But with Soviet communism gone and the cold war over we can more easily face up to what U.S. hegemony means and how our power is, and could be, exercised. A person who actually practices hegemony, namely, Henry Kissinger, who was national security adviser and secretary of state under President Richard Nixon and is a consultant to the rich and powerful, tells us: "The first thing to say about American foreign policy is that when the United States is accused of being a hegemonic power, I would grant that that is true. It is a hegemonic power in the sense that the disparity between the U.S. and other nations in military strength, economic power, and cultural reach is unprecedented. This, inevitably, evokes a desire by others to reduce that hegemonic position. That inevitable fact of life does not change our position."[14]

What we have experienced is corporate globalization under U.S. hegemony. It is a particular pattern of increased interdependence under which market relations have dominated, governments have been disempowered (or so it would seem), and many ordinary people are overwhelmed by the speed and extent of the changes. Hegemony, not simply that of the United States government but of U.S.-based transnational corporations and international financiers, guides how our government shapes globalization. So it is not really that globalization rules. It is that the rules of globalization are set by the powerful and imposed on the rest of us, who, if we don't like these rules, have to be serious about mobilizing the broad support necessary to change them. In this book I will suggest that there are a lot of changes needed and that the central political struggle of the twenty-first century will be for a democratic globalization from the bottom up, in place of top-down globalization. Americans have a special responsibility in this. We live in the country whose government more than others controls this process and pretty much makes and enforces the rules. Henry Kissinger has told us that "what is called globalization is really another name for the dominant role of the United States." He should know. And we can agree with him that the United States is certainly the hegemonic power in this era of globalization.

Kissinger's own role in setting this country's policies around the world has resulted in his winning a Nobel Peace Prize. It is also the reason he can rarely give a speech without an angry group of demonstrators calling him a butcher and other un-friendly names. I am not here concerned with the specifics of how Kissinger as President Nixon's national security adviser and then secretary of state exercised U.S. power, although, having invoked his expertise, I should say Kissinger's war crimes and other offenses against international law and human decency in-clude conspiracy to commit murder, kidnapping, and torture. Following, in 2000 in London, the House of Lords' denial of the "sovereign immunity" defense for state crimes in the case of Chile's former head of state General Augusto Pinochet, Chris-topher Hitchens wrote, "Many if not most of Kissinger's partners in politics, from Greece to Chile to Argentina to Indonesia, are now in jail or awaiting trial. His own lonely impunity is rank; it smells to heaven."[15] If Americans who did the work of the rogue operations that are normal operating procedure for the imperial state were held accountable to the same law "as losers and minor despots in relatively negligible countries," as Hitchens put it, then Kissinger should certainly be tried as a war criminal and as a serial killer. Mr. Kissinger is perhaps the most famous face of what is often called American imperialism, the active interven-tion in the affairs of other countries by the United States using military and other means to put in place policies and govern-ments that are amenable to the interests of U.S.-based corpora-tions. Although the military side is not of central concern here, it is an integral part of how corporate globalization is shaped.

A case can be made that the actions of international financiers and the global state economic governance institutions are subject to charges similar to those addressed to Mr. Kissinger. Indeed, there are those who think these entities are guilty of far more than even Henry Kissinger. As Ken Livingstone, London's mayor, has said, "Every year the international financial system kills more people than World War II. But at least Hitler was mad, you know."[16] These activities are presented in mainstream discourse such that discussions of international trade and finance serve the interests of the powerful and are given the positive spin of normalcy, making them a story of an unproblematic flowering, an onward and upward march of human progress. This, I think, represents an unacknowledged moral judgment, one that is extremely misleading. Part of the ability to exercise hegemony is to call your descriptions accurate ones and others' interpretations, especially when they accuse you of wrongdoing and immorality, as grossly biased and obviously beyond needing response. Both Mr. Kissinger and the IMF have set themselves up as being above criticism. Each has recently seen a lessening in their power to constrain debate over the meaning of their actions.

At the same time that the United States has frequently intervened to preserve or establish the peace we desire in a particular situation and played the key role in setting up tribunals to put individuals on trial who are accused of war crimes in places like Rwanda and the former Yugoslavia, we are nearly alone in opposing the establishment of a permanent international criminal court, which is endorsed by 120 other nations. We oppose such a court because these other countries have been unwilling to exempt Americans from its jurisdiction. We claim a special exemption from the rules of the law of nations in the economic realm as well, although this stance is undergoing slow change as U.S.-based transnationals see benefit in having laws that apply to the United States as well as other countries so that they can treat this country as just another profit center. Chauvinist politicians and other patriots who put nationalism above international solidarity might want to watch for further betrayals by liberal corporate internationalists. They might want to rethink whether the sort of small-scale competitive capitalism and national autonomy they desire is possible in a world dominated by transnational capital, and they might want to rethink the critiques of the Global Justice Movement, and the desirability of the alternatives it proposes.

In the 1980s and 1990s, as we entered the age of globalization, the market attained a hegemonic status of which Mr. Kissinger and President Nixon at the height of their powers could only dream. The "free" market can be said, although it would be wrong to do so, to have triumphed over politics. The market is widely and repeatedly declared to be replacing governments. Interference with its judgments (the market is always personified in this fetishized fashion) is declared bad under almost all circumstances.

The term *free market* needs comment, since we generally think freedom is good, and so the use of the term gains some credibility through this association. Most markets are not in fact "free" in the sense the models presume. A perfectly competitive market is one in which there are many competitors, all too small to affect price, and there is ease of entry in and out. Competitive markets are said to allocate resources more efficiently, hence the argument is made that regulating markets is bad, and keeping markets free of government regulation is good. But even if they were free and competitive in ways approximating the model, to many people there are other more important criteria. Are markets just? Is it enough that they allocate resources based on the initial distribution of income among buyers in the market when that distribution of income itself reflects structural inequalities and extensive social injustice? Even where outcomes are well understood to be unfair, free markets are said to further innovation and to be the source of rising productivity upon which everyone's eventual increasing living standard depends.

It is an uphill battle to introduce any qualifications to this story, and yet this is what the Global Justice Movement attempts to do. The movement's position is that the global marketplace is not an atomistic one that consists of many competitors, none of

whom can control markets. It is a reality that transnational corporations and international finance have guided the market and
prevailed on governments to change rules in ways that favor
business interests, businesses that in important ways harm the
quality of life on the planet.

One reason for the widespread acceptance of the "free" market view is that most discussions of globalization begin with
technology, and it is of course true that the apparatus of information technology such as the fax and the cellular telephone
make it much easier to "reach out and touch someone" on the
other side of the planet, to move a billion dollars out of one
country and into another, or to place an order for a new clothing
design with a factory on the other side of the planet. Globalization in this view is about how innovations in container shipping
and overnight air delivery make movement of goods and people
much faster and easier, improving all of our lives. Such an approach to how the world political economy is shaped is not
wrong. But to say simply that globalization has been driven by
technology and the market is to ignore that technology is a social
relation. It is not neutral. It is not natural. The ways scientific
possibilities are pursued and technologies constructed are based
on the power relations of society.

Those celebrating the wonders of modern technology are frequently blind to or undervalue the significance of the economic
and social realities that limit who can share, and in what ways, in
its promise. There are people who have easy access and there are
people who are more controlled by, rather than controlling of,
the technological possibilities. There are people for whom, because of their place in the world system, these technologies are
basically irrelevant. When President Clinton visited a remote
village on a trip to Africa in 1998 he urged the school there to
connect to the World Wide Web. He did not appear to notice
the school had no electricity. Commenting on the incident,

Bruce Cummings has written, "Using the Web I can find satellite photos of this village, learn the ethnicity of its inhabitants and count the number of homes with running water. But the villagers cannot see me or the World Bank employees who catalogue such information. And because knowledge is power, they are less free than before the advent of the computer."[17]

Technology can be a weapon for those who control it, and allows the continued exploitation of the have-nots and the have-less by the control-mores. Because we tend to accept the world as it is as being in some sense natural, and can hardly look at every familiar social relation with new eyes each moment of each day, most of the time we simply accept things as they are. One of the things the Global Justice Movement asks us to do is to step back and consider that—rather than making life better in some simple, unambiguous way—science and technology might also contribute to the deterioration of the life-space of landless Brazilian peasants as well as the emergence of a new agricultural proletariat in the Unites States, reducing life possibilities thanks to the advance of agribusiness both abroad and at home. Such phenomena are a matter of bargaining power and of the class relations that bracket all exchange under capitalism and of the forms such unequal exchanges take in an era of corporate globalization.

Global Governance and the One Superpower

While the media have presented globalization from a corporate perspective as good for everyone, the polls show that people fear job loss, condemn the use of child labor and exploitative working conditions in foreign factories that supply the brand-name products we consume, and worry about the environmental impact of the way corporations do business, and they thus want regulation of business behavior in these and other respects.

Greater awareness of the global state economic governance institutions like the IMF, which has acted as the debt collector for
the banks and imposes a punishing austerity on the poor of the
debtor nations, and like the World Trade Organization, which
has forced poor countries to accept arrangements that are widely
seen as unfair, have energized many Americans to demand that
our country use its predominant influence to change the way
they operate, to pursue speedy debt forgiveness for the highly
indebted poor countries, and to encourage the adoption by these
organizations of basic labor rights and environmental protections.

These institutions mediate the interests of U.S.-based transnational corporations and financial institutions, and to some degree
both obscure what is happening in the international political
economy and legitimate it. Thus it is possible to interpret the role
of the United States in guiding global state economic governance institutions in terms of an essentially benevolent domination. *New York Times* columnist and resident globalization expert
Thomas Friedman claims that "America truly is the ultimate be-
nign hegemon and reluctant enforcer."[18] It does not look this
way to many people in the world. Increasingly many of us here
at home are having doubts as well. If hegemony is having so
much power that everyone knows it and no one talks about it,
what does it mean to say, and we seem to say it over and over,
that the world is globalizing? What is globalization given the
reality of U.S. hegemony? For surely globalization is the
buzzword, a crucial keyword of our time. How it is used divides
Americans. It is a case, as Raymond Williams would have it, in
which "each group is speaking its native language, but its uses are
significantly different, and especially when strong feelings or important ideas are in question."

The U.S. government has always seen international law as
something that applies to others when we want to force said

others to do something they don't want to do or to punish them for doing something this country does not like. But we have always refused to allow application of that law to us and ours. "How can the United States get away with this?" the British financial publication *The Economist* rhetorically asks. "The answer, as in many other things, is simple: it is the world's only superpower. Its allies, recognizing that position, and aware that law alone cannot preserve the peace (or their interests), usually grant it wide latitude . . . and know well that it would not take much notice if they didn't."[19] *The Economist* thinks the world would be better off, and says the United States would be too, if we were seen as international law's champion rather than a nation that regards itself as beyond the law. The publication offers hypotheticals, asks but doesn't tell. "If America must be the world's policeman, a role it often plays only reluctantly, and quite often against a chorus of criticism, is it better served by being seen as international law's champion, or as a nation which regards itself as beyond the law?" The tone the *Economist* takes is indicative of its desire to convince the powerful by arguing that it is in the hegemon's best interests to choose an alternative to the option they are otherwise inclined to choose. For many other critics of U.S. behavior, which increasingly resembles, in the view not only of Third World revolutionaries but of many staid European government officials, a unilateral imposition of imperialist designs on the rest of the world, it is necessary to actually confront the only superpower, or perhaps, like Lilliputians, to attempt to tie down the giant, with many threads, and attack its abilities to do damage, limiting and perhaps even controlling it. I would myself call attention to the ways government officials in different places cooperate with the United States and transnational capital both because they see little alternative and because they too benefit from such cooperation. Blaming the United States for everything that is not liked about globalization, as we shall see, is too easy and finally mistakes the basic problem of corporate globalization.

Nonetheless, when faced with a single world superpower many governments have concluded that the global state economic governance institutions offer a place where problems with collective action can be addressed for the good of all, where discussion can take place, and where different positions can be presented. Such institutions provide a framework for the creation of norms the hegemon may over time be influenced by and follow, where potentially influential assumptions of multilateralism and normative priorities can flourish. As the theorists tell us, norms channel and regularize behavior; they often limit the range of choice and constrain action. And it is true that norm shifts can have profound impacts on what we allow ourselves to think and do. There is pressure to conform to norms. By changing norms new incentives can be imposed. But the question is, Whose behavior is likely to be changed in this way—the hegemon, who controls the organization, sets its agenda, and has a unilateral veto, or the less powerful, who find themselves constrained in new ways by such collective action rules?

Global State Economic Governance Institutions

In recent years the international agencies that we are calling global state economic governance institutions have been granted greater powers to decide such matters. Thus, such institutions, which include the World Trade Organization, the International Monetary Fund, and the World Bank, have taken on qualities of "stateness." They are governing what is and is not allowed, and they are settling disputes between and among nations in a host of vital areas having to do with economic matters. They are not accountable to the United Nations, but instead they were established as separate, competing, parallel institutions. They removed from U.N. jurisdiction the most crucial levers determining the well-being of member nations. Where the General Assembly runs on a one-country–one-vote basis, in these alternative forums votes are proportional to power and wealth. Thus the large contribution by the U.S. to the International Monetary Fund means all other members combined are unable to outvote the one country with veto power, the United States.

Global state economic governance institutions have been presumed to be technical bodies in which experts on trade or exchange rates established rules for a smoother operation of the international economic and financial system. Formerly, most people did not know what these organizations were or what they did. In recent years, however, and especially since the media coverage of Seattle, the situation has changed. More people know about these institutions, and polls show the majority agree with the demonstrators in their criticism of the way they function. Globalization is now better understood as a contested process over how the rules of economic integration shall be established, what these rules shall be, and how they will be enforced. The front line of this contestation is the nature of the global state economic governance institutions, and this is why the Global Justice Movement targets them for special attention. The transnational corporations and international banks influence the positions taken by such institutions, such as when the World Trade Organization says that labor rights and, more broadly, human rights and environmental concerns should not be allowed to interfere with "free" trade. Working through such global state economic governance institutions, transnational capital also indirectly, but effectively, appropriates elements of "stateness" in order to serve bottom-line purposes.

If companies like Monsanto produce genetically modified organisms without what many would see as proper observance of the precautionary principle (a principle to be discussed more extensively in chapter 5), do the rest of us have to allow ourselves to be the guinea pigs for such experimentation? Must citizens in other countries allow these products to be sold in their country? If corporate leaders and their friends in government have no problem with mad cow disease, do we have to allow the sale of questionable beef here? What happens to the rights of consumers when farmers in some of the far-flung reaches of the empire use pesticides that are banned here, and the WTO says there is no scientific evidence of danger and that we must import fruits and vegetables that have been thusly sprayed? What can we insist that governments do? And what power does the WTO have to tell our governments to do something different and contrary to our wishes? Must we accept a "free trade über alles" dictum? Who decides such international disputes, and on what basis? The answer we have been given is that the World Trade Organization's experts decide.

The WTO came into existence in 1995 as a successor to the General Agreement on Trade and Tariffs (GATT), which itself took on many of the functions that were to have been the province of an international trade organization that the United States and the United Kingdom designed as the Second World War was ending to create a new trade regime for the postwar era. The details of this history are not important here, but whereas the U.S. Congress in the late 1940s refused to accept what they saw as an organization that compromised U.S. sovereignty (even though the plan had been drawn up by the executive branch of its own government), by the 1990s transnational capital had become hegemonic in U.S. politics to the point where the nationalist-isolationist elements could not muster the support to prevent the creation of the WTO. Today the WTO acts as the battering ram breaking down the great walls of China for U.S. investors and it limits the ability of citizens here to impose social regulation on transnational capital.

In the realm of monetary affairs, which were less well understood and did not alarm a domestic constituency in the same way that national corporations feared import competition under the proposed International Trade Organization would, the internationalists had greater success. The IMF was set up in 1944 in Bretton Woods, New Hampshire (as was the World Bank, then called the International Bank for Reconstruction and Development, which was designed to help war-ravaged European economies recover), after extended negotiations between the United States, the acknowledged new hegemon, and, mainly, the British, the declining hegemon. Both believed the failure to maintain fixed exchange rates had caused a prolonging of the Great Depression. The Fund was designed to prevent competitive devaluations and financial instability. It was authorized to make temporary loans needed by debtor countries running balance-of-payments deficits and set rules for devaluations of currencies when they were judged necessary. The British had wanted more flexibility for debtor nations (they ended the war as a major debtor). The United States did not. It was the major creditor and wanted a system structured to favor creditor over debtor nations.

The IMF was designed to promote the U.S. version of what was good for the world, which is to say, what would help remake the postwar world in the interest of the United States. This is what hegemons do. They employ lofty rhetoric, but self-interest is paramount, even if there is disagreement among elites as to what exact policies are best in order to achieve maximization of wealth and power. However, this is not necessarily bad for others in all respects. Stability is better than disorder. But there are different ways of achieving and maintaining what is considered stability. In some patterns benefits are shared more broadly. In others the powerful gain far more and the costs to others are underestimated or ignored, and their voices go unheard. When the hegemon's interest changes, so do the rules by which it demands everyone must play. Yet to say the United States is hegemonic is not to say that citizens of this country are "bad" or that our government is more unscrupulous than other governments. We may be more idealistic or less; these are not the issues. The point is that all countries pursue their self-interest as it is defined by the most influential elements of society. The United States has far more power than other countries, and hegemons get what they want most of the time.

When a hegemon gets in trouble and markets produce unpleasant outcomes that are undesired by participants, hegemons have more ability to shift the costs of adjustment onto others. Due to the inability of the United States to support the value of the dollar, the result of inflation that was created by attempting to pay for the unpopular Vietnam War without raising taxes, President Nixon in 1971 unilaterally ended the Bretton Woods system of fixed exchange rates. Without consulting our allies and partners he devalued the dollar unilaterally. (That says something about how balanced a partnership other nations can have with a hegemon.) The world then moved to its current system of floating exchange rates. Every day the value of the world's currencies moves up or down depending on the supply and demand for them, unless governments intervene in foreign exchange markets. Under a floating exchange rate regime it was widely thought the world no longer needed the IMF (since exchange rate movement would keep the currency's price at its true market value). However, no bureaucracy likes to see itself without a function, and as the debt crisis of the developing countries grew, in the wake of irresponsible lending by private banks recycling the petrodollar (income from oil sales) surplus, the U.S. Treasury and State Departments, along with international banks, found a new function for the IMF, one its bureaucracy was more than happy to adopt rather than shut down operations. It turned out that floating exchange rates brought not stability but a greater instability to international financial markets. Due to financial deregulation vast amounts of "hot" money were free to move at a moment's notice in search of quick profit, acting like so many cannonballs rolling from one side of the deck to the other, destabilizing and threatening to capsize a ship. The United States, which was the generative center for most of the speculative loans, came to see the value of using the Fund to prevent default by debtor countries. As the largest stockholder in the IMF, the United States used its influence to encourage the Fund to bail out the banks and bondholders that were owed money, and to impose conditionalities on debtors that would enable the Fund to achieve its goals of forcing debtor nations to open their economies to foreign capital on better terms. Often the reforms desired by foreign investors were not necessary to ensure debt repayment and sometimes they in fact prolonged the crisis. Reforms were primarily directed at structural transformation of economies, so as to favor the interests of foreign capitalists.

Over time the IMF found itself lending to more and more countries in the developing world. Most of the world's economies are now or have been under IMF conditionality. As will be discussed in the next chapter the IMF persisted for decades in imposing on debtor nations policies that are now collectively known as the Washington Consensus, and that are understood to constitute the neoliberal agenda that has been so unpopular and that is now acknowledged as a failure from a development perspective. The Fund used its power to impose high interest rates and austerity, and to force devaluations and privatizations. It demanded a contraction of the public sector. It ordered reduction of government budgets to make funds available for transfer to foreign creditors. This has meant such things as the closing of health care clinics and the dramatic underfunding of public education. These policies failed to produce economic growth in these economies. But they have succeeded in extracting funds from these poor countries for Western creditors.

The World Bank is in a somewhat better position, because its mandate is to help the poor countries develop. It has paid for harbor installations and airports needed to integrate economies more effectively into the global system. It has paid for oil exploration and mineral extraction projects, among other activities. The Bank is instructed by those who fuel and finally control it to help the poor by creating a climate in which the market can do its magic.

The Bank, like the Fund, embraced the Washington Consensus and has been particularly active in its demands for the privatization of the provision of goods and services. Under withering criticism, however, it has shown itself to be more flexible, although it remains uncompromising on the matter of reliance on market solutions and privatization. Thanks to pressure from civil society, the World Bank staff has in the wake of widespread criticism recommended a broader approach to fighting poverty. In the past it was enough to fund roads and other infrastructure to make the country more attractive to foreign investors, on the philosophy that the way to improve living standards was to more efficiently extract the country's natural resources and send them abroad. This has been the Bank's basic approach for fifty years. However, as the global economy grew by 2.3 percent a year between 1965 and 1998, the gap between the poor and the rich became ten times wider, as measured by per capita gross domestic product, and income distribution within as well as between countries has grown substantially. There seems to be something wrong with the pattern of growth.

There are many ways of looking at why this is the case. The Bank for most of its history focused on lack of capital. It now stresses the level of corruption within the poor countries themselves, which has interfered with the benefits expected from financial liberalization. This new perspective focuses on local elites extorting funds from foreign investors. Such rent-seeking makes foreign capitalists hesitant about committing their funds. Markets, it is said, don't work because the locals are cheaters and some regimes are no more than kleptocracies. Now that the cold war is over, these dictatorial governments, which for the most part were put in place and sustained by the West as part of an anticommunist crusade to prevent national liberation struggles, are no longer needed. The anticorruption campaign is first and foremost a restructuring so that local elites will get less from exploiting both foreign investors and their own people. The longtime encouragement of and collusion with these regimes is left unexplored.

The Debate

Globalization produces contested terrain. At first neoliberalism seemed to carry the day as the rationale for a corporatist globalization. However, as the adverse impacts of this unrestricted freedom for markets became more evident, resistance grew. It became confusing to many Americans, and others as well who might be convinced that in principle globalization was a good thing. They just did not like a lot of what it was doing.

United States citizens as a whole are certainly not free traders (although elites tell them they should be because "we all benefit"). Only 10 percent describe themselves as free traders. Most of us tell poll takers that we are *fair* traders. Fairness to all the people involved is more important than free markets. People are the ones who need freedom and that freedom includes access to a decent job at decent pay so that we can enjoy other freedoms with a full stomach and a sense of security. As *Business Week* comments, reporting on one typical poll, there is "a gnawing sense of unfairness and frustration that could boil over in the future." Stephen Kull, the director of the University of Maryland's Center on Public Attitudes, explains that a strong majority of the American public "feels that trade policies haven't adequately addressed the concerns of American workers, international labor standards, or the environment."[20] This explains why there is such support for the Global Justice Movement among the general public. Its anticorporate outlook mirrors a significant undercurrent in the society at large.

C. Fred Bergsten, of a transnational corporation–sponsored free trade Washington think tank and advocacy shop, tells us that "globalization can perhaps be given credit for annual increases of about 0.5 percent in overall American productivity growth over the last five years."[21] That may not seem like a lot but it is about half the standard estimate of the total increase in productivity for those years. Thus, if his math is well founded, globalization substantially increases productivity. He also thinks globalization has reduced unemployment by about 1 percent and has helped low-skilled workers back into the workforce.

Is he right? Other estimates of trade's impact offer grounds to doubt the "globalization-has-helped-Americans-at-the-bottom-to-do-better" story. First, real wages (spending power adjusted for taxes and price changes) have stagnated for most Americans over the recent decades of globalization. Second, because the United States at the start of the twenty-first century ran a large balance of current accounts deficit (we imported the equivalent of about 4 percent of our gross domestic product [GDP], more than we export), trade on net cost the U.S. economy millions of jobs. The low unemployment rate in the 1990s cannot be explained by increased trade. Rather it is the growth in debt that explains high domestic spending. We consume more than we produce and borrow from the rest of the world to pay for it.

Similar issues arise when we look at other presumed benefits of globalization. For example, U.S. agribusiness exports are said to feed the world's poor. But when low-cost U.S. exports enter a poorer country they undercut local farmers and drive many off the land because it is impossible for them to compete with the (subsidized) production capacity of U.S. agribusiness. Yet the IMF forces the opening of local markets to transnationals even as it demands cuts in social programs to finance foreign debt payment to international financiers. In 2000 in Brazil, when the Catholic bishops, trade unionists, and peasant organizations, among other members of Brazil's civil society, held a referendum on IMF policies, it is not surprising that the 5 million people polled favored breaking with the IMF. "These institutions are responsible for destroying our economy," Rogerio Mauro explained. He is from the Landless Peasant Movement, one of the sponsors of the poll. "We want to fight this hypocritical globalization of capital and instead globalize our struggle to determine the future of our own country."[22]

We do not get to hear the voices of people like Rogerio Mauro. It is hard for them to jump the Concorde and fly to Seattle or Prague to protest trade policies or loan conditionality. It is often only the financially better off who can come out into the street for such meetings, and this too often leads to mindless editorials that call them spoiled rich kids who presume to speak for the poor. These same well-paid media pundits must suppose it is better to leave matters to the far richer folks inside the meetings, those who make the decisions on behalf of the other, really rich folks who benefit most from the way the world is run.

Civil Society Versus Corporate Globalization

Many of the people who work for global state economic governance institutions think they are trying to help the poor and that all those demonstrators who appear rather often in front of their workplace and at their conferences do not understand them. They are employed as technical experts and, as such, are not political at all, they say. What they do benefits the poor even if sometimes they, like everybody else, can occasionally make a mistake. But they have a serious problem. They have a very hard time pointing to many, even any, countries where their programs have actually benefited the masses. As importantly, as Nicola Bullard of Focus on the Global South has written, "By presenting globalization as inevitable the Bank precludes discussion of the inherent class, economic, gender and ideological biases contained in almost every aspect of globalization." This inevitability, at the rhetorical level, has helped produce a more sophisticated misrepresentation of globalization, says Bullard, one that "absolves the Bank from assuming responsibility for its own part in creating a world where fewer people have more wealth, produced by the exploitation of more people with less wealth."[23] It ignores the political reality as well that poverty in our century is not, as it once was, a problem of scarcity and the inability to do something about it. Rather it is a function of the economic priorities and the system under which we live.

During the Vietnam War there was also a great divide between official policy and the perceptions of many Americans that the war was wrong. Globalization divides us in a similar fashion. Globalization from the top is widely perceived as driven by transnational capital and international finance and to be unjustly devastating to millions. But its advocates say "no, it is a good thing, and you'll see in the long run it will make things better." This is reminiscent of how, during the Vietnam War era, the military and the civilian policymakers explained they were bringing freedom, while the demonstrators said the policymakers were bringing death and destruction and serving the interests of foreign investors and a cold war view of the world, one that denied ordinary people the right to make their own history. To-

day, as the *Wall Street Journal* points out, not only are IMF economists and policymakers unpopular in the same way but "it turns
out that many youths in the new millennium view the IMF the
same way antiwar protesters viewed the Pentagon in the 1960s."
Since the folks at the IMF, like the folks at the Pentagon, view
themselves as serving on the side of the good guys, such criticisms
are hard for them to accept. The *Journal* commiserates with their
feelings. The poor economists are "bewildered, resentful and
frustrated."[24] It is true that we tend to demonize the people with
whom we strongly disagree. The *Wall Street Journal* does this
regularly. It denounces those who protest against its preferred
version of free-market globalization and does so in a fairly offensive manner. Such disagreement is predicated not on the belief
that those who hold the opposing view are evil or stupid or not
expert enough to understand the issues, but on matters of self-
interest, political and economic philosophy, and sometimes on
who one works for.

Academics who talk about these issues tend to be realists (although not all are members of the realist school, a distinction
important to political scientists, but one that we can ignore here).
Most see themselves as realists in the sense of understanding very
well that the powerful rule and that economic power in a capitalist world system in an era of globalization is central to, if often
the unacknowledged absent center of, policy discussion. Being
good guys and gals they suggest that setting up institutions that
set rules that the rich and the poor must both follow will constrain the powerful and help the weaker countries and groups.
Some even say that of course the rich will have power over these
institutions, what else would you expect? Why else would they
allow them? So we should expect that global state economic
governance organizations will be controlled by the U.S. executive branch and serve the interests first and foremost of U.S.-
based transnational corporations and banks. Still, the realists

contend, having such institutions is better than not having them, as they place some restraint on the naked exercise of power.

In the popular mind, transnational capital comes in for increased criticism for its association with corrupt and brutal local rulers. The wide publicity given to the role of Shell in Nigeria— its complicity with the killing of the Ogoni activists who resisted the depredations and environmental genocide of their lands— has led to a major effort by the company to salvage its reputation. Nike, having long argued that it followed local rules, has awakened to the fact that its labor policies, including those of its exploitative subcontractors, cost them money once their customers knew about them. Such disastrous public relations debacles have led, albeit fairly late and only after powerful campaigning, to at least a rhetorical claim to being concerned. Supporting corrupt governments and allowing unacceptable labor and environmental practices has become costly. This leads transnationals and their governments to accept the need to promise a certain degree of reform. If they fail to do so convincingly, they will suffer in the marketplace. If enough corporations are shown to have disregard for human rights and environmental concerns, it is possible that what is now an anticorporate movement could become anticapitalist, a much more dangerous situation for the system.

Has the worry over profits lost and corporate morale destroyed led to fundamental policy changes for global capital? There is no reason to think that as a general proposition it has. We still must rely on voluntary compliance. Unless there are serious legal limits and enforcement of laws with meaningful punishment, corporations will look for cover and public relations solutions. The Global Justice Movement is having an impact, but it has entered a more tricky period in which the corporations, after having stonewalled critics, wish to be seen as repentant former sinners who are now members in good standing of a responsible, caring community. Maximum publicity of wrongdoing has constrained corporate behavior, but it still needs to be used as a means to the end of the establishment of international rules that have real teeth, and that are enforced effectively. It turns out most U.S.-based transnationals are not willing to sign on to serious standards because they are afraid they would then be held accountable at the level of those standards. Public relations spin is one thing, but if people started to sue them for breaking laws, that would be quite another. Of course, if the people in their companies who decide to break the law go to jail the same way muggers do, we would see very different treatment of workers and the environment. Part of the discussion in this book will address ways to turn the gains made by social movements into ongoing and irreversible global changes.

The costs of actions taken by governments at the urging of the global state economic governance institutions need to be examined as well. The Washington Consensus is now widely rejected, as we have noted, but the damage it has done still needs to be assessed and, where justified, compensation paid to its victims. One area where this is actively an important task is with regard to privatization programs. When national assets are sold to private investors the test is whether the majority of service recipients are better off. This is not the same as simple service improvement. Affordability and universal provision are the important criteria. We do not solve a problem of service provision when we transfer to a pure market solution if there are negative redistributional impacts. The underside of the market is that when resources are allocated by ability to pay rather than by need, the poor are priced out of the market. If you can't pay more you don't receive the higher-quality service. The free market, for example, allocates housing efficiently in the private sense. The rich get great housing, the middle class get middle-level housing, low-income people get shabby trailer parks and urban slums, and those with the least income get to sleep on the street. This is fair in a market sense. When the market delivers water or electricity it does so to maximize profit. This is even worse when what was a public monopoly becomes a private monopoly when the ownership is transferred, often to politically connected investors.

As a wise man once said, the law in its infinite majesty allows both the rich and the poor to sleep under the bridges at night. Every person has the same abstract freedoms and every dollar should be treated the same in the market. You can have what you can buy. In real life, markets are not perfect, of course. There is monopoly power on the part of corporations that control the terms by which employment is given and products are sold. There is discrimination based on race, religion, national origin, and other factors. But even in a perfect market utopia, so long as there are wide disparities of income and wealth and the government does not actively create an effective housing policy, there will be homeless families living in the streets and scrounging food from trash bins. How much redistribution is allowed depends on the politics of a country. How much freedom a country has to pursue the social and economic policies it prefers depends on the larger global forces constraining it. It depends in part on the hegemony of capital versus the counterhegemonic capacities of working-class popular organizations to address these constraints creatively and equitably.

The attacks that destroyed the World Trade Center and damaged the Pentagon created a climate of fear, anger, demand for revenge, and set in motion military responses that inevitably produced more fear, anger, and demands for revenge—making social justice campaigns both more difficult and more necessary. The Bush administration's rhetoric that ours is a war of good against evil echoed the terrorists' certainty that theirs was a just cause supported by God. There was a stunning lack of awareness or concern for why these "cowards" acted in this heinous fashion except that the president said they hated democracy, which the

United States represented. For many—and not only in the Middle East—such rhetoric from the world's only superpower, whose blockade of Iraq was blamed for the deaths of half a million to a million mostly women and children and whose contribution of planes and helicopters had been used to massacre helpless Palestinians under Israeli control, was seen as, at best, hypocritical. The scale of violence unleashed on September 11, 2001, and the U.S. response to these events changed the context in which the struggle between corporate globalizers and social movements takes place. It made reasoned discourse and dissent to official policies and structured inequalities more difficult even as it increased the need to reassess long-standing U.S. attitudes and practices. These horrendous developments do not make the work of the Global Justice Movement less important but, rather, expand its mandate and reinforce the need for activism.

Responding to Corporate Globalization

There are a lot of ways to react to the costs globalization imposes, ways that go beyond a war on terrorism and the wider use of tear gas, rubber bullets, and the deployment of riot police to discourage citizens who are exercising their right to free speech and to protest. In short order following September 11, the fact that some people threw rocks through Starbucks' windows, and Jose Bove, a French farmer, took his tractor to the local McDonald's seemed almost quaint. The actions of self-proclaimed anarchists, a "black bloc" of individuals, possibly including police provocateurs, are now also a feature of such manifestations, even as their violence against property and willingness to attack police undermine the possibilities of the nonviolent movement. Such activities go beyond peaceful protest. But it is also clear that most protesters have not been violent and that the governments of the world cannot cope with the size and determination of such protest. They may rather see benefit in initiating police violence to keep the numbers of those willing to peacefully protest down. There is a serious problem from an "establishment" point of view in this revival of activism and the emergence of an energized civil society. In the context of a "total war" on terrorism social justice activists must adjust to the dramatically different situation.

The movements of global civil society that claim our attention hold to a political philosophy of inclusiveness, which is at variance with mainstream economics and the understandings it offers of globalization. (This contrast will be drawn more fully in the next chapter.) The Global Justice Movement presents a moral critique that leads to the questioning of the legal framework created by corporate power and imposed on societies around the world. (This is the subject of chapter 3.) The movement is thus about a counterhegemonic view of the world and the construction of social activism to realize this alternative vision of globalization from below through the conscious activity of individual citizens joined together through organizations of civil society. It is a big area and the diverse groupings within it hardly speak with a single voice. It includes religious groups, tenants organizations, Jubilee Debt Campaign (formerly Jubilee 2000), which campaigns for debt relief for the poor nations of the world, and it also includes, we must remember, the National Rifle Association (NRA) and the militias who have armed to defend white America against the United Nations and its black helicopters. The discussion here follows Mary Kaldor's suggestion that what we might describe as global civil society "would be the interaction of these groups, networks, and movements who provide a voice for individuals in global arenas and who act as, to paraphrase a well-know dictum, the transmission belts between the individual and global institutions."[25] Our focus throughout this book is on the progressive, left-leaning elements of global civil society.

The protests, the movements for an alternative globalization from below, and the popular organizing around the world in recent years—all of which we collectively call the Global Justice Movement—have focused on the serious problems of labor rights and (more broadly) the meaning of effective and participatory democracy as well as on the environment and how to protect it. Chapters 4 and 5, respectively, address these issues. There is another big issue that should command greater attention than it has and will, I think, become more central to our thinking about globalization in the coming years. Put crudely, there are a large number of very rich people getting richer by cheating on their taxes and, more importantly, by having (through lobbying and influence pedaling) tax laws written to serve their interests. Although there is nothing new in this practice, increased globalization, improved information technology, and lack of international agreements on money laundering have now made it possible for former dictators who have been forced to flee their countries on short notice, Russian oligarchs who have sold their country down the river, Colombian drug lords who launder money—not to mention U.S. corporations who use transfer pricing and wealthy individuals who use dummy corporations—all to more easily avoid taxation. This means social services get worse as revenues fall or that their expense must be shifted on to those who are less globally mobile. This produces tax resistance and a whole antigovernment bandwagon attacks government as ineffective. The current round of financial liberalization has its origin in the United States's unilateral abandonment of the Bretton Woods fixed exchange rate system, and in the deregulation of financial markets that produced fragility for national economies everywhere and was instrumental in bringing on financial crisis (as shall be discussed in detail in chapter 2).

These too impact on the ability of the public sector to address basic needs.

The normalcy or naturalness of power, which after all is what hegemony means, necessitates that those who challenge neoliberalism have to confront it from the outside. When workers first formed trade unions the system declared labor organizations illegal restraints of trade. When progressive movement pressures forced the passage of antitrust legislation, conservative courts said the law applied to workingmen's associations but not to corporations. When civil rights activists sat in at lunch counters or tried to take the first available seat on public buses in the segregated South they were arrested for breaking the law, which of course they were doing. Unjust laws and norms concede nothing without a struggle, and demonstrators will be jailed and beaten, teargassed and shot with rubber bullets or with real ones. The law that needs questioning these days is the wider juridical–political framework that Stephen Gill calls "the new constitutionalism of disciplinary neoliberalism." This encompasses trade and investment rules, the nature of "private" property, and the management of social interdependence. It treats of macroeconomic policy—for example, the desirability of independence for central banks from political "interference" and other mechanisms that lock out democratic controls over key economic institutions and policy making.[26]

The pressures that have long been applied to the rest of the world are being applied more vigorously at home by transnational corporations, who see all locations as competing profit and production centers and no longer privilege their formal home countries. Each jurisdiction must bid with lower taxes and better incentives if they want jobs and other revenues. This brand of competition is what is meant by equal treatment, creating a level playing field, and the other rhetorical tropes of the new constitutionalism of disciplinary neoliberalism. The basic idea of neoliberalism, as Anthony Giddens writes, is that "markets are in almost all respects superior to government. Markets not only provide for a rational allocation of products and labor power, they foreclose the need for any kind of program of social justice. You don't need, and you can't have, policies of social justice when—if the market is given full and free play—everything is bought and sold at its true value." As he points out, "The idea of minimal government flows directly from this. Government is needed only to provide a legal framework for contracts and for defense, law, and order."[27] What is important from the neoliberal perspective is to allow the market freedom of competition and the ability to innovate. Typically such freedom for capital must be imposed on an unwilling civil society. The crucial weapon in successfully imposing this set of policies is ideological hegemony, the ability to pass off the interests of the elite as the interests of the society as a whole. The Global Justice Movement began with demands on the IMF and the World Bank for debt cancellation for the most highly indebted and poorest countries, and for basic labor rights and environmental protections, which have been undermined by the WTO. But the logic of its criticisms is such that it leads inevitably to powerful connections, to the awareness that the global system is as oppressive at home as it is in the poorest and most exploited areas abroad. It is the purpose of this essay to make those connections more clearly.

The noisy folks in the streets who don't like the policies (or the rule by the corporate elite in the first place) are roundly criticized and told that in order to have influence they must play by the rules and stay within the system, a system that grants them no influence—a socioeconomic catch-22. Given the extent of the power of transnational corporations and international financiers over governments and international decision making, one wonders about what democracy does and does not mean. It is not enough to say that with all its faults ours is better than other systems. As is, it is surely not the best of all possible systems, and it should be possible to change and improve it through a more participatory democracy. Change that takes place outside the constraints the powerful set can lead to unexpected changes inside the usual channels. Students of norm change understand that it has taken deliberately transgressive acts, such as organized civil disobedience, which often entails social ostracism or legal punishment, to send a message. Framing an issue through mass protest is always a messy business, but it is a necessary one if there is to be progress. After the fact, it is often the case that the same people who resisted the changes, who called for jailing demonstrators and who condemned their "bad manners," will say, "See, the system works." Having to listen to their unself-conscious hypocrisy is an annoying additional price movement folk have to pay to make a difference.

We can draw on Pierre Bourdieu's understanding of this conservative revolution of our time as one that has produced a paradoxical *doxa*. Bourdieu expects we understand that doxa, from the Greek, means "belief," and so a doxastic principle of the sort he invokes is a principle governing belief, setting out conditions under which our forming or abandoning a belief is justified. This concept of a hegemonic conservative doxa is a powerful and insightful one since it ties what at first appear as the disparate evils of our time together into a counterhegemonic understanding of the ideological terrain on which these struggles partly take place. For Bourdieu,

> this *doxa* is conservative but presents itself as progressive; it seeks the restoration of the past order in some of its most archaic aspects (especially as regards economic relations), yet it passes off regressions, reversals, surrenders as forward-looking reforms or revolutions leading to a whole new age of abundance and liberty (as

with the language of the so-called new economy and the celebratory discourse around network firms and the Internet).

All of this can be clearly seen in the efforts to dismantle the welfare state, that is, to destroy the most precious democratic conquests in the areas of labor legislation, health, social protection, and education. To fight such a progressive-retrogressive policy is to risk appearing conservative even as one defends the most progressive achievements of the past. This situation is all the more paradoxical in that one is led to defend programs or institutions that one truly wishes to be changed, such as public services and the nation state, which no one could rightly want to preserve as is, or unions or even public schooling, which must be continually subjected to the most merciless critique.[28]

Bourdieu criticizes the false universalism of the neoliberal doxa, with its formal (and false) cosmopolitanism, and offers instead an international solidarity rooted in the progressive elements of global civil society. Corporate globalization from such a counterhegemonic position is a false universalism that serves the interests of transnational capital while attempting to isolate the separate struggles of those who are harmed by its mode of expansion by asserting that there is no alternative to what is alleged to be a natural and inevitable process. It is this assertion that the Global Justice Movement consistently challenges.

2
Economics and Political Economy

The editorial writers of the *Financial Times* declared in the wake of yet another massive protest against the logic of the global state economic governance institutions that "a small number of protesters against global capitalism have, as expected, graced the annual meetings of the World Bank and International Monetary Fund in Prague with their ugly presence. How should the world respond to these uncivilized representatives of 'civil society'? With contempt is the answer."[1] As is now traditional in such editorials, the demonstrators, almost all of whom were peaceful, are accused of being violent and unreasonable beyond endurance. "How can anyone deal constructively with people who believe that throwing stones is a proper response to world poverty?"[2] *The Economist* asks, "Are citizens groups, as many of their supporters claim, the first steps towards an 'international civil society' (whatever that might be)? Or do they represent a dangerous shift of power to unelected and unaccountable special-interest groups?"[3] There can be little doubt which they think.

These publications are enunciating a theory of democracy in which important decisions are left to elites and are not to be questioned. But if history is a guide, such warnings, condemnations, and dismissals of popular grassroots activism that is demanding social and economic change and that has reached the size and degree of mature consciousness that the Global Justice

Movement has are unlikely to be effective. Rather, they are likely to be the first stage in what is a typical three-step process. New ideas and critiques of business are first ignored for as long as possible by the powerful, who claim "TINA," an acronym, popularized by Margaret Thatcher, that stands for "there is no alternative." Activists are ridiculed as unrealistic and as being outside of the frame of respectable opinion. But if activists do not go away, and if their ideas begin to have influence, in a second-stage response they may be repressed, sometimes jailed, and even shot. If that doesn't do it, a mild version of their ideas is embraced as "just plain common sense" by the establishment, which then wants to take credit as forward-looking innovators facing new problems in a creative, yet responsible, way. How close the final outcome is to the original status quo versus how much real change the transformational movements wanted is a matter of struggle. Reform can be closer to the one or the other depending on whether the powerful grasp that they must make peremptory concessions. If they hang on too long to an untenable position, they threaten to provoke a more radical outcome. If the governing coalition cannot suppress, and doesn't or can't respond effectively, it runs the risk of being swept aside.

Intraelite struggle is often between those who urge some concession to the radical movements for social change—concessions that dilute their strength for the purpose of showing a willingness to listen to the protesters' views—and those who think such talk will only encourage, legitimize, and strengthen antisystemic forces. The movements for social change face similar tactical questions, questions of combining willingness to talk "inside" with a determination to keep up the pressure "outside." The problem with sitting down at the table is that while the conversation may be friendly enough, it takes place largely using a vocabulary and within a frame of thinking that is resistant to grassroots-movement ideas. Efficiency, cost minimization, and property rights are keywords of the privileged. It is hard going to force the conversation onto another track, which requires an equally well worked out frame and a redefining of the counter-hegemonic meanings of keywords. Movements for social and economic change face not only the power of corporate capitalism and government but also the economistic mode of thought, which is central to the way the powerful do business. Behind corporate power is the ideology of mainstream economics.

Many who have studied introductory economics are dismayed to find that economists reduce all values to those of the marketplace, all issues to the narrow measure of efficiency. People who come away thinking they don't understand economics usually can't accept the assumptions of economists' models and so don't see how to apply them given their own values and purposes. In Economics 101, phenomena are understood in terms that are constant over time and across social formations. Little energy is spent on the ways core economic assumptions of maximizing individual utility in free markets ignore the role of institutions, the functions of democratic dialogue in changing preferences, and the constraint of class position on choices available to individuals. There is more most people want to say about the relationship between values and knowledge than many economists are willing to discuss.

In mainstream economics, problem-solving generally involves one of two sorts of tasks. The first is to show why markets work better than any other way of deciding how resources should be distributed and how, in the real world, markets naturally win out. Existing social relations either go untheorized or are presumed to be subject to methodological individualist behavior models in which atomistic actors and not social groups, surely not classes, compete and cooperate based on their place within existing material conditions, the group consciousness as it develops in an historically contingent manner, and identity politics, which may develop out of the life space people occupy. None of this is to say that an encounter with a sophisticated economics course, even a fairly conventional one, cannot be enriching and that a capacity to understand economic models (to understand how economists think) may not be useful.

An economic theory built on logical analysis of profit-seeking behavior by large numbers of well-informed, independent individuals in competitive markets that are governed by legal systems that enforce contracts and ensure the property rights of owners is certainly a fair first take for many analytical purposes. But if we do not ask about the origin of property in violent appropriation, the perpetuation of certain definitions of property rights through the exercise of bribery and coercion, the use of wealth to protect and increase wealth, and the manipulation of these presumably well-informed, independent individuals by advertising and pressures from a culture of possession (which measures self-worth on the basis of the ownership of status items), we surely miss a lot of the real story.

Mainstream economics starts from given endowments and preferences and sees freedom from extramarket "coercion" as defining the good society. Those who start from a social justice perspective accept that there is such a thing as society (something methodological individualism in its rigorous form denies) and so understand freedom in the positive sense of empowerment. In this egalitarian perspective the community should help provide the means for people to gain capacities to function effectively. But because of the wealth distribution in real existing communities, the development of the capacities of their members, their tastes and their preferences, along with the incentive system of the market, can be seen as privileging some values at the expense of others. The market in most real-world situations is not a neutral means of allocating resources but rather one that has built into it—in a society of unequal power and wealth—systemic

biases that reinforce status quo relations. Unless there is positive
social intervention, inequalities can be reinforced, and certain
people through no fault of their own will be victimized by the
"natural" workings of the system. To the extent that workers
lack education and training, proper health care and other basic
needs, and are forced to take any job no matter how substandard
the conditions or excessive the demands on health and well-
being or how inadequate the compensation to allow a life of
basic dignity, these individuals and the society are poorer for it.

Perhaps the purest example of the economistic way of seeing
the world is to be found in a now (in)famous memo written by
Lawrence Summers (now president of Harvard University). Toward the end of 1991, when he was chief economist at the World
Bank, he distributed to his staff an explanation of why the institution should welcome and encourage more migration of environmentally hazardous industry to the less-developed countries.
It is useful to reproduce most of the memo here, since it so
accurately reflects the often unstated premises of market logic as
applied by powerful policymakers.

"1. The measurements of the cost of health impairing pollution
      depends on the foregone earnings from increased morbidity
      and mortality. From this point of view a given amount of
      health impairing pollution should be done in the country
      with the lowest cost, which will be the country with the
      lowest wages. I think the economic logic behind dumping a
      load of toxic waste in the lowest wage country is impeccable
      and we should face up to that.

"2. The costs of pollution are likely to be non-linear as the initial
      increments of pollution probably have very low cost. I've
      always thought that under-populated countries in Africa are
      vastly UNDER-polluted, their air quality is probably vastly
      inefficiently low compared to Los Angeles or Mexico City.

Only the lamentable facts that so much pollution is generated by non-tradable industries (transport, electrical generation) and that the unit transport costs of solid waste are so high prevent world welfare enhancing trade in air pollution and waste.

"3. The demand for a clean environment for aesthetic and health reasons is likely to have very high income elasticity. The concern over an agent that causes a one in a million change in the odds of prostate cancer is obviously going to be much higher in a country where people survive to get prostate cancer than in a country where under 5 mortality is 200 per thousand. Also, much of the concern over industrial atmosphere discharge is about visibility impairing particulates. These discharges may have very little direct health impact. Clearly trade in goods that embody aesthetic pollution concerns could be welfare enhancing. While production is mobile the consumption of pretty air is a non-tradable.

"The problem with the argument against all of these proposals for more pollution in LDCs (intrinsic rights to certain goods, moral reasons, social concerns, lack of adequate markets, etc.) could be turned around and used more or less effectively against every Bank proposal for liberalization."

After the memo was made public, Brazil's then–secretary of the environment, Jose Lutzenberger, wrote Summers, "Your reasoning is perfectly logical but totally insane. . . . Your thoughts [provide] a concrete example of the unbelievable alienation, reductionist thinking, social ruthlessness and the arrogant ignorance of many conventional 'economists' concerning the nature of the world we live in. . . . If the World Bank keeps you as vice president it will lose all credibility. To me it would confirm what I often said . . . the best thing that could happen would be for the Bank to disappear."[4] As it turned out it was Mr.

Lutzenberger who was soon fired. Mr. Summers did leave the Bank, but he did so for a job in the Clinton administration, where he rose to be secretary of the Treasury, the office that establishes policies for the World Bank and the IMF on most important matters. The memo is in fact a clear statement of the market logic that undergirds private and most public decision making. As we'll note in chapter 5, while some call the disproportionate siting of toxic waste dumps in low-income minority communities environmental racism, economists just call such occurrences the result of cost minimization. These are the communities where land costs are lowest. We wouldn't expect toxic waste dumps in Beverly Hills. The land is too valuable. It is all simply economics. Is there something wrong with this picture? We do not have estimates of the Love Canal–like situations that may occur in the poorest "underpolluted" countries that correspond to Mr. Summers's offer, but most people reject the immorality of such "efficiencies." Mainstream economics has a lot to answer for.

The problem with this sort of market metric is that the poor, who have few choices, may sell the very life space they occupy for short-term reward. They have after all what economists call a high rate of time discount. As one worker in a chemical plant told a reporter who asked if he minded working without protective equipment, "Hell, I'd jump in the damn vat if they told me I had to to keep my job." This represents choice in only a very limited sense. It is also true that hungry people sell their children into slavery. This is a free choice by people who love their children when they have others who would die without the food such a free market exchange between willing participants allows. It is in such a sense that Lawrence Summers's memo is not wrong.

In another instance of the economistic logic of cost-benefit analysis, a study commissioned by Philip Morris and produced by the consulting firm Arthur D. Little International explains that in 1999 the Czech Republic's government gained $147 million as a result of people smoking in that country. It seemed that because people died earlier from lung cancer and other diseases that are caused by smoking the government saved on pensions and health care, compared to if these people had not died prematurely due to cigarette smoking! When the *Wall Street Journal* did a story on the study and California senator Dianne Feinstein and others picked up on this outrage, Philip Morris, attempting to defuse a widening public relations debacle, issued a statement saying "We understand that this was not only a terrible mistake, but that it was wrong."[5] According to the Centers for Disease Control and Prevention, tobacco is expected to become the biggest killer in most developing countries over the next two decades, causing more deaths than malaria, tuberculosis, homicides, suicides, auto crashes, and AIDS combined. Think of the money this will save!

When the Bush administration beat back South Korea's attempt to raise tariffs on foreign cigarettes in the summer of 2001, White House spokesman Ari Fleisher said the case had nothing to do with public health. "It was a straight trade issue," he said. The U.S., which at home sued the tobacco companies for misrepresenting the health risks of cigarettes, forced open Asian markets during the Reagan and first Bush administrations. President Clinton demanded a reduction in Chinese tobacco tariffs as one of the conditions for supporting China's entry into the WTO. While the United States insists that countries not bar U.S. tobacco products or limit the tobacco companies' rights to advertise their wares, if current patterns hold, half a billion people who are alive today will be killed by tobacco.

Aside from the social justice concerns, marketization has political consequences. As more resources are allocated through the market, those who benefit or may potentially benefit have more resources and more reason to pressure governments for more concessions. As this is being written, President George W. Bush is pushing a plan for (partial) privatization of the now public retirement pensions, namely, Social Security. The reasoning is that if more people owned stock, they would be more inclined to demand policies that would help Wall Street. For example, when layoffs are announced, a company's stock price goes up, but when labor is strengthened profit shares are likely to be reduced. Therefore, if more Americans relied on stocks for their retirement income, it is assumed that they would move politically toward procorporation and antilabor policies. Efforts to discipline monopolists would likewise meet with greater resistance. As the quality of and coverage by public services decrease, the antigovernment constituency increases, and it becomes easier to reach agreement on tax cuts that go overwhelmingly to the already-rich. When markets rule it is easier to remove social protections of all sorts.

Trade and the Global Economy

We are repeatedly told that free trade is good for everybody and should be adopted as widely as possible. But trade theory does not in fact tell us that free trade is good for everyone (or that it is bad for everyone). Free trade and liberalization generally both create and redistribute income. Some gain from trade and others lose. Unfortunately, the question of what should be done about redistributional impacts is approached in a very strange way in the mainstream literature. That is to say, a hypothetical is asked: Are the gains from trade sufficient for the winners to compensate the losers out of their gains and still be better off? If so, free trade or liberalization in the particular instance is justified whether or not compensation is actually paid. Redistributional questions are especially troubling in a country like the United States, where trade theory tells us that labor with specialized skills in demand (for example, people in computer science, finance, and so on, who fit the needs of the transnational corporations) will be rewarded more generously as the market expands through more trade, but that textile workers and others with less education and who face greater global competition from even lower-paid workers will be made worse off. That there are gains to the first group, whose wages are bid up, and losses to the second group, who see "their kind" of worker in oversupply, is important. That macro indicators show average income rising is perfectly consistent with extreme distress among some groups and for many workers.

Even if one supposes that free trade and unrestricted capital mobility may eventually result in global-factor price equalization and international equality, the transition may take centuries. As J. Mohan Rao writes: "Meanwhile, many areas of pressing global concern can be successfully addressed only through international collective action. But can effective and efficient solutions be found if questions of distribution, equity and justice are sidestepped?"[6] From the viewpoint of the efficiency model, advocates of "nontrade" values and issues are seen as complicating the trade regime with what are at best extraneous concerns (like human rights and environmental protection) and at worst using these social regulations to achieve protectionist goals by other means. However, there are no pure trade issues, and for many Americans other issues are more important than efficiency concerns as defined by economists.

Trade is not so much about one country winning or losing but rather about some people in each country winning and others losing. There may be important gains from trade but the central issue is how those gains are distributed. From a working-class perspective protectionism may not be a good solution because the cost per job saved may be great. Because the resulting higher cost of living may not be worth it, some alternative and at least equally effective way of helping workers who may be displaced is desirable. There are better ways of dealing with the problems trade creates. The preferred solution is not protectionism but protection of vulnerable people in socially equitable ways. For most people, if not for many economists, fairness needs to be taken seriously and made integral to the evaluation of international trade policies. But market economies are not inclined to pursue justice issues as part of economic analysis or trade policy. Negatively affected workers realistically see tariffs and other simple ways of preventing competition as their best shot. While they are second-best choices, in many cases they are the only hope of the working class. Because of the difficulties "fairness" entails (it is, after all, subjective), and because retraining is typically a sop and a shill, workers can be better-off just saying "no" to any change that will adversely effect them.

The poorer countries have problems with the way corporate globalization has imposed priorities based on market power. In response, many developing countries in the 1960s and 1970s supported the U.N. Code of Conduct for Transnational Corporations as a way of making transnational corporations more accountable to local needs and priorities. Trade theorists saw such proposals then, and analogous ones today, as exercises in rent seeking, attempts by locals to extract resources from foreign capital. Other critics of such regulation see these efforts as harmful to the interests of the developing countries themselves, arguing that they ignore "the basic fact that trade remains the most viable path to escape poverty" and that because trade and investment offer the best chance for these countries to overcome their poverty the activists are showing "apparent hypocrisy" in rallying against the WTO and demanding codes of conduct for corporations and labor and environmental standards. The battles of the 1970s for a new international economic order along the lines of a new deal for developing countries—better terms of trade for their primary products, technology transfer, and respect for local state development options such as local content rules—have mostly been lost. Countries now compete to attract foreign capital and do so on terms increasingly favorable to investors. As shall be argued, there needs to be a reversal of this trajectory and more consideration given to strengthening local development in a just and sustainable manner, to the fairness of the distribution of gains from trade, and to imposing control over something as mundane as the system of taxation.

Free-trade advocates are insistent that no regulation that interferes with "free" markets can be accepted. But corporations would still invest if they had to act in a more socially responsible manner, and trade flows might not be so different. Income would be more equitably shared and the environment better protected, thus increasing well-being. Although philosophical stances are complicated and often inconsistent, there are three clear tendencies in the debate. There are proponents of free markets, who favor deregulation, an end to attempts at social engineering by the World Bank and other global state economic governance institutions, strict market accountability, privatization, and the reduction of the role of the IMF so that it does not bail out financiers who have made bad loans and governments that have followed wrongheaded policies. They want the World Bank to be restructured as a development lending-agency, making loans only to those very poor countries that do not have access to private financial markets. The Bush administration is sympathetic to such reform priorities. It is less interested in advancing international regulation and the legalistic framework that was pursued by the Clinton team, and it is more inclined to think too much authority is ceded to global state economic governance institutions. It is better in the Bush approach to leave our options open rather than commit to multilateralism as the operating framework.

Third Way neoliberals of the Tony Blair–Bill Clinton school want modest changes having to do with greater transparency, better information supplied by countries, and monitoring by international agencies to avoid bad investment decisions and financial crises. But they also see value in maintaining global-state-economic-governance-institution leverage over developing economies to move them toward the market-friendly policies of open markets and access for foreign investors to their economies, without prejudice. The Third Way neoliberals see carrots as essential for behavioral modification and fear the costs to all of uncontrolled markets. Because of pressure from key parts of their political base they are more ready to accept at least rhetorical commitment to labor rights and environmental protection. The Bush people are not.

The activists of global civil society address the vacuum on the electoral center-left, which has proven incapable of responding effectively to corporate globalization and instead appears to accept TINA, offering only an "I feel your pain, but I sadly cannot do anything that will make much of a real difference" response. Leading political figures have talked about Third Way alternatives between a straw-man left (central planning Soviet-style) or the old-style welfare state (one that protects people and makes their lives better). Yet their bromides barely cover their capitulation to neoliberalism. Pointing to the most high-profile of such efforts by the leaders of Germany and the United Kingdom, Will Hutton observes that "the document that [Chancellor Gerhard] Schroeder and Blair presented in June 1999 as their model of updated social democracy was an astonishing statement of neoliberal principles. It continues to have a naive trust in markets. It explicitly argues that the job of politicians is not to change, reform, or manage these markets; rather it is to attempt to improve the empowerment of our citizens to do better in these markets."[7]

To the left of such positions, more progressive viewpoints include the call for strict labor and environmental standards and for regulation of international speculators in the interests of stability, along with a pattern of inclusive development and a focus on increasing the capabilities and political power of the poor. Those who support these goals are divided between "fix it" and "nix it" positions on the global state economic governance institutions. Some favor their reform because international forums and organizational infrastructure are needed to achieve equitable and sustained development and to renegotiate better terms between rich and poor in areas of trade and investment to further such goals. Others see these institutions as hopelessly compromised, nothing but the tools of transnational capital and international finance, and argue that they should be abolished. Sorting through the various positions requires evaluation of how these institutions have functioned and can be made to work in the future, given different politics.

IMF Conditionality

Developments are moving faster in the post-Seattle period. What the impact will be for the kind of globalization we shall see in the twenty-first century is still far from clear. The discussion here focuses mainly on the IMF, criticism of its role as lender of last resort, and the conditionality it imposes. For some time the IMF asserted that it did not control the actions of its clients. It said it offered advice that countries were free to incorporate into plans submitted for structural adjustment to the Fund. The IMF wanted the countries to own the plans, and the fiction that they came from the borrowers was seen as necessary to preserving their dignity and the illusion of sovereignty. However, as country after country failed to meet the conditions of these agreements and failed to recover under IMF tutelage, conditionality became more and more blatant and detailed in the form of demands by the Fund. Some time around the end of the twentieth century a turning point was reached. Under various pressures, ranging from those exerted by nongovernmental organizations (NGOs) to those from within the U.N. system, the IMF changed its stance of leaving the protection of the poor up to the governments involved in its programs. Its missions now discuss distributional aspects with governments as part of their remit in the preparation of programs and conditionalities. Policy framework papers are to include measures to protect the well-being of vulnerable groups. Such a change on paper, it is to be hoped, may impact the real world as well. But doubts remain. Programs at their core appear to persist unchanged. Countries must impose austerity. The poor suffer painfully.

The extent to which the IMF intervenes around the world and continuing dependence on the IMF over decades have become matters of widespread concern. Rather than the IMF needing to intervene at rare intervals when a particular country had balance-of-payment problems, a permanent overlord relationship has developed. As a result, there is growing awareness that these problems are structural, that they are integral to the way the global financial regime works. Most countries in the world are, or in the recent past have been, subject to IMF control or conditionality. Their indebtedness has been the occasion to force changes in policies preferred by international financiers under the guidance of the U.S. Treasury Department. Systematic disadvantage in a world of unequal power relations has created structural dependence.

For Marxists and other radicals this is hardly surprising. It is the way imperialism works and it seems clear enough that we are living through an internationalized version of dollar diplomacy, the control of weaker economies by the United States as it uses finance as a weapon, similar to what it imposed at the start of the twentieth century. That was a time when imperialism was not a bad word and imperialists were proud of their activities. As explained by President William Howard Taft, "The policy has been characterized as substituting dollars for bullets. It is one that appeals alike to idealistic humanitarian sentiments, to the dictates of sound policy and strategy, and to legitimate commercial aims. . . . The United States has been glad to encourage and support American bankers willing to lend a helping hand to the financial rehabilitation." At the start of the twentieth century the United States would send its experts on missions to debtor countries and they would draw up a plan to restore fiscal order and the repayment of debt to U.S. banks and bond holders. Dollar diplomacy for Taft embodied "a dream of rising living standards for all, boosted by ever-larger volumes of goods within a trading network greased by predictable financial infrastructure."[8]

To others of course it represented "imperialist domination and exploitation, fashioned by greedy bankers, financial experts who acted as proconsuls, and sometimes marines who would be dispatched to do the bidding of both."[9] If necessary, the marines set up at the customshouse to collect taxes. When the debt was paid the marines went home. If there was instability or perception of unwillingness to stay the course laid out by the American economists, the marines might stay longer. When they did leave they left in place a local government deemed amenable to U.S. interests. This was the nature of U.S. imperialism and gunboat diplomacy a century ago. As Emily Rosenberg writes in her study of these financial missionaries to the world, "Dollar diplomacy was a controversial U.S. policy that attempted to use private bank loans to leverage the acceptance of financial advisers by foreign governments that U.S. officials and investors considered unstable."[10]

There was little question then, at least in the minds of the bankers and the imperial state, that it was the job of the advanced

races to discipline the more backward. The United States as the
rising hegemon took over from no-longer-so-great Britain. The
transition from the late nineteenth century onward reflected as
well a change in emphasis from free trade to the rule of finance.
A similar change has been evident in the post–World War II
period as first trade and competition for export markets dominated the policy debate, and then, by the 1980s, debt and financial crises became the mechanism of increased U.S. dominance.
Gallagher and Robinson coined the term *free trade imperialism* to
describe the imposition by the British government, in the second
half of the nineteenth century, of the doctrine (and the enforcement of the practice) of free trade on unwilling trade "partners,"
in this the age of Britain's undisputed industrial monopoly.[11] In
this spirit we may speak of neoliberal imperialism in describing
the imposition by the global state economic governance institutions of the doctrine of free mobility of capital on unwilling
weaker economies in the contemporary era of globalization.

Transnational capital appreciates an enforcer of the rules, an
agency twice removed from their visibly direct manipulation of
the world political economy. The global state economic governance institutions are once removed from decision making in the
major economic powers' governments. The corporations who
fund elections and guide politics in areas central to their interests
are thus twice removed. At a first level of distancing, while it
would have appeared unseemly for the United States to openly
intervene in elections in, say, Russia, when a widely discredited
Boris Yeltsin was in danger of not being reelected, the head of
the IMF simply rewrote the Fund's rules to ease credits for Russia and went on Moscow television to announce the extending
of a $10 billion loan in what was understood as an endorsement.
The international financiers had much to fear if the corrupt and
incompetent Mr. Yeltsin, drunk much of the time and seriously
ill as a result of his lifestyle, was not kept in power, and they were

relieved when the Russian president was reelected. As the *New York Times* said at the time, "Although the monetary fund is not supposed to take sides in elections, the extraordinary deal—the second largest loan in the fund's history—was driven by the West's desire to impede the comeback of the Communist Party in Russia."[12] Thus international capital acted through the major economic powers, who then directed the intermediations of the IMF, keeping two steps removed from responsibility for the policies from which they benefit.

The Russian loan, along with close to $18 billion to Mexico the year before (also at U.S. insistence), amounted to half the Fund's outstanding loans, a dangerous concentration. Rules were bent to accommodate the United States even though these loans far exceeded the Fund's lending limits and were made without consultation with the twenty-four-member board, the IMF's presumed governing body. The IMF's own internal evaluations are understood to have been critical of these policy steps, but they are kept secret. Board meetings are closed. The minutes are sealed. Many of the important details of what the Fund does are not available to any outsiders. It does not believe in the transparency it urges on others.

It would seem obvious that the IMF undermines democracy by imposing its policies and that these policies have not been effective in achieving their professed goals. Joseph Stiglitz describes the way they work:

> When the IMF decides to assist a country, it dispatches a "mission" of economists. These economists frequently lack extensive experience in the country; they are more likely to have firsthand knowledge of its five-star hotels than of the villages that dot its countryside. They work hard, poring over numbers deep into the night. But their task is impossible. In a period of days or at most weeks, they are charged with developing a coherent pro-

gram sensitive to the needs of the country. Needless to say, a little number-crunching rarely provides adequate insight into the development strategy for an entire nation. Even worse, the number-crunching isn't always that good. The mathematical models the IMF uses are frequently flawed or out-of-date. Critics accuse the institution of taking a cookie-cutter approach to economics, and they're right. Country teams have been known to compose draft reports before visiting. I heard stories of one unfortunate incident when team members copied large parts of the text for one country's report and transferred it wholesale to another. They might have gotten away with it, except the "search and replace" function on the word processor didn't work properly, leaving the original country's name in a few places. Oops.[13]

Before he was fired, Stiglitz was chief economist at the World Bank, and so when he judges the IMF economists to be frequently third-rank, though from first-rate universities, and often not as good as the better-trained local economists upon whom they impose policies, one has to listen. Stiglitz is not alone in thinking their models are inadequate or bad and certainly "out-of-tune with reality." "It's not fair," he writes, "to say that IMF economists don't care about the citizens of developing nations," but he thinks they "act as if they are shouldering Rudyard Kipling's white man's burden." After delivering a scalding criticism and considering why they seem to have screwed up so badly, he asks: "Were some of the IMF's harsh criticisms of East Asia intended to detract attention from the agency's own culpability? Most importantly, did America—and the IMF—push policies because we, or they, believed they would benefit the financial interests in the United States and the advanced industrial world? And, if we believe our policies were helping East Asia, where was the evidence? As a participant in these debates, I got to see the evidence. There was none."[14]

Jeffrey Sachs, director of Harvard University's Center for International Development, writes that "the truth of course is" that the IMF and the World Bank are "the instruments of a few rich governments, which hold a majority of the dollar-based votes and would rather pretend that all is well in the world than ask their taxpayers to address the urgent problems of the poor." His scathing judgment is that "the IMF and World Bank have been the mouthpieces of this deceit, with their charade of analyzing the 'debt sustainability' of the poorest countries. These analyses have nothing to do with debt sustainability in any real sense, since they ignore the deaths of millions of people for want of access to basic medicines and nutrition. Money that could go towards public health is instead siphoned off to pay debts owed to Western governments and to the IMF and World Bank themselves."[15] This is precisely why many activists have joined the "Fifty Years Is Enough!" campaign, and what brings other groups such as Jubilee Plus to call an end to this punishment of the poor. American officials have often been frank about all of this as well. Former U.S. trade representative Mickey Kantor has explained, with regard to the way the East Asian financial crisis was used to manipulate the countries of the region, that "the troubles of the Tiger economies offered a golden opportunity for the West to reassert its commercial interests. When countries seek help from the IMF, Europe and America should use the IMF as a battering ram to gain advantage."[16]

Sometimes a battering ram can level a whole country. In Russia, where the IMF's economic program went into effect at the beginning of 1992, within five years the country had lost nearly half its national income. The Russian government followed the IMF's prescriptions on monetary and fiscal policy and on privatizing industry with the result that they were inflicted by a plague of organized crime and corruption. There has been a dramatic decrease in life expectancy and a shrinking Russian population as a result of the economic disaster and its social fallout. But the cost was deemed acceptable by the United States and the IMF, given the goal, which was to ensure at any cost that the Communists or any other opponents to extreme liberalization and the quick sell-off of state assets was prevented from successfully challenging the transition. This meant that the West worked with the most corrupt and criminal elements, known as "the oligarchs," or the handful of men who appropriated for themselves through a variety of dishonest measures the wealth of the country. Extreme wealth inequality and lawlessness are the result of the policies the West put in place.

IMF–World Bank (WB) financial and technical assistance programs to former Communist countries stipulated that recipients could neither place restrictions on foreign direct investment nor encourage state development banking. "In its 1996 negotiations with Bulgaria and Bosnia, the IMF explicitly tied the continued receipt of financial support to creation of currency boards. . . . In the early 1990s, the Polish, Hungarian, and Czechoslovak governments were forced by the IMF to abandon plans to pursue non-neoliberal economic programs involving economic development strategies and state financing mechanisms," writes Ilene Grabel, detailing the specific interventions that were used to guide the transitions of the former Communist countries of Eastern Europe. "The Polish case is particularly dramatic in this regard: the terms of a WB loan agreement constrained the ability of the Polish Development Bank to issue direct, subsidized industrial loans. Moreover, these multilateral institutions have even barred former Communist countries from pursuing gradualist reform or state capitalist models."[17]

It is not just the former Communist states. The IMF and WB cannot point to policy success in any part of the world. Moreover, comparing the twenty years of Thatcher-Reagan–Washington Consensus to the two decades that preceded them, it is clear that global growth was far slower under the neoliberal regime. The causes for the slower growth are of course a matter of debate, but the deflationary bias of the austerity imposed and the redirection of capital to speculative activities are surely important factors. Why then did the IMF persist in forcing liberalization of capital markets? We have already quoted Joseph Stiglitz on the role of U.S. financial elites. Jagdish Bhagwati, a leading advocate of free trade and a professor at Columbia University, has answered this question: "Wall Street has become a very powerful influence in terms of seeking to open markets everywhere. Morgan Stanley and all these giant firms want to be able to get into other markets and essentially see capital account convertibility as what will enable them to operate everywhere. Just like in the old days there was this 'military-industrial complex,' nowadays there is a 'Wall Street–Treasury complex.'" In a similar vein, Allan Meltzer, a professor of political economy at Carnegie Mellon University, visiting scholar at the American Enterprise Institute, and chair of the commission appointed by the Republican-dominated Congress to recommend reform of the IMF and WB writes: "Most of the demonstrators oppose the 'Washington Consensus,' the long list of conditions that countries must accept in exchange for financial aid. They are right to do so. Many of the conditions are intrusive and of little value."[18]

The rationale for bailing out the foreign investors and speculators was so that there could be a quick return to large-scale short-term lending. But this lending is itself undesirable, for the most part. Short-term debt, as is now more widely appreciated, is intrinsically a risky form of finance, made more dangerous when it is undertaken in dollars or other foreign currencies. When market psychology changes, the money pours out faster than it came in, loans are not renewed, debt must be paid immediately, and, since the local currency loses a large part of its value as investors panic and exit the economy, the debt burden of local borrowers in real terms increases dramatically, just as capacity to repay evaporates. We see this same painful cycle over and over again. It has brought crisis to more than fifty countries in the last decades. Self-control on the part of either local elites or Western speculators is rare. The incentives to overlend and overborrow are just too great. The history of repeated debt crises and speculative bubbles and mishaps are a part of the way capitalism has always operated. Making creditors bear a greater share of the adjustment burden would perhaps moderate these cycles, but that is not politically easy to achieve given the power relationship involved. It is easier, and more profitable, to force "belt tightening" on peasants and workers in the debtor nations, and, when this approach reaches its limits, to then tax the affluent nations to fund the global state economic governance institutions, so they can bail out the creditor banks and bondholders who profit from the disasterous imposition of financial liberalization. The main advocate and enforcer of international financial market deregulation was Robert Rubin, U.S. secretary of the Treasury from 1995 to 1999, who came to government service from Goldman Sachs & Company, where he was chairman. After leaving his government post he went to a key position at Citigroup, another major winner from financial deregulation. Citigroup is a merged entity made possible by banking reforms Rubin himself had pushed through Congress.

Larry Summers, Mr. Rubin's successor as the secretary of the Treasury (author of the World Bank memo cited earlier) responded to these attacks by proposing a scaling back of the role of the IMF, to meet the criticisms that its "mission creep" had so expanded its role that the richer governments of the world (and most especially the U.S. Congress) were unwilling and probably unable to enlarge its resources in line with the rapid growth of available private financing. The huge and growing amounts being put at risk could not be insured through IMF bailouts. In attempting to do so, the Fund had created a huge moral hazard problem. Lenders acted irresponsibly in the belief that if problems occurred the IMF would make monies available to make them whole. The Fund's lending to Russia, undertaken at U.S. prompting, came in for particularly withering attack by congressional Republicans who were looking for partisan advantage. Summers thought the Fund should do more to collect and disseminate timely information to financial markets, focusing on its "core competence," and leave lending to private markets in the case of those middle-income countries with access to private capital. While this was a retreat, it was also consistent with the IMF having achieved its goal of moving these countries, through its loans and conditionality, into a position where foreign lenders could do normal business in these economies. The Fund had broken the back of nationalistic alternative development models and globalization had proceeded to the point of integrating these countries so fully that they had no real choice but to play by American rules. The Bush administration made this clear early on in the statements of its secretary of the Treasury, Paul O'Neill, who denigrated the role of the global state economic governance institutions and urged reliance on the market. Whether he would be willing in practice to take a hands-off attitude awaits his first major international financial crisis.

Much of the criticism of the international lending agencies in terms of their "bureaucratic bungling" and the need for change was hogwash, intended solely for public consumption and designed to place blame on the institutions rather than on those who set their policy. The IMF, as Amity Shlaes, the *Financial Times* columnist, suggests, "is less a grand power" than "the servant" of the U.S. Treasury and Congress who "find the status quo quite convenient. The Treasury likes the IMF because it tends to execute Treasury commands without the Treasury having to take direct responsibility. Congress wants reform, but it likes having a punchbag even better."[19] Allan Meltzer, in a similar vein, says: "The Treasury uses the language of reform to protect the status quo—to use the IMF as its own slush fund. The Congress likes to rail but it doesn't want to take responsibility for agreeing to finance particular actions." Indeed, the pontificating and posturing in the post-Seattle environment may be seen as a casting around for reforms that can increase the perceived legitimacy of neoliberal policies without doing very much to change either the way decisions are made or the incidence of who bears the burden of adjustment costs in the world economy.

The Economist reports disapprovingly, "The IMF, long regarded as impermeable to outsiders, now runs seminars to teach the NGOs the nuts and bolts of country-program design, so that it can better monitor what the Fund is doing and (presumably) understand the rationale for the Fund's loan conditions. Horst Köhler, the IMF's new head, has been courting NGOs. Jim Wolfensohn, the Bank's boss, has long fawned in the direction, but in the Bank too the pace of bowing down has been stepped up."[20] The Economist, dedicated to preventing any weakness in the free-market front, is very critical of any concessions to the anticapitalist globalization forces and defends its position on the basis that higher labor or environmental standards would hurt the poor ("sweatshops would simply move somewhere else leaving workers without jobs"). The idea that poor people and poor countries cannot afford standards is hardly new. Defenders of business interests have long been solicitous of the poor, such as when reformers first objected to child labor, and during the limiting of working hours in England and the United States. But the poor should be free to sell themselves at the going price, and any interference in the "free" market hurts those who would willingly and out of dire necessity sell themselves into the worst forms of wage slavery.

Such views never die. Defenders of these positions always see those who call for social legislation and programs of redistribution as anticapitalist. Perhaps we are. When I arrived in the South during the 1960s civil rights movement I was accosted, if that is not too strong a word for it, by an elderly black woman who wanted to know whether I was a Communist. I was taken aback for a moment and she went on, "I sure hope so. We read all about Communists in the local paper and that they were coming to help us get our rights to vote. I sure hope you're one of them." And so it turned out I was. We can expect that those who fight for global social justice will be denounced by the media defenders of the status quo. And perhaps like the early Christians who followed Jesus and shared what they had, the activists in faith-based groups like Jubilee Plus can aspire to be truly "communists."

At the same time we should not mistake the grounds for disagreement within the establishment. One wing, represented by the Clinton folks, presents bailing out the Wall Street lenders as good for the people of the debtor countries and for the stability of the world, seeing the painful conditionalities as necessary to ensure that the bankers and bondholders got their money. The Republican critics represent the other wing of the establishment, which believes that this amounts to social engineering, that capitalism needs the market to do its work, and if speculators make bad loans they should not be bailed out. Bailouts undermine the effectiveness of the market mechanism, which is harsh but fair. If governments do not intervene, bankers will be more careful about who they lend to and governments that borrow unwisely will have to take their medicine. Neither wing cares much about the people of the debtor countries, who bear the burden either way. The Clinton side represents an internationalist management style of indirect control through the proxy of the global state economic governance institutions. The Bush folks represent the laissez-faire style of domination. They also see dangers in encouraging social engineering, since it opens the possibility of legitimating debt forgiveness, and redistributional measures of other sorts that undermine market discipline.

The IMF has reacted to the attacks from civil society by responding in a variety of ways, with the intention of fostering the perception that it is committed to a new level of accountability. It has agreed to set up an independent watchdog to monitor its activities, a permanent evaluation office that reports to, but is, or so it is planned to be, structurally independent of the board. "The decision," we are told, "will mark a decisive break with the past practice of self-evaluation by operational departments, supplemented by occasional reports commissioned from outside consultants."[21] The recommendation came from a group of board directors as a way "to enhance its credibility with outside observers." That is, they are trying to walk the line between the conflicting approaches of the establishment, tacking strategically as power balances change under the pressures of global civil society.

The Development Banks

The World Bank responded to NGO critics by accommodating some twelve hundred citizens' organizations from sixty-five countries in a dialogue and on-the-ground evaluation of the World Bank's in-country programs. The Structural Adjustment Participation Review Initiative (SAPRI) is designed to produce evaluations and recommendations to the Bank and governments for changes in structural adjustment programs and economic policy more generally as it affects the poor of these countries, people who are the majority of their citizens. The extent to which these initiatives will legitimize local knowledge and priorities and the degree to which they prove distractions and simply the demobilization of righteous anger remains to be seen.

The hope is that they will empower movements for progressive social change. The fear is they will lead to cooption and not to change of the fundamental direction of policy, from the top down. In the triangular struggle between Third Way left-centrists, right-center free marketeers, and the radicals of the Global Justice Movement these agencies attempt to finesse strategies that serve to legitimate the workings of corporate globalization.

But even by appearing to respond to all demands, the appearance of commitment to stronger social policy has worried those such as the *Wall Street Journal* and *Financial Times* columnists, who see this as cozying up to anticapitalist movements, granting them harmful real influence and legitimizing their perspectives. For example, whereas the free-market ideologues call for more deregulation, studies by the World Bank point to the need to combat economic insecurity after an era of liberal reforms, suggesting that conventional unemployment insurance and public works programs are needed (although they stress self-insurance as the preferred approach because administrative capacities are limited). In one such report World Bank researchers note, "Perceptions of economic insecurity run high in the region" (the report is on Latin America). "Indeed, there is a widely held view that economic insecurity has become so pervasive that it could undermine social and economic support for the ongoing reform process, and even bring it to a halt."[22] The writers are aware that the way they can achieve change in this, as in all other matters, is to argue that the powerful will benefit from the proposal. "You will be hurt unless you give the oppressed and exploited a little," otherwise you encourage their organization and give them nothing to lose by rebelling. "It is cheaper to buy them off with some token concessions," could be a cynical translation.

It is easy to be distrustful of the people who administer the global state economic governance institutions. Their activities have accompanied a grave deterioration of the life condition of countless millions. I would not myself, however, want to demonize such individuals. I cannot know, but it seems to me that to take a job in such an institution requires a certain concern for the well-being of the poor. But the sort of people who qualify live in a bubble of taken-for-granted affluence and live lives far removed from the conditions of those they are paid to help. Over the last two decades evidence of the failures of the neoliberal theology has mounted to the point where there has been a real questioning. Thus when Tadeo Chino took over as head of the Asian Development Bank (ADB) in 1999, it was against the background of two years of crisis in the region during which, as he said, "Millions have lost their jobs and cannot find work. Women, children, and the disabled and the elderly are suffering the most. Many are malnourished; more are prone to illness."[23] Mr. Chino, who most had considered "just another Japanese bureaucrat," made the goal of achieving a poverty-free Asia the overarching aim of his term at the bank.

Of course what such priorities mean in practice is a different matter. To focus on infrastructure, as such regional development banks do, doing things like building roads and airports to encourage economic growth, may or may not have much direct impact on those who have suffered most from the collapse of the financial bubble in the region. That the ADB has opened a dialogue on poverty and is acknowledging that equity is a more important issue than the bank had previously emphasized, when its focus was single-mindedly on economic growth, seems like a good start. But, still, in the minds of the region's activists, the ADB has been slow to implement change. Ana Maria Nemenzo, a vice chairperson of the National Anti-Poverty Commission in the Philippines, urges the bank to get around to understanding the nature of the political economies of the region, which structurally practice social exclusion and make the reproduction of poverty a natural part of the way economics works. "Poverty is not just material deprivation but a lack of opportunities and access to power to enable an individual to fully participate in the life of the community or nation," she says.[24] The Philippines is not the only country where a small group controls the wealth and exercises the power. For the Asian Development Bank, or its counterpart in any other region, seriously fighting poverty would require a commitment to social revolution, which is highly unlikely despite the best will and sympathy for the plight of the oppressed and the exploited, people who are excluded and marginalized in systemic fashion.

I would like to think that Mr. Chino, Mr. Wolfensohn at the World Bank, and the others involved are most sincere in wanting to help the poor. How far they go depends on those powerful groups and individuals who control the resources, and on how much pressure they feel from the Global Justice Movement and the broader public. With prodding from civil society, the World Bank has announced a number of initiatives. For example, at the World Education Forum in Dakar in April 2000, James Wolfensohn declared that the World Bank stood ready to lend "multiples" of the $2 billion it was currently devoting to education programs each year. The resources would be focused on poor nations that produced comprehensive programs for enrolling more children in school, for eliminating illiteracy, and for ensuring that girls have equal access to education. The commitment came at a time of "unusual public pressure"[25] on the Bank and the IMF to do more to alleviate poverty and protect the environment. It was followed a week later by another proposal, aimed at fighting poverty at the grassroots level through a focus on empowerment, an approach that stirred the ire of the free-market-defending pundits.

In many ways the debate over empowering the poor is reminiscent of the war on poverty struggles of the Lyndon Johnson presidency. The government, trying to respond to the civil rights and black liberation struggles, called for empowerment as a strategy, and it began war-on-poverty–funded government services that did things such as provide offices to help the poor help themselves. Whether this represented progress or cooption depended on one's viewpoint. It was attacked by conservatives as social engineering and as a dangerous pandering to the unreasonable activists. The government poverty warriors saw it as social justice. The politicos in the Democratic Party saw it as cooption and solidifying the party's urban base. But as the independent movement lost steam it turned out to be fairly easy to shut these programs down. They were called ineffective because the token amounts of funds they had at their disposal did not change the inequalities of what many saw as the institutional racism of the American system. It was said that progress could be better left to the market, and so it was. Poverty levels, which had declined in the 1960s—in some measure thanks to the investment in inner cities, in their children, in job-creation programs, and in other measures—soon started to rise again.

Martin Wolf recently reminded the World Bank that "it is not Oxfam." The Bank cannot, he declared, "run with both the progrowth, pro-market hares and the anti-growth, anti-market hounds. It has to choose between them." The Bank, in questioning whether the sort of economic growth the free market by itself provides was enough to help the poor, had sinned, according to the *Financial Times*'s most influential columnist. The Bank's 2000 *World Development Report* was misguided, and the Bank had better watch its step. The draft had, in Mr. Wolf's view, downplayed the benefits of rapid growth. Equally, it had questioned the benefits of market-oriented liberalization. "In short, it came closer than is either right or sensible to the anti-development, anti-liberalization position espoused by many NGOs." In Wolf's view, the world's poorest countries must go for growth above all else. "The World Bank must represent the views of its shareholders, not those of non-governmental organizations that are suspicious of economic growth, the market and globalization."[26] The World Bank had crossed the line. *The Economist* agreed, stating the hard-line free-market position with admirable clarity: "There is no prospect whatsoever of appeasing the marchers, who will be satisfied only by an outright repudiation of capitalist development. By tending in their direction, rather than defending liberalization and globalization on their merits, the Bank is only empowering (as you might say) its enemies and helping them to recruit allies from the middle ground. Meanwhile, the development message the Bank has rightly been pressing gets increasingly blurred."[27]

The Bank was criticized by the social movements as well, and its officials felt frustrated that their attempts to meet criticisms had not been reciprocated. "These are issues that need to be debated around tables," says Caroline Anstey of the World Bank. "It is hard to debate them in the streets." A Friends of the Earth spokesperson responded, "We have been trying to reform the IMF and the World Bank from both inside and the outside for over a decade. . . . We have tried lots of dialogue, and it has got us nowhere."[28] The two-sided criticisms reflect the position of the global state economic governance institutions. They are established by the powerful to pursue an agenda. The agenda is perceived as seriously harming the many for the benefit of the few. Activism against their activities increases. They respond by trying to patch things up without actually abandoning their mission, as it is seen by those who pay their bills and ultimately control their agenda. As a result they are then seen as both making overly substantial concessions and not doing enough to reform themselves. They claim to be for real democracy, but the financial press sees them as skirting real concessions to the anti-systemic forces too closely.

From the antisystemic side, it is said that "The World Bank and the IMF are all for democracy as long it doesn't go too far. When people start saying the system doesn't work for them and they want something that serves their interests, these external donors get nervous. That's a definition of politics they don't want to hear."[29] Bank reformers must ward off those suspicious of its activities as cooptive as well as those who see them as making unwarranted concessions to antisystemic forces. Which perspective is correct? I would think both to some degree. If the people at the base struggle, they win concessions. The more effective their struggle the more substantial the concessions will be. The extent to which the system can make cosmetic changes early enough, it wards off demands for more fundamental changes. To the extent to which market ideologues insist that no concessions be made, the less change will appear to be possible, and the more that pressures may at the same time build up, to the point of explosion. Such a dialectical tension is always at the heart of struggles to change the system. For all of its professions of good intentions and lessons learned, the independence of the Bank remains circumscribed by the power of the United States. The Bank has made massive loans at the behest of the U.S. Treasury and State Departments while insisting that borrowers meet "objective" standards. As Robert Wade commented in early 2001, "The need to manage the inconsistencies makes hypocrisy a way of life at the Bank—saying different things to different audiences and making declarations of intent that cannot possibly be carried out."[30]

After Seattle

Divisions are evident among those who unite to demonstrate against the global state economic governance institutions. Not only are their priorities different—labor rights, the environment, community development under local control, debt forgiveness, and so on—but some think institutions can be reformed, whereas others wish to abolish them. Some look for a new consensus. Others see any presumed consensus as ultimately unfair to smaller, less powerful countries who will be browbeaten by the major powers. In the post-Seattle environment, there has been a casting around for a new institutional formula. The criticism of the G-7—the group of major industrial powers that includes the United States, Canada, Japan, Britain, France, Italy, and Germany, and that is the peak organization for global decision-making—has gotten louder. Why is Italy a member, but not China? Why Canada and not Brazil? The old imperialist club does not speak to twenty-first-century reality. The United States has played with the idea of a G-20, consisting of the G-7 and a small group of what are called "systematically significant" economies, including China, South Korea, and Indonesia. Something like a G-20 may prove to be the venue for expanding the informal dialogue between the United States and an expanded group of "serious" players in the global economy. Whether such a change is "enough" remains to be seen. Certainly it will not be enough for the social movements, either in the "smaller" countries or generally, movements that do not see the governments in those countries as representative of the interests of the majority of their citizens, that see them as beholden to the business community and "bad" on issues of social justice. The situation remains fluid and is complicated by the multiplicity of actors and the two-level game of simultaneous international and domestic negotiation and the "third dimension" that is added by the activism of global civil society.

It may have been the business community's fear of the demands for social regulation of the economy that led to the widespread opposition to Clinton-Gore despite the reality that they pursued free trade and liberalization of the global economy to a greater degree and perhaps with more success than could have been achieved by a Republican administration. What a Democratic administration single-mindedly committed to the goals of U.S.-based transnational capital can achieve is great, because it is more difficult for the party's base to go into opposition. Yet to achieve these goals they must take some steps to meet the demands of that base if they are to achieve their greater designs. What the Clinton administration was proposing by way of reform may have been too much for many in the U.S. business community. As the centrist, Third Way state actors and global state economic governance institutions look for greater legitimacy and workable reforms, "U.S. multilateral companies prefer talking to individual developing world governments rather than going through a long, multilateral process. This," says Bruce Stokes, a senior fellow at the Council on Foreign Relations, "gives business an unfair advantage."[31] Stokes is concerned that unless the World Trade Organization gets it together and comes up with workable dispute-resolution mechanisms the transnationals can live with they will abandon the organization.

Reeling in the aftermath of the Seattle shock, as the costs of "free" trade were driven home by turtles and teamsters, by complaints from developing nations that their agenda had been ignored, and by deep division among the United States, the European Union, and Japan, the WTO lost momentum. Criticism focused on the United States and the ways in which it had mismanaged the Seattle meetings and attempted to force its agenda down the throats of all the other participants. The World Bank, while it had made a greater effort to involve civil society, found its new focus on good government meeting political resistance from client states, and it found its emphasis on political empowerment met with suspicion by free-market conservatives. The steps it took to meet its NGO critics were met with suspicion as well. The establishment seemed divided on what was to be done. In the United States, the Bush electoral coalition was oriented very much toward business, rather than toward Wall Street, as the Clinton administration was. Bush also owes more to social conservatives and is less in tune with the liberal wing of the establishment, which typically supports multilateral approaches such as those pursued by Clinton. George W. Bush is, of course, not beholden to support from labor or the environmental movement. As soon as the election was over, this compassionate conservative was unmasked as the most conservative president the country has known since Calvin Coolidge, or possibly William McKinley.

Fearful of the breach with much of the Democratic Party's base on the eve of the 2000 presidential election, Mr. Clinton called in an interview in Seattle during the WTO meetings for sanctions to enforce environmental protection and labor rights. The assumptions of the Clinton approach have been well stated by Robert Lightizer, a trade lawyer and deputy trade representative in the Reagan administration, who found that while in fact President Clinton failed to lay out a specific proposal, "Mr. Clinton's statements are important nonetheless because he implicitly admitted that a global free market will not by itself raise standards throughout the world. It cannot be assumed that businesses and countries will get rich and do the right thing."[32] While Mr. Lightizer understood that the road to enforceable standards will be a long one, he said, "Only negotiated enforceable minimum standards can solve problems in basic areas like protecting workers and the environment. The World Trade Organization is a long way from addressing these issues; it has virtually no regulations governing either."[33] That of course is why the demonstrators were there. It is unlikely the president would have made the statement otherwise. Clinton had traveled some distance on the issue, though pushed every hesitant step of the way by the popular movements in the streets, by the NGOs, and by their supporters who compose a large part of the Democratic Party's electoral base.

Given the opposition to the North American Free Trade Agreement (NAFTA) a newly elected Bill Clinton had had to wait to submit the treaty to Congress until he had completed side agreements, which he claimed offered mechanisms to protect the environment and labor rights in the setting of free trade and investment with Mexico. Given the furious reaction to the GATT's tuna-dolphin decision, NAFTA specifically stated that the provisions of international agreements on endangered species, hazardous waste, and ozone levels take precedence. The Commission for Environmental Cooperation set up to assess environmental impacts allowed nonbusiness participation and greater process transparency. A number of NGOs, including the Audubon Society, the National Resources Defense Council, and the World Wildlife Federation, endorsed the NAFTA agreement as a result of these concessions. Others, Public Citizen and Friends of the Earth among them, continued to strongly oppose it. The support President Clinton received from environmentalists was critical to NAFTA's passage. While congressional Republicans continued to strongly oppose inclusion of either labor or environmental standards, and many governments of developing countries opposed them fearing that sanctions would be used to punish their economies in a disguised protectionism, the movements of civil society, both in the rich and in the poorer countries, supported such measures, and they put pressure on the Clinton administration and social democratic governments in Europe.

The election of George W. Bush signaled a change in tactics from Clintonesque multilateral negotiations to a simpler America First exercise of naked power. The Clinton administration, before leaving office, concluded a trade agreement with Jordan that included both labor and environmental provisions and announced that its agreed-upon pact would be a model for future ones with Chile and Singapore. The Bush people rejected such a tying of these standards with trade. They moved ahead with a Free Trade Area of the Americas, encountering huge Seattle-style demonstrations in Quebec in the spring of 2001 as they sought to move this project forward in meetings with hemispheric leaders. Bush changed the terms of the debate dramatically. He had chosen as his secretaries of labor and the environment individuals who were anathema to unions and environmentalists, women firmly opposed to the Clinton approach, which was at least rhetorically reconciliatory. The Bush U.S. trade representative was a man who eschewed the social engineering approach of the global state economic governance institutions and followed policies that relied more directly on free-market forces in areas in which the United States had a strong position. The Bush strategy was to as fully as possible marginalize the NGOs and to move quickly into new arrangements to liberalize trade and investment bilaterally and through expanding a North American free-trade zone. There was less interest in any development strategies for the poorer countries, other than those that relied on the unalloyed market mechanism.

Shortly after Mr. Bush's hundred-days-in-office marker, on Earth Day (April 22) environmental groups highlighted Mr. Bush's decisions to reject an international agreement on global warming, abandon a pledge to reduce carbon-dioxide emissions, soften new efficiency standards for air conditioners, and delay rules relating to arsenic in drinking water. Probably no issue has caused more political damage to the president than arsenic. His decision to delay the arsenic standard was a boon to the mining industry, a main contributor not only to arsenic in our groundwater but to the Republican party. Of the $1.7 million the industry directly contributed to candidates and committees, more than 80 percent went to the president's party. Of the smaller amount of money environmental groups donated, more than 90 percent went to the Democrats.[34] It was payback time.

After George W. Bush took office the U.S. Chamber of Commerce, which represents thousands of small and medium-sized companies, had a now receptive White House to which to argue for the total separation of trade agreements and pacts on labor and the environment. But the Chamber does not speak for transnational capital. The big companies, aware that fast-track authorization was unlikely without some concessions to labor and the environmental movements, began to jump ship. The solid front of business interests was breached as companies such as Kodak, Motorola, and others with major export markets at stake sought compromise rather than risk imperiling the trade agenda they wanted from the Bush administration. It was clear to many of the leading U.S.-based transnational exporters that it was essential for the president to accept labor and environmental standards to prevent congressional Democrats from holding up free-trade agreements and to get fast-track authorization.

CEOs and their advisers were debating how far they would have to go. As Peter Scher, who had been a deputy trade representative under Clinton and was representing several big companies under Bush, explains, "It's clear that there is little hope for enacting any new trade deals without addressing labor and environment, and business knows this."[35] For companies like Boeing and Caterpillar, acceptance of some level of recognition of the Global Justice Movement demands is just good business sense. Many of the same corporations who lobbied hard in the 1997 fast-track fight, which they lost, have changed sides. "The E.U. [European Union] is poaching on our turf in Latin America," complains Johanna Scheider, spokeswoman for the Business Roundtable, which represents 180 of the country's biggest companies. "Our CEOs are concerned that we'll fall behind."[36] The corporations are looking for "mushy" provisions that, like the side agreements Clinton came up with to ensure the passage of NAFTA, while they end up not meaning much, are enough to win the support needed to pass the legislation. It remains to be seen how the advocates of strong and meaningful environmental protections and labor rights respond to these overtures. As in debt cancellation, a topic to be discussed in the next chapter, commitment in principle to the concerns of the Global Justice Movement does not necessarily mean adequate progress will be made. What these developments do show is that when well-organized social movements in civil society successfully mobilize public opinion they can effect policy and change the world, to some extent. How great their impact will be is a matter of how sophisticated they and their opponents are in mobilizing the resources they can bring to bear.

3

Debt, AIDS, and Today's Colonialism

While global state economic governance institutions create a new neoliberal constitutionalism that protects their expanding rights as it disciplines countries who do not cooperate in the progress of corporate globalization, a small number of giant corporations are growing more and more powerful through mergers and takeovers that are transforming the structure of global markets through cross-border alliances. At this point in world history, there is a basic conflict between those who celebrate these twin developments and those who worry about the far-reaching authority of nonrepresentative and nonelected governance institutions and the growth of monopoly power. In this latter group are those who see the need for international enforcement of antitrust laws, as well as those with a more radical, antisystemic critique who see such mild regulations as inadequate to the scope of the problem. In the more radical group are those who see imperialism, or a new colonialism, at work, and those who decry the control, by the transnational corporations and the United States government, over the global state economic governance institutions. There are also those who see the globalization process as basically a positive process and who welcome the role of the United States, seeing the process not as recolonization but as a necessary and positive integration that needs to be speeded up because it is the only hope for the poorest countries.

Representing the Global Justice Movement perspective, Ignacio Ramonet writes, "The world is experiencing a new age of conquest, reminiscent of the days of colonialism. But whereas the protagonists of previous phases of conquest and expansion were national states, this time the drive for global domination is coming from big companies and conglomerates, major industrial groupings, and the private finance sector. Never before have the world's masters been so few in number and so powerful." Ramonet observes that "these groupings have their bases within the 'triad' of the United States, Europe and Japan—but half of them are based in the U.S. What we are seeing is fundamentally an American phenomenon."[1] From this Global Justice Movement perspective what is needed is an alternative model of globalization that addresses demands for social justice and the redistribution of wealth on behalf of a more democratic and inclusive world society. Advocates of corporate globalization, on the other hand, see the market bringing real choices, better choices, to people who up to now have not had them. They see capitalism and democracy as a package; market freedom as requiring political freedom; political democracy and the rule of law as protecting property rights and setting the conditions for economic success.

At such a level of generalization each argument becomes a closed thought system and there can be little in the way of productive debate between them. Because there is some truth to each, some conversations go by each other, and others remain confused. The issue of whether poverty, exploitation, and alienation are produced by exclusion from the world system, or by the way peoples and economies have been incorporated into the world system, divides the partisans at a basic level. It is unlikely that such differences can be reconciled. Yet, is it possible to acknowledge, on the one hand, that the freer the market the greater range of choice, while at the same time to admit that too many people do not have the resources that would allow them to exercise much freedom in the market? Can we on the one hand say that the global economy produces more wealth, while at the same time say that the manner in which it works re-creates poverty? Can we agree that there is a very serious lack of political freedom in many of the poorest countries and still concede that the dictatorships that exist and the divisions that dominate were nurtured by the colonial powers and later by the needs of the great powers during the cold war? Is it possible to say that autocentric development through delinking with the global economy is neither possible nor desirable and still reject the free-market version of investment in which the foreign investor's bargaining power allows a disregard for the needs of citizens and the priorities of local communities?

From a global state economic governance institution's perspective the need to become more intrusive to foster democracy serves the function of making penetration easier and more profitable for transnational corporations by creating class rule by a new modernizing elite tied to foreign capital. Such a local governing class, they think, ensures freer markets and more efficient allocation of resources. Democracy and free markets together, they say. But what is produced, say movement activists, is precisely elite rule, which solidifies the hold of foreign capital by putting a smiley face on systemic oppression and privilege. This is hardly the same thing as fostering grassroots democracy, in which money does not buy elections and all citizens are encouraged to participate in discussion and policy making. From the Global Justice Movement perspective, this is the problem with reforms from outside and above. They serve the interests of elites and do not empower the people. Such reform from above is consistent with continued mass poverty. With these differences in mind, we consider one of the key issues for many members of the debt-cancellation coalition.

It is surely the case that the frequently unacknowledged problem that nation-states lack meaningful sovereignty, on the one hand, and, on the other, that they may be ruled by incompetent, venal, and brutal elites leads to the argument that to give such countries more resources is simply to enrich the moneyed and the corrupt, while doing little to help the poor. It is possible to conclude that it would be a good thing if the global state economic governance institutions were to make the encouragement of good governance a priority. By insisting, to the extent that their substantial leverage allows them to, on a rule of law, procedural transparency, and honest administration, they could enable the growth of democracy and help foster conditions in which a free market could operate. Still, however, to demand democratic reform under such circumstances often has the effect of allowing a modernizing elite to replace a rent-seeking one.

One of the difficulties that world poverty presents to concerned progressives is that many poorer countries are run by dictators who do not care about their people. Much of the debt burden they face is the result of corruption by local elites (albeit in collusion with Western bankers and governments). How are the people to be helped without feeding the corruption that is systemic in many of these countries? How is one to best criticize without feeding the "what can you do" pessimism concerning aid from the rich to the poor? This chapter examines these questions. It suggests that the history that led to the present situation is important if one is to understand the very radical changes that are needed.

The political order under which the people of much of the world now suffer is the legacy of colonialism and of the greed of foreign investors. The cold war was excuse for supporting this order, indeed for putting in place brutal and undemocratic regimes that, armed by outside interests, now fight frequent civil wars over the spoils of diamonds, oil, and other riches—little of which trickle down to the people. In recent years a new scourge,

AIDS, is crushing Africa and is spreading fast in Asia, Eastern Europe, and elsewhere, devastating the development possibilities, as bleak as they already are, in many of these places. Corporate globalization and the neoliberal policies of the global state economic governance institutions have been responsible for the creation, perpetuation, and failure to adequately address all of these problems to a significant degree. It is important to spell this out so that the discussion of "debt forgiveness" and other aid can be seen in a broader context and the question of what role now exists for the global state economic governance institutions can be discussed.

The condition of many of the world's "failed" and "failing" states, especially in Africa, is a matter of great concern. Charles Onyango-Obbo, who is editor of the *Monitor* newspaper of Kampala, Uganda, writing in the *East African,* published in Nairobi, Kenya, in the summer of 2000, tells of a friend who has given up on the Kampala government. Nothing new there, of course. What struck Onyango-Obbo are the reasons for his despair. He says everyone understands the Kampala government is corrupt, but what his friend can't comprehend is that it lacks the vision of a "good" corrupt government "because it is not doing anything to help people produce more and create more wealth so that it has something more to steal tomorrow." He encounters the same despair in reports in the British press of the murderous rebellions in Sierra Leone. These reports quote local people as begging the British to return and recolonize the country. "It was for the usual reasons. Unlike the British colonialists, past and present Sierra Leonean leaders and rebels raped the wealth of the country and put nothing back. In between bouts of looting, they passed the time chopping off the hands and legs of the people they had robbed." In Onyango-Obbo's opinion, "The British at their worst as colonists were still better than past and present

Sierra Leone rulers at their best, some people reasoned, obviously driven to that extreme position by desperation."[2]

The danger in such an argument is that in stressing internal mismanagement, gross corruption and brutality, the role of foreign capital, the plundering of slavers and enslavement through colonial rule, other things—such as imperialist exploitation, the current reign of international enforcement agencies, the deterioration in the terms of trade (the purchasing power received per unit of agricultural and extractive exports), and the militarization of the continent during the cold war and its lethal aftermath—are not stressed enough. The Atlantic slave trade lasted four hundred years, European colonialism another hundred, and, after colonialism officially ended (from the late 1950s to the mid-1970s), the African states soon fell under the tutelage of the IMF and WB. The analysis of the 1981 World Bank study of the collapse of the African economies (known as the Berg Report) declared that Africa's problem was excessive state interference in the market. By the mid-1990s the whole region had adopted a structural adjustment package of programs pushed on them by the IMF and WB. But the problem has not been too much state intervention, but the absence of an effective state. The problem is state incapacity and state collapse, a reality the World Bank has only belatedly recognized.

The legacy of the cold war, a period when the United States armed dictators, empowered military tyrants, and arranged for the assassination of popular leaders who favored a nationalist alternative to continued neocolonialism, has been of particular importance to the creation of the current situation. It was the thoroughness with which the colonial powers closed off alternative paths that accounts for the present state of so many countries, most especially in sub-Saharan Africa. The arms-pushing and continued support of dictatorial rule, which outlived the cold war, the refusal to address the essential unsustainability of the drain of debt repayment, and the refusal to consider liberalizing agricultural imports to Europe and the United States to protect domestic interests, all play a part in the tragedy. So of course do local elites in many African countries. There is plenty of blame to go around.

Even with regard to slavery, it needs to be remembered that the Atlantic slave trade involved the participation of Africans who enslaved and sold other Africans, and that slavery today— brought to public attention in April 2001 with reports of a ship off the coast of Benin carrying more than two hundred children into slavery in West Africa, and evinced in efforts by religious groups to buy slaves their freedom in the Sudan—is about Africans enslaving other Africans. If we accept Anti-Slavery International's definition of a slave as someone "forced to work under physical or mental threat, and where the owner or employer controls the person completely—where a person is bought and sold," then slavery is the state for millions of people who are now enslaved. Slavery is a very real and widespread problem, and surely not only in Africa.[3] In most areas, such slavery is both the legacy of the poverty in which the vast majority of formerly colonized persons find themselves and of the attitudes of ruling elites that were inherited from their colonial masters.

Because I write from a U.S. position in the world system and tend to emphasize the role of my own government, it is perhaps all too easy for me to "background" or ignore how oppressive elites in many impoverished countries can be and how oppressive British, Dutch, French, German, Portuguese, and even Italian colonialisms were, not to mention the legacies of governance structures, personnel, class domination, and dependency they left in place, along with the continued interventions of Western governments in their former colonies. The British foreign office exerts pressures on the Commonwealth countries long after the flag has been lowered and its sun has set. John le Carré's *Constant*

Gardener is the truest kind of fictional tale of transnational capital. In this novel the immorality and murderous practices of the giant pharmas (pharmaceutical companies) and the supporting role of the British government drive the plot. Indeed, as the book was being published the *Washington Post* in late 2000 broke a story about Pfizer's use of the experimental drug trovafloxacin (commonly known as Trovan) to treat a 1996 meningitis outbreak in Nigeria's Kano district. At issue was the company's alleged breach of global ethical guidelines on pharmaceutical trials. It is claimed that, as in le Carré's novel, a new drug was tested on children without their or their parents' knowing it was a trial for an experimental drug. Children died. Many others were left with disabilities, an eerie echo of the le Carré novel in which Kenyans (not Nigerians, as in the Pfizer case) are allegedly used as guinea pigs by a greedy Western pharma. In both cases governments with cozy relationships to foreign capital are blamed for collusion in rubber-stamping the trials without due diligence.[4] We can look to press clippings of French paratroopers restoring or overthrowing some Francophone government to be reminded of some of the more obvious interventions of the colonial powers in the so-called Third World. The use of torture and deliberate killings of guerrilla suspects by colonial authorities have been widely documented, as has the business profitability achieved at all costs, of interventions in the affairs of formally independent former colonies. The reality of such cynical, crude interventions matches any fictional accounts.

The core capitalist nations, the colonial powers, the imperialists, and the adventurers who extracted the wealth of the continent and framed its developmental possibilities along with their local collaborators and allies have a great deal for which to answer. During Africa's liberation struggles the United States backed the colonial powers, and late in the game they still continued to do so (as in Angola and Mozambique) as these societies struggled to expel the Portuguese. This country wanted to hold on to NATO bases in Portugal and so backed the pro-Portuguese terrorist militias. Through the cold war the United States installed and maintained dictators in what are today some of the most undemocratic countries on the continent, including not only Uganda and Sierra Leone but the Sudan, Zaire, and others, giving weapons and aid to governments with horrid human rights practices. It is well understood that the poorest countries with the worst development prospects are those that have been most heavily involved in wars and civil wars. It needs to be remembered that the United States supplied the weapons and the training in eight out of the nine currently warring countries. The number of poor in Africa rose by almost 50 million during the 1990s. When you force open such economies to the world market they do not compete well. And if the scramble for Africa a century ago involved military face-offs among the great powers, these interimperialist rivalries continue today as embassies jockey for local influence in pursuing better deals for "their" corporations and collude when the privilege of foreign capital in general is challenged by local governments. Opening to the free market is as much a process controlled by foreign economic interests as was the subjugation of these nations by colonialism and neocolonialism after formal independence.

When it is said, "Why can't these people govern themselves honestly and efficiently?" all of this history and continued dominance is a large part of the answer. There is an unfortunate path of dependence at work. It surely should be obvious why, when the same people who are responsible for the problems say, "We are here to help you," there is widespread suspicion of their motives. Solutions that will perpetuate structured inequalities and allow a new basis for surplus extraction are thus expected. Both the existing and future division of wealth and poverty are related to the way in the past colonialism and imperialism constructed a particular mode of capital accumulation and created a social structure to support its goals. Today debt is being used to further concentrate wealth and power on a global scale and demand economic restructurings favorable to foreign investors. This is perceived as injustice in the same way that colonialism and enslavement in earlier eras were.

While Africa is very much in the news as this is written—and we shall focus on the AIDS crisis there because it is a prism through which we can discuss a number of related issues of importance—its people are not the only ones who suffer from the manner in which the world system operates. Of the 6 billion people on the planet a quarter live below the international poverty line, a level below which a minimum nutritionally adequate diet plus essential nonfood requirements are not affordable. The *United Nations Human Development Report* indicates that a third of all human deaths each day are poverty related, that the growth of two of five children in the developing world (as it is called) is stunted, and that hundreds of millions of people are chronically malnourished. Two billion people live without electricity and a billion without safe water. The number of people who live on a dollar a day or less increased to more than 1.3 billion over the past decade. They live in countries that have been important sources of raw materials and human chattel, which has been a basis for the accumulation of wealth for the advanced economies. As income from their agricultural and extractive industries that is available for national development has decreased, many of these economies have been going backward. They are not developing economies so much as failed and failing nation-states. Debt cancellation would seem a minimal demand if these problems are to be effectively addressed.

The International Labor Office in Geneva reported in 2000 that child poverty has risen sharply in the world since the mid-1960s. There has been a breakdown of families, unemployment has increased, and there has been widening of income inequalities. The vast majority of the population in most developing countries has no social protection at all.[5] The *Human Development Report* showed the accelerating income inequalities between North and South to be growing more rapidly than at any time in the previous two centuries. In the summer of 2000 Oxfam, the respected NGO development agency, reported that there would have been 1.7 million fewer deaths that year had the world's governments met pledges they had made at the 1995 social development summit in Copenhagen. It foresaw that none of the targets promised for the year 2015 would likely be met. If present trends continue, 8.5 million children will die that year, more than half of them in Africa.[6] Sub-Saharan Africa accounted for 38 percent of total child deaths at the end of the twentieth century but their share will rise to 57 percent by 2015 unless there are changes in the expected trends.

The Oxfam report called for a "bonfire" of the tariffs and nontariff barriers that so disproportionately affect the poorest countries. Nicholas Stern, the chief economist at the World Bank, agrees. "Industrialized countries' protectionism is indefensible: it is estimated to cost developing countries more than they receive in official aid each year."[7] The twenty-nine rich countries who are members of the Organization for Economic Cooperation and Development spend more each year on agricultural subsidies (to the detriment of the poorer countries, who are unable to export products as a result) than the total gross domestic product of each country in sub-Saharan Africa. The tariffs maintained by the rich countries for their agriculture are highest where the poorer countries are most able to effectively compete. The rich also practice tariff escalation. Tariffs are even higher on processed raw materials in order to prevent the agricultural producers from being able to move into industrial processing based on their agricultural product's comparative advantage. Tariffs are particularly high on such labor-intensive products as textiles, in which the poorest countries have comparative advantage. The rich do not believe in free trade when it is inconvenient for them. Further, given that the price of non-oil commodities has declined since the beginning of the twentieth century, poverty is likely to keep increasing in countries that continue to depend on such products.

The issue of tariffs imposed by the rich that hold down the poor is finally receiving prominent attention, thanks in significant measure to the street protests and the educational efforts of the NGOs. Consider the case of sugar, which is in the news at this writing. When, post-Seattle, the European Commission took up a plan to eliminate trade restrictions on imports from the forty-eight least-developed countries in the world, they encountered stiff resistance from European agricultural lobbies. The sugar industries in Britain, France, and Germany were opposed. The producers of rum, rice, and some fruits and vegetables likewise resisted. For the sugar producers, who enjoyed restrictions and subsidies that allowed them to keep sugar prices at three times world levels, giving in without the most serious fight was unthinkable. But this seemingly straightforward leveling of the playing field to help the poorest of the poor is not so easily managed.[8]

From the other side, a country like war-ravaged Mozambique has received help from the World Bank, which lent it money to construct sugar mills and sees a promising future for the industry in that very low-income country. But the IMF, where free-market orthodoxy reigns, told Mozambique it must stop subsidizing its sugar industry and remove its tariffs, which protect it from foreign sugar from the United States (where subsidies to Florida's high-cost sugar producers are also destroying the Everglades, at taxpayer expense; the leading firm in Florida is run by two brothers, one who is a major funder for the Republicans,

the other to the Democrats). Matters are as bad in the United
States as they are in Europe, where subsidies are at approximately
the same high levels. As Oxfam spokesman Seth Amgott observes, "When only poor countries have to open their markets,
it's not free trade, it's global plantation." "We're not a bit concerned that the IMF supports free-market policies for sugar," says
Amgott, "but it's dogmatic and ideological to advise Mozambique to stop protecting its low-cost sugar producers if you do
nothing about the U.S. and European Union protecting high-
cost sugar producers."[9] The IMF argued, along proper lines of
pure comparative-advantage-theory logic, that Mozambique
shouldn't waste its money competing with subsidized foreign
producers but instead should take "advantage" of their cheaper
sugar. Because other countries subsidize their industries doesn't
mean Mozambique should. It insisted Mozambique quickly
phase out its subsidies.

The World Bank disagreed, and it continues to offer financial
aid. It sees the industry as a success in a country with few suc-
cesses and knows that if it shuts down, the workers employed
therein will not automatically be able to switch into some other
industry that will, as abstract trade theory with its assumption of
full employment would have it, automatically absorb them. Simply saying the free market will provide seems hollow, inadequate, and irresponsible. After embarrassing publicity, Horst
Köhler, as the new head of the IMF, overruled his economists
and allowed Mozambique to develop its sugar industry. Indeed,
a study by World Bank economists finds that, in the short term,
greater openness to trade by the poorer economies slows income
growth among the poorest 40 percent of the population. Even
though there may be long-term benefits from freer trade, the
costs of adjustment are borne predominantly by the poor.[10] Despite the oft-made claim to the contrary, the benefits have not
gone to them.

In the poorest countries the impact of the IMF's harsh course of treatment was simply to encourage a downward cycle of economic decay and death. Because the debt overhang meant an extended period of austerity, it produced capital flight rather than encouraged investment. Educated citizens looked for better opportunity abroad. Those with money took it out of the country to the point where perhaps 40 percent of the investable wealth of Africa is now outside the continent. It is the restoration of locally healthy conditions, and an expanding economy, that will attract investment and produce economic growth. Yet the austerity imposed by the debt collectors produces just the opposite conditions. In Africa, governments spend 40 percent of their national budgets on interest payments on a foreign debt that will never be repaid, and they have done so for a long time.

In Latin America, according to Ricardo Haussmann, chief economist at the InterAmerican Development Bank, commenting in 2000, "Latin Americans are in a state of worrisome pessimism and perplexity." Polls show that Latin Americans believe that "their countries are in bad shape economically, that people lived better in earlier generations, that poverty increased a great deal, and that income inequality is unjust." Helped by greater computer power and access to more usable information at the end of the 1990s, researchers were finding that inequality was hurting growth. Nancy Birdsall, a senior researcher with the Carnegie Endowment for International Peace in Washington, commented that "it is one of the big reasons Latin America is growing so slowly. It is not surprising if half the population isn't on the production and productivity bandwagon."[11]

As we saw in the last chapter, the IMF has made the situation worse. In Brazil in 2000, when a new government announced it planned to spend more than $22 billion on social programs over the next decade, the IMF argued the monies would be better used to reduce Brazil's indebtedness, rather than to do things like fight poverty. The IMF's representative in Brazil, Lorenzo Perez, said the government's plan "established a precedent that could be dangerous." Mr. Perez said, "Brazil already spends a significant amount of money on social programs. The money has to be used more effectively." After a national and international uproar, it was not only the leaders of the powerful and militant Brazilian Workers Party who called for Mr. Perez's expulsion from the country. Mr. Perez backpedaled and declared that "after further study," he "did not think the plan carried macroeconomic risks."[12]

The cost of decades of debt is writ large in the health and education budgets of impoverished countries and in the deterioration of public services and quality of life generally. An unsustainable burden that was initiated by banks lending irresponsibly and that is attributable in many cases to rulers who stole these same monies outlasted some of the worst of the cleptocracies. For decades the IMF has been squeezing debt repayment out of debtors at the expense of the poor and has not regarded external debt burdens as a major impediment to the development prospects of these countries. Fund officials assumed that the discipline of debt repayment served a positive function of encouraging these nations to adopt better (i.e., neoliberal) economic policies. The structural adjustment programs that went along with debt rescheduling were a key development strategy from the IMF's perspective. Successful growth would result and thus ease the burden of remaining debt. After two decades and more, for some countries, this has, however, not proven to be the case. Under pressure from debtors, from Western NGOs, and from broad public opinion, and especially from the debt-relief campaign spearheaded within the religious community, and facing the reality that the debt is just not payable, the IMF and World Bank have reacted. The G-7 initiated debt relief, but it has been a slow process, heavy on rhetoric and short on achievement.

It took more than twenty years from the time of the Latin American debt crisis and the other crises addressed through IMF conditionality and World Bank structural-adjustment programs before the leaders of the G-7 accepted that, for many heavily indebted poor countries (HIPC), the debt was simply not payable. In October 1996 the World Bank and the IMF agreed to the first comprehensive debt-reduction plan for these poorest nations. The promises initially proved disappointing, because the conditions imposed to qualify for limited debt forgiveness were stringent. No country was able to meet them for some years after the first "generous" steps were taken by the global state economic governance institutions. Debt relief was held up by the U.S. Congress, which did not approve its share (a mere 4 percent of the wealthy nations' total, or $920 million over a four-year period). Small as the amount was, the noncooperation of the United States stopped the process from going forward. The goal of debt forgiveness for twenty of the poorest debtors during the Jubilee year, 2000, was initially met with skepticism in Washington and by IMF officials. But pressure from the pope, from rock stars, and from millions of ordinary citizens around the world pushed the process forward, making it harder and harder for the politicians and staff economists to deny the campaign.

The Debt-Relief Initiative for Heavily Indebted Poor Countries (the HIPC Initiative) was announced at the 1996 Group of Seven Summit. A half dozen years later it had made very little difference for most of the forty-two poorest Third World nations the debt-relief plan was supposed to help. Even if fully implemented, it would reduce each of these countries' debt service by an average of only 37 percent. A majority of the countries that have gotten reduced-debt payments continue to spend more toward debt repayment than they spend on health or education. The current official debt load of the forty-two HIPCs is now $175 billion, which they cannot pay. Reducing the debt to "sustainable" levels given their situations leaves them with very great burdens and is very different than debt cancellation, which is what the Drop the Debt coalition is demanding. They point out that the standard of living of these HIPCs in 2000 was 25 percent lower than it was two decades earlier.

The basic assumption of the HIPC Initiative is that the global state economic governance institutions cannot cancel debt. They concede the debt owed by the poorest countries is unpayable but do not want to use their own funds to absorb the losses. They therefore are waiting for the G-7 to come up with the money to pay off these bad loans. Critics on the political left suggest that the global state economic governance institutions and the U.S. Treasury refuse the demand for debt cancellation "not because of the cost, which is peanuts to these institutions, but because the current mechanisms keep them in control of the economies of developing countries. If the debt were canceled, people in these countries would be free to implement their own economic policies, and they would be much less likely to accept the demands of the IMF. Thus, by supporting refinancing the current system, as opposed to debt cancellation, one supports refinancing the system of oppression."[13]

More free-market-oriented critics are also critical of the loans and endorse the proposal made by President Bush to turn loans to the poorest countries into grants. The International Development Association, the division of the Bank that makes forty-year loans that carry an interest rate of 0.75 percent to the poorest countries, in effect is making these countries a gift of 75 percent of the money (if we calculate the opportunity cost of the loans over this period at market rate, and calculate its present value). George W. Bush's suggestion is that monies for education, health care projects, and other investments with high social returns be termed grants and thus go to countries that show they use the money effectively (he has suggested educational testing and other results-oriented yardsticks be applied). The World Bank estimates that, if 50 percent of the loans were turned into grants, the United States would have to double its annual commitment to the Bank if the amount the Bank was able to extend to the poorest countries was not to diminish. The United States currently spends only one-tenth of 1 percent of its gross domestic produce on foreign aid, less than half the proportion it spent just ten years ago. This country is far less generous than other advanced countries on a per-capita-share-of-income basis, and most other countries oppose the idea of grants in place of loans unless the Americans commit additional funds at the same time, something the Bush administration has not offered to do. In fact, the IMF and World Bank are doing little to lift the burden from the poorest countries, and the U.S. and G-7 countries have been slow to bring any new monies to the table.

This has led to a certain cynicism on the part of those who believe that none of this should be surprising unless one takes at face value the claims of the global state economic governance professions that they are there to help the poor. They suggest that if we accept as a working hypothesis that these are agencies of imperialism, their actions appear consistent with their true mission. Hiding this mission, pretending they are there to help, makes it easier to do the bidding of transnational capital more effectively. You may not agree. But in many minds the evidence of their activities suggests that the imperialist-tool theory is not without merit and the "we are just do-gooders who occasionally go astray" interpretation—while not unreasonable at the level of individuals who may remain idealists while working for these agencies, and who may not be totally without merit—when applied to their institutional, structural role in pursuing corporate globalization, challenges credulity.

In support of the idea that the Western democracies are not doing much to help the poorest countries, there are a number of issues that are raised by the way debt relief is presented. First, there is far less generosity than meets the eye. Most of the debt would not have been paid back in any case. The money lent is gone and the economies of the debtor countries are too weak to afford repayment now or in the foreseeable future. As the *Economist* points out, "If there were a secondary market these loans would be trading at no more than a few cents on the dollar."[14] The large face value of the loans is therefore misleading and bears no relationship to any realistic expectation of what might have been repaid. Most importantly, to date there has been very little real debt relief, even measured by the face-value standards of the global state economic governance institutions. As Robert Naiman, senior policy analyst at the Center for Economic and Policy Research in Washington, wrote, in response to Horst Köhler's claiming credit for the IMF's debt-forgiveness program, poor countries approved for debt relief "are still paying more in debt service than they are spending on health care for their own people. One country, Zambia, will be paying even more in debt service in the future than it did in the past."[15]

The IMF is engaged in its own public relations and lobbying campaign. Part of its new approach, as we have noted, is to put boilerplate directives on poverty eradication more centrally into its policy. Indeed, as part of the new approach, each country, in order to borrow from the IMF and WB for macroeconomic stabilization, now produces a poverty-reduction strategy paper (or PRSP), in which it outlines plans for growth and poverty reduction. The letter of intent the country signs with the global state economic governance institutions has a list of benchmark indicators to measure progress in both areas. But the new procedure looks to many very much like the old one. The governments complain that there are long lists of conditions that must be met—only now they are more about poverty-reduction matters. They say such conditionality and the supporting documentation that is required slows the process of resource transfer. The IMF is still obsessed with inflation reduction, even though there is little evidence to indicate that moderate rates of inflation, below, say, 20 percent, damage growth in poor countries, rather than encourage it, as many think. NGOs and other representatives of civil society acknowledge that the global state economic governance institutions are now more willing to consult with them, and that there may be less arrogance, but they are not ready to say any of the recent changes make a significant difference in how these institutions basically operate.[16]

Debt forgiveness raises issues that have generally not been addressed by campaigners and progressives who implicitly or explicitly assume that debt-forgiveness-freed monies will be spent on human services. As the *Zimbabwe Independent* editorializes, "Will canceling these debts free Africa's toiling masses from years of economic bondage? We think not. There is no guarantee that leaders, once given a reprieve, will not persist with the same habits that got us into this mess in the first place." The editorial asserts, "What is the point of further aid and loans that simply relieve recipient governments of having to decide where priorities should lie? Why should Zimbabwe's rulers, for instance, stop spending $142 million on defense every year when they know gullible Western donors are prepared to underwrite health care and rural infrastructure?"[17] The newspaper urged selective debt cancellation conditioned on political and economic reforms that would be predicated on transparency and accountability, the rule of law, and so forth. They were not alone in seeing the greatest obstacle to economic development as not the debt but the political class that had squandered or stolen their people's resources. The pattern of perks for the top leaders, the subsidies that favored them and their friends and families, and the failure to collect taxes from the local elite in basically corrupt regimes means that there is no guarantee or, in many cases, any likelihood that the money made available will be spent on the needs of the poor. At the same time, efforts to closely constrain debt forgiveness through conditionalities have produced complex politics. It is true that meaningful aid, wisely delivered, would be the better course. Blanket, unqualified debt forgiveness does not guarantee how governments will use the breathing space granted them. Yet desperately needed debt forgiveness has been delayed by those attempting to work out such new conditionalities.

Anne Krueger and T. N. Srinivasan, two leading trade and development economists, suggest that "it would make far more sense to allocate resources directly to areas such as education and health through nongovernmental organizations with a proven record rather than forgiving debt. If foreign aid is received only upon demonstration that education, health, or other appropriate social expenditures are being undertaken, there is no way that government can funnel the resources to other uses."[18] But of course the rich countries have not been willing to extend funds for foreign aid. The desperate need for help has been overwhelmingly clear for some time. But with the end of the cold war the hardheaded policy makers in the advanced countries, especially in the United States, have turned their attention elsewhere—to Star War proposals and other big weapons systems, for example. Even during the cold war years, economic development was only the most minor part of geopolitical thinking. Debt forgiveness, as difficult a campaign as it may be, is easier than facing the essential nature of the odious debt that was contracted by elites and foreign bankers over the heads of the debtor nations' people. Debt cancellation, given the conditions under which the debt was contracted, is more appropriate in many cases. As to foreign aid targeted to meeting basic survival and developmental needs, a real commitment to meaningful levels of resource transfer has proved politically impossible. Debt forgiveness of essentially unpayable debt is a minimal concession.

It does not address the depth of the structural problems the poor face. It is not intended to do so. Its purpose is to legitimate unequal exchange in the world system, disarm critics of capitalism, and coopt liberal reformers.

Increasingly, Americans favor foreign aid to the world's disadvantaged. About six in ten favor giving aid to foreign countries (as of 2000, that number is up from fewer than half of Americans who favored foreign aid in the late 1970s). However, as has been noted, the United States gives only 0.1 percent of its national income in bilateral foreign aid and only 0.02 percent of its national income to the least developed. On a per capita basis each American contributes only about $29 a year to international development, compared to a median amount of $70 in other developed countries. Moreover, the congressional budget resolution provides for no growth in the foreign affairs budget from 2002 to 2011.

The United States's aid is based on realpolitik criteria, not on need or effective utilization of funding. Only 5 percent of U.S. aid goes to the least advantaged countries. Half goes to two countries, Israel and Egypt. Most of the rest goes to other client states who are not low-income countries but rather who have some strategic importance to U.S. foreign policy makers or who are important to domestic constituencies in the United States. In total, American foreign aid declined by an average of 8 percent each year in the 1990s, and it is the lowest among the rich donor nations as a percentage of gross domestic product. It is only because the campaign for debt forgiveness has been so effective that its critics now talk about better ways to do the job and get an audience. The United States has touted a "trade not aid" policy orientation but, as has been noted, puts up barriers to exports to U.S. markets from the poorest countries (as do the Europeans). Taken as a whole, sub-Sahara's exports are overwhelmingly agricultural and, as noted, face stiff tariffs in Western markets. Foreign transnationals profit from the misery of the poor in many areas, from mineral extraction to arms sales.

If the executive branch targets most of foreign-aid funding for geopolitical security reasons, the Congress earmarks foreign assistance as payoff to domestic constituencies, which support reelection of those who control key committees. Thus, Republican senator Mitch McConnell of Kentucky was one of the leading critics of U.S. foreign aid. He believed that USAID should be abolished until the Republicans took control of Congress in 1994, and he became chair of the Senate Appropriations Foreign Operations Subcommittee, the panel that funds aid programs. He used this position to channel funds to Kentucky contractors, including the University of Louisville and Western Kentucky University, as well as to the Mitch McConnell Conservation Fund.[19] Over the years Senator McConnell allocated hundreds of millions in aid to Armenia, and although there are fewer than three hundred Armenian Americans in Kentucky, out-of-state Armenian Americans and their organizations were among the most generous of the senator's supporters. It was a good investment. By donating a couple of hundred thousand dollars a year in campaign contributions, they win millions in tax dollars for economic aid to Armenia. Indeed, the Armenian Assembly, the group that spends such amounts lobbying, receives millions in USAID grants. Roughly a third of its income comes from the U.S. taxpayer through the foreign-aid program, money that is earmarked to set up training programs for private organizations in Armenia.[20]

Alternative proposals, from within the United Nations system, for "adjustment with transformation," proposals that stressed sustainable development and increased assistance to disadvantaged countries, and that spoke to the need to reduce inequalities between the more developed and less developed countries on a less politicized basis, have not gotten much of a hearing in Washington. Similarly, rather than let multilateral development lending be arranged through the United Nations system, the United States prefers the World Bank, where it exercises more direct control. Lending to debtor nations that face crisis is done through the IMF for the same reason. Setting up the IMF and WB outside the control of the United Nations and with a decision-making structure of "one dollar–one vote" was done precisely to enable the rich and powerful to control the international economy without input from the majority of the nations of the world, those who had different ideas on how the governance of the global community might be structured. The debt crisis was addressed in Latin America so as to necessitate the dismantling of import substitution industrialization and to force open markets to foreign corporations and financial institutions. The transformation from communism was guided by these institutions to ensure that the most free-market version of capitalism was adopted, despite the social costs of shock therapy and the dismantling of the social safety net. In East Asia, the financial crisis was made worse by IMF-imposed conditionality, such that foreign capital could gain control of local assets at bargain prices and the state-led model, which had been so successful, could be undermined to the benefit of the transnationals.

The Political Economy of AIDS

The South African economy is predicted to be 17 percent smaller in ten years than it would be without AIDS. By 2010, there are expected to be 2 million AIDS orphans in South Africa. According to UNAids, the disease will cut Kenya's gross domestic product by 15 percent by 2005. Zambia has lost the equivalent of ten years of growth. In Malawi, between 25 and 50 percent of teachers will have died from AIDS by 2005, by which time 60 percent of the health budget will be spent on AIDS-related illnesses.[21] In

Zimbabwe, a personnel officer confessed to a visiting journalist that he had hired three people for each semiskilled job he had to fill, expecting two of them to die in training. Half the executives in a company turn down promotions because an HIV test is required.[22] Husbands infect their wives and mothers infect their unborn babies. Families are destroyed. Breadwinners fall ill, and others must take care of them. Meager savings are used up, and without money for food the uninfected grow weaker. Many AIDS orphans, ostracized by their communities, turn to prostitution to survive. Governments spend more and more resources on the spreading social costs of AIDS-caused problems.[23] Businesses steadily lose skilled workers and face higher and higher absentee rates and medical costs. And the disease has not yet peaked, even though 17 million Africans have already died of it. As globalization integrates the world and travel and migration accelerate, infection spreads rapidly. AIDS is not just in Africa but in Asia, where HIV infections in India, though now relatively low, may, not so far in the future, surpass those in Africa. The disease is also spreading rapidly in Russia and in Eastern Europe. It is only when AIDS threatens to undermine profit opportunities in these areas that the plague receives attention.

U.S. officials have reached the conclusion that the impacts of AIDS are so vast as to constitute a threat to U.S. national security. Seeing the plague in these terms, the United States's National Security Council, which has never before been involved in combating an infectious disease, is directing a rapid reassessment of the government's effort and asking for a doubling of its budget request to combat AIDS overseas.[24] At the same time, the United States is challenging South Africa's efforts to make lower-cost AIDS drugs available to its people as a violation of the intellectual property rights of U.S.-based pharmaceutical companies. The United States, which had written trade rules and patent-enforcement provision extensions to maximize U.S.

transnational profit making, was faced with the stark cost of such profits-before-people policies. The most striking instance of this brand of profit seeking is the effort by U.S. transnationals to prevent AIDS drugs from being sold at low cost in Africa. Governments are harassed when they act, within their legal right, to require compulsory licensing for local production and pursue parallel importing of drugs from lower-cost sources, instead of paying prices demanded by Western pharmaceutical companies.

The law that received the ire of the U.S. trade representative was passed by the South African parliament in 1997. It applied to all medicines, but the focus of the debate has been on AIDS drugs. The law allows the importation of commercial drugs from third countries, where these drugs are available at lower cost, and it calls for compulsory licensing, which allows local companies to produce generic versions of drugs. The WTO allows both practices under certain conditions, which the South African government asserts are being met. But American trade officials challenged South Africa's right to allow such practices, declaring the law is written in too broad a manner, and they have threatened retribution to force the South Africans to abide by rules the United States prefers.

Then–Vice President Gore, the Clinton administration's point man in helping the pharmaceutical industry make money off AIDS drugs, was met by hundreds of chanting demonstrators on the campaign trail who were shouting "Gore's greed kills" and waving signs in front of TV cameras. The vice president, locked in a close campaign, arranged for a delay in U.S. actions and a quick, if vague, compromise. The drug companies too looked bad. Some of them promised to negotiate steep cuts in the price of AIDS drugs with South Africa and other poor countries in the region. This had the advantage of not committing them to any concession on intellectual property rights claims. The Clinton administration backed away from attempting to

punish South Africa for hurting the profits of U.S.-based pharmaceutical companies. President Bush's very first foreign policy
action was to defund international public health and family planning by not allowing monies to providers who also offer repro-
ductive health information and abortion services using money
from other sources. His next action was to review Clinton's executive order supporting the right of African countries to import
or produce generic AIDS medicines that are still under U.S.
patent.

The United States received favorable action from the WTO
for its request that a panel be established to decide whether Brazil
was in violation of WTO intellectual property rules in its AIDS
program. Brazil had slashed the number of AIDS-related deaths
by 50 percent in five years. Brazil spends an average of $4,716 per
AIDS patient per year. The same treatment costs about $12,000
in the United States. The drugs are produced at low cost by a
state-owned pharmaceutical laboratory. U.S. drug makers are
unwilling to lower their prices enough, so the Brazilians prefer to
make their own drugs for distribution and, in doing so, lowered
the cost of the AIDS drugs by more than 70 percent in a few
years.[25] The outcome of such cases will depend on what pressures the WTO and the drug companies are under. Some prominent economists have raised the question of whether it is even
the WTO's remit to deal with intellectual property. Jagdish
Bhagwati of the Council on Foreign Relations suggests that intellectual property rights protection "is for most poor countries a
simple tax on their use of such knowledge, constituting therefore
an unrequited transfer to the rich, producing countries." He
thought that the WTO was turning, "thanks to powerful lobbies, into a royalty-collection agency, by pretending, through
continuous propaganda that our media bought into, that some-
how the question was 'trade related.'"[26]

The Global Justice Movement and key NGOs did not let the

issue drop. In early 2001, Oxfam, the Oxford, England–based campaign against world hunger, initiated a separate campaign to force the transnational drug companies to cut prices on life-saving drugs to poor nations, accusing the companies of "waging an undeclared drug war" against poor nations by keeping drug prices high and continuing to threaten trade sanctions.[27] They were joined by such groups as Doctors Without Borders and ACT-UP, the U.S.-based AIDS activist group. At GlaxoSmith-Kline, the world's largest pharmaceutical company, which had been targeted, shareholders became nervous and morale dropped among employees. Large institutional investors threw their weight behind the campaign. Oxfam accused GlaxoSmithKline of systematically using patent rules to squeeze low-cost copies of branded medicines off the market and urged it to forgo patents in Ghana, Uganda, and South Africa, where it said the company was using legal maneuvers to block the import of cheap medicines.[28]

The drug companies were attacked by an energized and redirected candidate Gore toward the end of the 2000 U.S. presidential campaign, when Gore, who had been falling behind, turned populist briefly (and inadequately) in the hope of winning working-class votes. One of the reasons the pharmaceuticals backed down to the degree that they did on the AIDS issue in Africa was that people at home were beginning to draw a more complete, and not very flattering, picture of the industry. It did not escape notice that at the start of the twenty-first century Americans pay the highest prices in the world for prescription drugs. Elderly people here spend more on medicine than on doctor bills. By 2000, drug expenditures had doubled from 1993 and were expected to double again by 2004 (according to a study by the Health Insurance Association of America). Health plans cut back on drug benefits and many Americans are not covered at all, paying high prices from limited incomes and making this a life-and-death issue for millions of Americans. The AIDS crisis focused attention on such larger issues concerning the total irrationality of treating health as a commodity and what that means in a world that contains striking class inequalities.

Not only have the multinational pharmaceutical companies actively obstructed every national and international reform effort on drug supplies and sales, they have lobbied the U.S. government to withhold contributions to the World Health Organization because of the WTO's drug policies that are aimed at the development of generic supplies. As Meredeth Turshen, an Africanist who has followed the issue, reports, "The World Bank brought a halt to the innovative work on a public drug sector at about the same time it displaced WTO as the leading international agency setting the global health agenda."[29]

The pharmaceutical companies say that the high costs are necessary to finance the expensive research and development that goes into producing the miracle drugs that have become so valuable to extending lives and making them more comfortable. But this oft-repeated claim does not stand up to scrutiny. As Merrill Goozner reports, "Every independent study that's ever looked at the sources of medical innovation has concluded that research funded by the public sector, not the private sector, is chiefly responsible for a majority of the medically significant advances that have led to new treatment of disease."[30] Much of the research by the pharmaceutical companies is devoted to copying drugs already on the market from competitors, the drugs they create making no greater contribution than those already available. For our purposes, it is important to note that most drugs for treating AIDS are the result of government-sponsored research. While Glaxo Wellcome claims that it developed AZT, it was the National Cancer Institute working with the staff of Duke University that developed the technology for determining both that AZT could suppress the live AIDS virus in human cells and in what concentration it would affect humans in the desired manner. The private company was not the one to first administer AZT to humans with AIDS, nor did it perform the first clinical pharmacology studies on patients. It also did not perform the immunological and virological studies. They have however grown rich from the patent of drugs developed by government and university researchers.

In contrast to U.S. actions to prevent countries with medical crises from importing generic substitutes, Canada awarded a contract to a non-licensed manufacturer of Cipro during the anthrax attacks in the fall of 2001, thereby ignoring Bayer's patent. The German drug company said it would be willing to supply Cipro (their trade name for the antibiotic used to fight anthrax), but to no avail. Although it hadn't yet experienced a recent case of anthrax, Canada was nevertheless willing to infringe its patent laws due to an announced medical emergency. This sent powerful reverberations through the pharmaceutical industry, which was defending patent protection for AIDS medicines in poor countries. The U.S. quickly followed Canada's lead, in its case using the threat to buy generic substitutes to force major price concessions from Bayer. Only a handful of people in the U.S. had died when the government asserted the very rights it had denied to countries that had been decimated by AIDS. Much of the world was quick to see the hypocrisy. And some also warned that the actions of the U.S. and Canada were shortsighted and would discourage research into new drugs: for if companies were to be forced to lower their prices they would not risk the vast sums necessary to develop them.

The pharmaceutical companies *do* invest tens of billions of dollars in research each year, but mostly in the hunt to find drugs to grow hair, relieve impotence, and fight fat. They are looking for drugs with large money-making potential. The National Institutes of Health, which spends about as much on research as the

entire private sector and is the source of much public-sector research in health care, is responsible for far more progress than the
corporations. A National Bureau of Economic Research study of
the twenty-one drugs considered to have the highest therapeutic
value of those introduced between 1965 and 1992, showed that
public research led to fifteen of them. Most innovative drugs
would have taken far longer to discover without research by
government labs and noncommercial institutions.[31] Patenting
in biomedical research enforces secrecy and slows sharing of
important results (since once a result is published it can't be pat-
ented).[32] Patents are also used to prevent competition, as companies patent alternative processes and whatever else they can to
preserve monopoly power. Further, unless substantial profits are
anticipated, there will be little or no interest in research. They do
not do work on malaria or sleeping sickness (a truly terrible disease whose name is totally misleading), since these diseases are
not a serious problem in rich countries, even though they are
devastating in poorer ones. Thus, diseases that affect the poor
are not studied by profit-maximizing pharmaceutical companies,
although should cows, pigs, or sheep face the same health problem there will be research, since the animal market is valuable in
the West. Most medicines to treat tropical diseases have resulted
from work done by the U.S. Army or financed by private companies that do research on livestock and pets. Since Africa accounts for 1 percent of world drug sales (while North America,
Japan, and Western Europe account for more than 80 percent),
Africa's poor lack "effective demand" and so are ignored by the
market. As James Orbinski, international president of Doctors
Without Borders, says, "He who can't pay, dies."[33]

Even taking drug company research expense claims at face
value, their marketing costs and profits far outstrip the monies
they claim to spend on research. GlaxoSmithKline reports to
investors that it spends 37 percent of its revenues on marketing

and administrative costs and only a third of that amount on research. After all costs, the firm has 28 percent of its revenues left as profits. GlaxoSmithKline is the world's largest manufacturer of AIDS drugs. For example, it has sold one such drug—Combivir—for about $7,000 per person per year in the United States even though it can be made from ingredients that cost about $240 on the generic market. Cipla Ltd., a manufacturer in Bombay, India, says it offers a finished generic version of Combivir for about $275. The $80 million the pharmaceutical companies spent on the 2000 congressional campaign, a record for any industry, could be amply funded from such profits. Such contributions were an investment in trying to retain its privileged position and to keep the public from understanding what the true economics of the industry look like.[34] The Europeans have sided with the poorer countries and the campaigners for cheaper drugs who favor a tiered pricing system that allows poorer countries to shop for cheaper generic drugs. The European Union is trying to prevent the fund from being turned into a subsidy for Big Pharma. The Bush administration is trying to prevent greater use of generics.

But the story is more complicated. It has not helped that the most high-profile African elected leader, Thabo Mbeki, South Africa's president, has disputed the cause of AIDS, delayed recognition of the problem in his country, and questioned the safety of the use of AIDS drugs. President Mbeki was widely criticized for raising questions about the different nature of AIDS in South Africa and in the West. He asked how the conditions of poverty affect the way AIDS/HIV develops. While this is a standard epidemiological question, his rejection of mainstream Western medical advice has delayed South Africa's treatment program, while he explored dead ends. Yet the impact of bad water, malnutrition, and poor access to care highlight the wisdom of Louis Pasteur's comment that "the microbe is nothing, the terrain everything." Eileen Stillwaggon, a researcher who has written on the relationship between poverty, disease, and underdevelopment, has responded to the attacks on Mbeki by noting that "populations in poverty are also characterized by malnutrition, parasite infection, and lack of access to medical care and antibiotics for bacterial STDs [sexually transmitted diseases], which are important co-factors for transmission of HIV. To acknowledge the synergistic relationship among malnutrition, parasite infection and infectious disease is not to say that AIDS itself is a nutrition disease."[35] She is not alone in pointing out that AIDS also makes the body susceptible to secondary diseases like malaria, tuberculosis, pneumonia, meningitis, fungal infections, and cancer, and that death from such causes is often attributed to AIDS.

Such complications suggest there may be serious questions about the figures on AIDS in Africa, which are based on the World Health Organization's definition of AIDS in Africa, and which are calculated based on a common set of symptoms: severe weight loss, fever, persistent cough, and chronic diarrhea (and *not* the presence of HIV). There are in fact serious problems with HIV testing in Africa, which often result in false positives. Malaria and tuberculosis kill larger numbers than does AIDS, and war-related violence and land mines cause more deaths, dismemberment, and disability.[36] There are questions, as well, as to whether immunization shots for children would not save far more lives per dollar (assuming the richer nations will only make very limited contributions to addressing Africa's health crisis). Because of the devastating experience of AIDS in the West there is an unbalanced and distorted discussion of health problems in Africa, one that ignores local priorities and is oblivious to the complexities of the local situations of other diseases and the impacts of poverty and underdevelopment. It must also be considered that the subservient position of women—who suffer under severe forms of patriarchy and are often the victims of rape and violence in many parts of Africa—only discourages males from being interested in taking precautions against the sexual transmission of disease. The shunning of its victims and the shame that leads to denial are major factors in the spread of the disease, such that the drug companies are only part of the story. And as U.N. Secretary General Kofi Annan has made clear, "Cheap anti-retroviral drugs, however vital, will not by themselves provide the answer." He has called for major project funding by richer governments and foundations. Even in the single-minded focus on AIDS, the United States contributed a mere $200 million, compared to the $10 billion the U.N. is seeking for the fight against AIDS in Africa, and the United States has insisted that monies be used to buy drugs from the U.S.-based pharmaceutical companies.

Jeffrey Sachs, director of the Center for International Development at Harvard University, suggested in early 2001 that "A realistic policy would go beyond fighting AIDS, committing to another $5 to $10 billion a year to a full-fledged fight on malaria, tuberculosis and other killer diseases that help keep Africa trapped in poverty. The rich countries could finance both this and the AIDS program—at between $10 and $20 billion a year—without breaking a sweat. Even the highest cost would be less than a penny for every $10 of their combined gross national product, which will be around $25 trillion this year."[37] The share for each of us would be the equivalent of a movie ticket, about $10.

Globalization calls attention to the interconnections between politics and economics, poverty and the appropriation of wealth through the exercise of power. It allows us to think about alternatives and to consider implications that are important to how the world works but that we may never have thought about before. This chapter has ranged over issues of debt and disease, economic violence, and the role of the imperial powers in civil conflicts. It has ended by making connections between the AIDS plague in Africa and the role of the U.S. government and pharmaceutical companies there and at home. Other connections and still more questions can be suggested. As drug companies merge and there are fewer competitors, it is even easier for the companies to collude in fixing prices. In the fall of 1999 six of the world's largest vitamin makers agreed to pay more than a billion dollars to resolve a class-action lawsuit that accused them of participating in a conspiracy to fix prices over the previous decade. The suit was brought by some of the world's largest food, beverage, and animal feed companies (who put vitamins in their products).[38] In markets where these big drug companies face individual buyers it would be difficult to mount such a suit successfully, given the resources of the companies and the cost of such a trial effort. Thus, since each of us loses relatively little and we have other things to do with our money (like buy the needed medicines), these international cartels, if they are able to buy off governments as they are, have little to fear as they divide up markets and share extortionist profits.

Dean Baker has made an interesting proposal based on some simple but suggestive mathematics. If the money the drug industry spends on socially useful research were to grow over the next decade at the rate it is expected to, spending would amount to about $240 billion over the next ten years. By comparison the prescription drug proposal Al Gore made during the 2000 presidential campaign would have cost $250 billion, about the same amount. If we did away with the patents on drugs and had the government supply the money for research, the American people could pay 75 percent less for prescriptions (since that is the cost once the monopoly rent from patents is taken out). Most seniors would end up paying less for drugs than if the Gore plan were adopted.[39]

The prescription drug industry has a lobbyist for every two members of the Congress. In an effort to fight a plan to legislate adequate drug coverage for seniors, the industry by 2000 had increased its campaign contributions by about 150 percent over its 1994 cycle of spending, which was already quite substantial. When criticized for such efforts to buy elected officials, the president of the Pharmaceutical Research and Manufacturers of America, the industry trade group, said all its activities were perfectly legal.[40] This may well be so, but it's a telling commentary on how powerful corporate interests have been able to have laws written. The drug companies spend millions of dollars to create seemingly independent groups that promote their agenda. For example, Citizens for Better Medicare was created by the industry association. According to David Magely of the Center for the Study of Elections and Democracy at Brigham Young University, Citizens for Better Medicare led the special interest groups in the 2000 congressional election with $65 million in spending, aimed generally at defeating Democratic Party candidates who supported expanding prescription drug coverage. His report suggested that this group, while claiming not to engage in election-related activity, ran up the vast majority of the commercials that clearly opposed or supported a candidate in that election.[41] Records unearthed by investigative reporters Jeff Gerth and Sheryl Gay Stolberg show the drug companies are the major backers of this "alliance," which describes itself as a coalition of nearly thirty organizations representing seniors, patients, medical researchers and innovators, doctors, hospitals, small businesses, and others.[42] Financial press pundits wonder why anticapitalist sentiment is growing in this land and around the world!

Globalization and the problems it creates suggest such questions and bring together various movements of global civil society: the antihunger coalition, AIDS activists, and those who think fifty years of the global state economic governance institutions is enough. As these connections are made, and groups come together, an alternative understanding of a different globalization—globalization from below—is possible. Debbie Field asks, "What would happen if a fraction of the funds now spent in the medical system were invested in ensuring that healthy food is available free or wholesale to the entire population? Or if agricultural policy were driven by a desire to reduce local hunger, increase healthy food production, stabilize the income of farmers and reduce environmental damage?"[43] What happens if a different agricultural model replaces or at least powerfully supplements the export-oriented one pushed on developing countries by the global state economic governance institutions? The AIDS crisis too provokes logical connections to U.S. foreign policy, to racism and human rights. Salih Booker, executive director of the American Committee on Africa, writes: "AIDS must be seen for what it is: a consequence of global apartheid, in which basic human rights, including the right to quality healthcare, are denied along the color line. . . . The real foreign policy priority for the United States is the threat presented by the structural inequalities that perpetuate war and poverty in a world where race, place, class and gender are the major determinants of people's access to the full spectrum of human rights."[44]

What the Global Justice Movement has done by holding up for scrutiny the various global injustices is to invite inspection of how they are woven together into the fabric of our economic and political systems. In the next two chapters connections to labor rights and environmental protection are considered in relation to how the globalized political economy operates.

4

Labor Rights and the Meaning of Democracy

As more of the global poor have been brought into the international division of labor, working in the new factories of the global assembly line, their desperate need and the coercion of their undemocratic, repressive governments have meant an expansion of sweatshop conditions. The Huffy bicycles you buy are made in Shenzhen, China, where workers put in fifteen-hour shifts seven days a week. Stride Rite shoes are made by Kunshan Sun Hwa Footwear, where sixteen-year-old girls apply toxic glue with bare hands and a toothbrush. Keds are made by workers locked in their factories behind fifteen-foot walls.[1] It is not adequate to say that people are better off under such conditions than under alternative conditions, or that efforts to improve negative conditions would lead to unemployment and starvation. The very small cost of increasing wages and improving working conditions would not raise the sales price of these products beyond what repeated polls show Western consumers are willing to pay to redress such exploitation. However, the laws of supply and demand, given the power of transnational capital and the willing collusion of local elites, make the race to minimize the production costs of such products logical and "normal." This is how capitalism works. Whether it needs to work this way or not is a question that divides movement activists. My own position is that we should continue to push for what we think is fair, and if a just economy requires changing the system, so be it. Corporate globalizers are prepared (if necessary) to accept reforms. If these reforms are enough for the movement, then the system has proved capable of the flexibility it has shown in the past when challenged. Should the movement make demands that call for deeper, more profound changes, ones that embody a different vision of how people deal with each other, the system itself will come under effective challenge. We will have to see how the situation plays out. How revolutionary the outcome will be depends on the consciousness of both the Global Justice Movement and the broader society, and on the abilities of capital to placate its critics. There is reason to think it may not be so easy to stop at mere token reforms.

There are 100 million unemployed persons in the world today (and street vendors and garbage pickers are categorized as employed, or they are not counted as part of the labor force). A billion people live on a dollar or less a day. As the homogenizing effects of globalization are felt, public policy turns away from attempting to incorporate "surplus" population into society. Without international standards, in the presence of a 30 percent unemployment and underemployment rate (the latter defined by the International Labor Organization as working, yet unable to attain a minimum living standard) for the world's labor force, desperate people are willing to sell themselves into wage slavery and parents to sell their children into literal slavery.

Only 1 percent of the projected growth in the global labor force in the next twenty-five years is expected to be in the high-income countries (according to World Bank projections). The power of capital under a regime of free markets over these years will grow dramatically and excessively so that discussion of the "unemployment problem" is likely to continue to be in terms of the need for more deregulation and labor-market flexibility. When Richard Freeman and Joel Rogers presented findings that only 15 percent of U.S. managers would welcome a union, business leaders responded that they wanted to know who they were "so we can get them fired immediately."[2] If higher-paid workers want jobs, they will have to have unique skills or be willing to work at competitive wages and in questionable working conditions. For those whose standards are pushed downward, racism, sexism, xenophobia, militia-style responses, and the practice of blaming immigrants may grow in intensity from the disturbing levels we already see.

As the discussion of unskilled labor in chapter 2 suggests, less-skilled, lower-paid workers in the United States suffer from greater trade openness and are not reabsorbed into the economy at comparable wages, and they are sometimes not reabsorbed at all. Indeed, as corporations shed labor through downsizing and plant closings and reemploy other workers as subcontractors—in satellite plants around the world and as temps at home—so local governments abandon the poor who need social services while new (unskilled) immigrants, the uneducated, and the desperate poor do jobs at the lowest rungs of an increasingly stratified society. Fairly well paid immigrant professionals are also having an impact on the U.S. job market, in computer hardware and software, medicine, and other areas. The positive role of both groups, the lower paid and the technical-professional, are usually underestimated. Immigrants today, as in other eras of U.S. history, contribute substantially to the country's development. Protecting immigrant rights is not only good for these individuals and their families but would protect other workers whose wages and conditions are threatened by the inferior treatment of immigrants.

In the United States the unemployment rate fell throughout the 1990s, but with declining job security, falling job tenure, and an increased cost of job loss. Flexibility produced a booming stock market and created more millionaires, but it also produced persistently worsening income distribution. At the end of the 1990s, the top half of 1 percent of all U.S. households owned, directly or indirectly through institutional investors, close to 40 percent of outstanding corporate stock. Eighty percent of U.S. households together owned less than 2 percent.[3] The record expansion of the 1990s did not lift all boats. The economic downturn that began in the fall of 2000 intensified following the events of September 11, 2001—their aftermath increased unemployment and compressed wages still further.

Along with the greater power of capital due to globalization has come a weaker trade union movement, especially in those countries like the United States and Britain where free-market ideology has the strongest grip. Only 10 percent of the private-sector workforce in the United States is covered by collective bargaining agreements, as a result of a powerful employer and government assault on the ability of workers to organize, which began in earnest in the early days of the Reagan administration when the new president fired and replaced air traffic controllers rather than bargain with their union.

Ironically, the United States, which campaigned under Clinton to pursue international human rights standards, has not fulfilled this goal at home. Its National Labor Relations Board (NLRB) did not favor workers' rights. The firing of organizers by employers to discourage unionization drives was not all that different than in the days of Clinton's Republican predecessors. "Without a major change in course," Roy Adams has written, "the large majority of American workers are likely to continue to be denied, against their will, what most of the world considers to be a fundamental human right—the right to collectively bargain, the right to a voice at work."[4] George W. Bush's NLRB appointments have been extremely antilabor individuals, and his Department of Labor's leadership is markedly antiunion.

Since the Reagan years, the minimum-wage law has meant

less and less. Violations of the minimum-wage law are in most cases costless to employers, who benefit, because enforcement is minimal, from paying workers tens of billions of dollars less each year than they are legally mandated to do. The Department of Labor has cut back on workplace inspections. "Voluntary compliance" is the watchword of our pro-business elected officials and their appointees. The United States's low union density, effectively the lowest among the advanced economies, might be considered a matter of worker choice except that it is so hard for workers to speak freely and organize without retribution. The threat and the experience of activists being fired is pervasive. Eighty percent of workers believe it "very" or "somewhat" likely that "nonunion workers will get fired if they try to organize a union."[5] There is ample evidence that most nonunionized workers fear victimization and that their fears are warranted. What for many middle-class activists is an involvement with helping address injustices perpetrated by U.S.-based transnationals abroad comes to include awareness of the harsh conditions of the Third World that is within our borders and the need to support unionization drives.

What starts as solidarity with the poor and oppressed workers of the Third World leads to a recognition of the conditions of workers in the United States—many of the most exploited of whom are immigrants, women, and people of color, though they also include white men—and to an examination of the labor regime in this country, which is among the most regressive of any in the advanced economies. Researching workers' exercise of labor rights in different industries, occupations, and regions of the United States, Human Rights Watch found that "freedom of association is a right under severe, often buckling pressure while workers in the United States try to exercise it" and that "any employer intent on resisting workers' self-organization can drag out legal proceedings for years, fearing little more than an order to post a written notice in the workplace promising not to repeat unlawful conduct."[6] When employers are ordered to pay back pay plus interest, any income received from other employment in the interim is deducted from the amount they need to return to the wronged worker. In any event, back pay is a small price for getting rid of union militants and organizers and it is considered a routine cost of doing business. "As a result, a culture of near-impunity has taken shape in much of U.S. labor law and practice," the report concludes.

Globalization has allowed corporations to effectively use the threat and the practice of runaway shops, that is, moving production offshore.[7] The dramatic increase in part-time and other contingent workers has weakened labor protections as well. At the same time, the frantic pace of the workplace, the long hours, the insecurity, and the low pay have produced a generation of workers who are more favorably disposed to trade unionism at a time when organized labor has shown a revitalized activism and interest in organizing the unorganized, especially the new immigrants, women, and people of color, who have been the most victimized of deregulated, "flexible" labor markets. Yet as conditions worsened for workers, unionization looked better to them despite the obstacles created by employers and government policy. By 1999, 54 percent of younger workers were "in favor of joining a union," compared to 36 percent of older workers. This number was up from 47 percent in 1996, according to a study by Peter D. Hart Associates.[8]

As we have noted, it is difficult for workers to join unions and to bargain effectively. This is especially true for immigrants, despite what is often their courageous and militant activity. As I write this, a march for workers' rights through the Bushwick and Williamsburg sections of Brooklyn, New York, organized by the Latin American Workers Project, is protesting the runaway, or "ghost," factories that sprouted up all over the neighborhood and then disappeared without paying their workers, who have sometimes not been paid for three or four months. They are also protesting the flagrant violations of minimum-wage laws and legal overtime requirements, as well as the racial discrimination, police harassment, and arrests to which day laborers are subjected for just standing on a street corner waiting to be hired for a job. The workers are also victimized by travel agents, lawyers, and others who, for thousands of dollars, offer to arrange residency papers and then tell the client the application has been rejected. The overwhelmingly Spanish-speaking workers of the neighborhood have organized for the right to live without fear as well as for fair pay and decent working conditions, and for decent housing, education, and health care, all of which services the city refuses.

It is to be hoped that as the Global Justice Movement labor-rights activists look closer to home they will join such struggles, for while it is true that conditions are typically worse abroad, labor-rights violations pervade the system everywhere. To take one example, Paul O'Neill, the Bush administration's choice to head the Treasury Department and the former chief executive of Alcoa, was reportedly confronted by Juan Tovar Santos, an assembly-line worker in a Mexican plant where he made $6 a day working for Alcoa. Tovar had been brought to an Alcoa stockholders' meeting by a Benedictine nun from San Antonio, Texas. Tovar told of conditions in the plant. Mr. O'Neill responded, "Our plants in Mexico are so clean they can eat off the floor." "That's a lie," said Mr. Tovar, and he produced newspaper clippings to prove his point. In the town where the Alcoa plant is located and where American companies get away with paying such miserable wages, these companies also pay such minimal taxes that "its schools are a shambles, its hospitals crumbling, its trash collection slap dash and its sewage lines collapsed." Half of the town's fifteen thousand residents use backyard la-

trines. A company spokeswoman said, "Wherever Alcoa operates around the world we take being a good corporate citizen
seriously." It appears the company pays no income, property,
asset, import, export, sales, or value-added taxes to the city, although with the Ford Motor Company it donated $52,000 to
build the Ford-Alcoa elementary school for three hundred students enrolled in six grades. Still, the lone teacher at the school,
when a reporter visited, complained that the roof leaked, windows fell out, and that the classrooms were surrounded by a sea
of mud.[9] Can there be a question that the goal of Ford, Alcoa,
and the other transnationals is to give back as little as possible of
what they take from the communities that create the wealth? It is
only the bad publicity their exploitative relations generate that
leads to such meager charity on their part. Social justice would
demand good schools (through fair taxation) for the children of
the working class everywhere these corporations set up shop.

The Global Sweatshop

The quality press is full of stories of class warfare, from the industrial export zones of the Third World to sweatshops in the
global cities of the core economies. As capital has gone global,
labor has learned that it must do so as well. In Las Mercedes, a
free-trade zone outside of Managua, Nicaragua, workers who
sew blue jeans are paid twenty cents for making jeans that retail
for twenty dollars in the United States. Their wages in 2001,
although exactly their country's minimum wage, meets only a
third of the cost of living. If the workers win their pay demand of
a 60 percent raise in basic pay, the impact would be eight cents
extra for each pair of jeans produced. The company fired leaders
of a strike and set up an in-house company union, saying it did
not want to deal with the strikers. The company that owns the
plant, Chentex, is part of a Taiwanese consortium called Nien

Hsing. Taiwan has given the country millions of dollars to build its presidential palace and other projects for the right-wing government of the country. When a Taiwanese journalist questioned the use of "dollar diplomacy," Nicaragua's president declared in a national radio address that he was a Communist spy.[10] The International Labor Committee based in the United States has made the case a cause célèbre, effectively publicizing the treatment of the workers and conditions in the plant. It has brought delegations to Nicaragua and workers from the plant to the United States to tell their stories. These actions have been effective. President Clinton's trade representative, Charlene Barshefsky, wrote to the Nicaraguan government demanding that conditions be improved at the Chentex plant and she threatened the loss of benefits under the Caribbean Basin Initiative, which gives Central American and Caribbean *maquila* products access to the U.S. market tariff-free. The Bush administration, however, did not follow up this initiative. Again, these are the two faces of the establishment as it defends capital. The reformist wing wants to take the edge off class struggle by addressing the worst abuses. The hard core says let the chips fall where they may. We have the power. To show weakness only encourages them.

But even where the U.S. government shows no interest in involving itself in such matters, the publicity generated by solidarity actions can produce results. The Workers Rights Consortium, which includes sixty-seven universities as members, sent a delegation to investigate a Nike contractor in Puebla, Mexico, in early 2001. It reported the factory violated child labor laws, fired strike leaders unjustly, and intimidated union supporters. The factory made sweatshirts bearing the names of many U.S. universities, including Georgetown and Purdue. Nike, having learned something about the impact such disclosures could have, said it was interested in resolving the situation "fairly and expeditiously" so that all the plant's workers are "treated with dignity and respect." It added that the Consortium's report was not objective.[11]

Whatever the outcome in any of these particular struggles it is clear that the solidarity movement has made progress. Better-known companies do not now wait for such organizing campaigns to target them. They have been stung in the past when the practices in their overseas plants have been publicized by labor-rights activists and they have learned that it is the better tactic to at least rhetorically pledge commitment to high standards for the workers in their subcontractors' plants. For many years companies profiting from sweatshop-produced goods simply said they did not control the overseas suppliers and would not give any information on which contractors they used, saying this was a company secret and they did not want to make such information available to competitors. It took years before the protesters began to be effective, publicizing these connections and the horrible conditions of workers sewing the clothes Americans bought. The campaign took root on college campuses. Slowly, resistant companies, which at first stonewalled, were forced to admit complicity and after saying there was nothing they could do about conditions in plants they did not own or control they were forced to take some responsibility. They mostly saw the situation as a public relations problem. The labor-rights movement would not let them escape the glare of publicity for substandard labor conditions. It has been a hard-fought battle in which the activists have stood up against some of the most powerful corporations in the world, but because brand names and corporate image are so important, by some estimates making up 40 to 50 percent of a company's market value, protecting these assets has become a major challenge to the corporations. They are vulnerable to activists publicizing their misdeeds. Companies like Eddie Bauer and Levi Strauss pulled out of Burma (Myanmar) due to widespread publicity concerning the military government's routine use of forced labor. The companies were under pressure from human rights groups and stockholder resolutions.[12] Consumers press chains like Wal-Mart and JCPenney, which buy clothes that are produced under the most oppressive conditions, to impose standards on their subcontractors.

Subcontractors are under tremendous pressure from the brand-name manufacturers to cut cost and speed deliveries. If they do not perform, they lose business. Contractors routinely violate workers' rights to meet the schedules and the cost requirements of the multinationals. Seasonal orders are particularly taxing. In the apparel industry such pressures are routine and constant. Subcontractors suppress the union movement at all costs, blacklisting organizers, having them beaten and jailed. They violate freedom of association, free speech, and the right to assemble, and they do so despite their ostensible espousal of corporate codes of conduct, visible on placards and sometimes handed out on beautiful pocket-sized laminated cards that are suitable for sending home to one's village, or giving to visiting journalists. Local officials set on maximizing economic growth hardly ever see reason to stand in the way of such practices, and it is easy to manipulate labor laws where they do exist. Yunya Yimprasert and Christopher Candland report that workers in Thailand putting in 80-hour workweeks for a subcontractor for Reebok do so with the company itself making two contradictory demands. Reebok wanted manufacturers to follow its codes and to fill orders. They note that "many manufacturers still seem to think that it is acceptable for workers in stitching lines to have their hands cut by sewing needles, for workers in assembly lines to have solvent spit in their eyes. Every day, workers complain of rashes, headaches, stomachaches, and nausea. Medical checkups, which are typically provided only once a week, if at all, attract lines of hundreds of workers. Serious accidents are common.

Most management turns a blind eye as they do with many other such occupational health and safety issues."[13]

Dexter Roberts, reporting for *Business Week* from Zhongshan, China, tells of a Wal-Mart supplier complete with a sign in its cafeteria explaining that if the plant was not living up to specified labor standards workers should call 1-800-WM-ETHIC (and presumably action would be taken to address problems). This was a plant where up to 80 percent of workers were skipping breakfast to save money. If they decided to quit their jobs and leave the factory, they would most likely not have money for a bus ticket home because they were forced to pay illegal fees and were receiving subminimum wages. Yet, overcoming fears of retaliation, they had marched to the office of the local labor officials. Given the presence of foreign observers, the labor officials ordered payment and fined the company.[14] But many such factories routinely break China's announced labor laws and violate the official policies of U.S. transnational purchasers. However, when investigators check the reality of these "protections," they often find them lacking. At the plants, conditions are often worse than the rural migrants drawn to them expected. In Chinese industrial zones their identity cards are taken by the management. They are virtually captives, risking arrest if they try to leave. Workers are beaten and fined if they do not work fast enough to please their bosses. Self-policing has been shown not to work in many such instances. Local officials collude, looking the other way or even helping to punish protesting workers, since these export plants bring revenues to the government and officials are not anxious to rock the boat, indeed it is in their interest to collude in intensifying the exploitation of workers.[15] Western monitors can sometimes catch these situations.

For many months Wal-Mart repeatedly denied any connection to a factory labor activists said was producing its products under inhumane conditions. Wal-Mart and Kathie Lee, the company whose bags were being produced in the plant, issued press releases saying reports that their products were connected to such practices or that their products were even produced in the plant in question were "lies" and insisted that they never had "any relationship with a company or factory by this name anywhere in the world." But after a three-month investigation *Business Week* reporters cut through the screen, got in touch with workers who smuggled copies of records out of the factory, and Wal-Mart was forced to concede its Kathie Lee line of handbags were indeed being produced there.[16] The company said after being caught that it had denied the truth because it was "defensive" on the sweatshop issue. Kathie Lee, along with Nike and others successfully targeted by labor-rights activists, responded by setting up an industry-financed and -controlled organization, the Fair Labor Association (FLA), brokered by the Clinton White House as cover from activists. It has its own monitoring, which certifies the good behavior of its members.

Student activists have demanded that their universities withdraw from participation in the Fair Labor Association, this industry-backed monitoring group that believes in announcing inspections beforehand and in not making public unflattering reports. It does not believe in fines and such for violators. Its executive director says its goal is not to expose but to remediate. It represents a major public relations effort by the companies who tout their new efforts. "Factory inspections—at $3,000 to $6,000 apiece—won't be cheap," said Reebok's vice president of human rights and an FLA director. "I hope the FLA can be a vehicle for communicating good news."[17] Students, unions, and religious groups left this industry-dominated group and started the Workers' Rights Consortium (WRC), which gets less than a quarter as much funding as the FLA and receives all of its monies from the dues of university members. But corporations put tremendous pressure on sweatshop activists and those who join the

Workers' Rights Consortium, independent of the industry. Nike has become infamous for canceling its contracts with universities, like Brown, that join the Workers' Rights Consortium. Phil Knight, Nike's CEO, withdrew $30 million he had pledged for a sports stadium at the University of Oregon after the school announced membership in the Workers' Rights Consortium. The University of Oregon then withdrew from the WRC and joined the FLA to please Mr. Knight. The University of Michigan, faced with the threat of losing a $28 million licensing arrangement with Nike after it joined the WRC, was forced, by Nike pressure, or rather the threat of losing so much money, to join the FLA. It now belongs to both groups, and that was enough to renegotiate its contract with Nike. Other universities may teach good citizenship, but they are hesitant to give up the free uniforms for their teams—"free" meaning they do not pay cash for them. They do carry the Nike logo and so endorse the company and its practices.

Such actions have angered and energized the student movement against sweatshops. The Clinton administration's role in covering for the corporations led to greater awareness by students of the role of their own as well as that of foreign governments in serving corporate interests. (The Bush administration is producing a new cohort of campus radicals.) The Student Alliance to Reform Corporations, started in the 1990s, in its mission statement, for example, makes the following condemnation: "The relentless pursuit of profit without conscience or regard to consequences has inflicted countless wounds on our people and our environment. . . . The era in which corporate interests take precedence over justice will end."[18]

There are those who do come out and say they are in favor of child labor. They say it teaches work habits and allows poor families to enjoy a higher standard of living. But generally the argument is more one of the high cost of making the transition before the poor are better trained, the economies in which they live more developed. Mainstream economists typically argue that the workers are getting the value of their marginal product. Markets are just. Compensation is fair and efficient. Indeed, the problem such economists see in all of this is unions and governments who force payment above the marginal productivity of workers and so are responsible for creating unemployment and hurting the poor. Matters are best left to the market. As productivity rises so will wages, and working conditions will improve through a competitive process of firms needing to bid for workers. (There is not much discussion of how the rapid expansion of the global labor force and the desperation of many of the unemployed and underemployed seeking jobs might long postpone this nirvana.) An alternative and more helpful perspective starts with the unequal bargaining power between capital and labor and suggests that social regulation of markets is necessary to raise standards and improve working conditions. The problem is how best to achieve this goal.

The stakes are obviously very high for the workers involved, but one should also consider the example these corporations set and the influence it has on the practices of others. Wal-Mart is the largest corporation in the United States (measured by sales). It is transforming retail globally because it is able to undercut competitors, forcing them to adopt its practices—which include not just the admired computerized inventory system but its antiunion policy and its use of sweatshop suppliers. As the *New York Times* reports, "Labor advocates say overseas factories that supply Wal-Mart are routinely among those with the worst working conditions. In addition, as Wal-Mart begins to compete with American businesses that are mostly unionized, labor unions, their members and some local government agencies are arguing that the company is big enough to exert downward pressure on benefits and wages across whole regions of the country."[19]

The lengths to which Wal-Mart will go to stay union-free are extreme, and until recently the company has thwarted unions at every turn. In 2000, when just eleven meat department workers in a Jacksonville, Texas, supercenter voted to join a union, the retailer approached a friendly judge in Bentonville who slapped the union with a highly unusual "national temporary restraining order." The order prohibited the union—the United Food and Commercial Workers, which had launched a recruiting drive—from soliciting workers inside its stores on the grounds that "union members were entering private store areas and potentially endangering public health." Although the judge was forced to recuse himself (the union found out he was a Wal-Mart stockholder), the order stayed in force.[20] Wal-Mart is not an extreme case, only one of the best known. The erosion of labor laws that in the 1930s were passed in this country under intense pressure from a mobilized trade union movement to protect workers, has transformed into emasculation in recent decades. It will be necessary to build a global workers' movement so that core labor rights can be made viable not only in Third World police states but here as well.

Some companies acted earlier and took the initiative to avoid the loss of reputation experienced by Wal-Mart and Nike. After sustained adverse publicity, the Gap, which had been resistant to such a move, announced it would undertake investigation and resolution of labor disputes in its El Salvador plants. Levi Strauss adopted new terms of engagement for its business partners, including those in the Pacific island of Saipan, a U.S. protectorate, a designation that enables Levi Strauss to put the "Made in the USA" label on sweatshop-produced products (a Levi Strauss contractor was underpaying workers and keeping them in padlocked barracks).[21]

The opponents of internationally enforced labor rights talk about "free trade" and say that regulating wages and hours will hurt the poorest workers. Advocates speak of workers' rights: the right to bargain, to organize freely to form unions, and to practice collective bargaining. They point to agreements already widely accepted against forced labor and child labor. Such core labor rights have been agreed upon. It is a matter of enforcing them. If workers in all countries could bargain freely they could fight for conditions appropriate and possible in their industries given local conditions. As G. Rajasekaran, general secretary of the Malaysian Trade Union Congress, has put the matter, "We are not asking for the moon, but very basic things. Workers' rights that are already universally endorsed, but simply not enforced."[22]

The five widely accepted core labor standards are elaborated in the International Labor Organization's Declaration of Fundamental Principles and Rights at Work (adopted in 1998) and are required of all International Labor Organization (ILO) members. Unfortunately, they are not enforced because the ILO has no enforcement powers. The WTO does, but it refuses to consider enforcing these rights as "trade related." What are these much-talked-about principles? The first promises freedom of association. Workers should be able to join together and to form organizations, including unions, of their own choosing. Governments may not dictate the form or internal operation of these organizations or suspend their operation. The second, following on the right to free association, is effective recognition of the right to collective bargaining. Employers may not discriminate against workers who join associations of their own choosing, or pay for the establishment of their own organization to "represent" the workers. It is incumbent upon governments to prevent such practices. Governments must also promote voluntary collective bargaining between workers' organizations and their employers (this is covered in the ILO's Right to Organize and Collective Bargaining Convention, Number 98). The third principle is the elimination of all forms of forced or compulsory labor, that is, labor performed under threat of penalty rather than voluntarily. (There are very limited exceptions for the military and in the case of national emergencies.) Fourth is the effective abolition of child labor. The Minimum Age Convention (Number 138) sets a baseline minimum working age of fifteen. If a country is less developed or if only light work is involved, the minimum age can be lower; for hazardous work the minimum age is eighteen. The fifth basic labor right speaks to the elimination of discrimination, which requires governments to establish national policies that eliminate employment and occupational discrimination on the basis of race, color, sex, religion, political opinion, and national or social origin. The Equal Remuneration Convention establishes the right of women and men to equal pay for work of equal value and other provisions applying to training programs and equal treatment at work.

Michael Moore, speaking before the WTO in Seattle, asked, "Who supports slave labor? Or prison labor? Who wants their children in factories rather than in schools? . . . None of us." In his audience was the ambassador from Myanmar (Burma), which a few months earlier had been banned from the ILO. The Burmese military rulers had also been condemned for imposing a "contemporary form of slavery" on their people. A 1998 ILO report states that government officials and the military "treat the civilian population as an unlimited pool of unpaid forced laborers and servants at their disposal" and that life under the current regime is "a saga of untold misery and suffering, oppression and exploitation of large sectors of the population." Forced labor is used to build roads, grow crops, and make products for international trade. Men and women are chained at night so they cannot escape, those who work too slowly are beaten and even killed. Yet Myanmar is a member in good standing of the WTO. When a 1996 Massachusetts law was passed that prevented that state from doing business with companies that do business with Burma, it was challenged for violating WTO principles. The lawless junta in Burma has the support of the WTO over and above those who object to the way it obtains comparative advantage in international trade. The rulers of Burma also benefit from other WTO services, such as a WTO-sponsored course titled "Internet Technology," held in July 1999 in Rangoon, the country's capital. Dennis Bernstein and Leslie Kean, reporting on this conference, noted that "the few citizens of Burma who can afford a computer are denied the right to have one. Those caught with an unsanctioned computer face imprisonment for as much as fifteen years."[23]

Child labor is often bonded labor. Children are sold into slave labor by their parents to meet debts. But most child labor is not forced labor in this way. It too is a result of family poverty in the context of a failure to create inclusive economic development. Most children who work do so in a family setting. If they are denied a chance for education and the opportunity to enjoy a childhood, it is by social, political, and economic structures of the societies in which they live, societies that are themselves embedded in global relations of inequality. But few of these children work for foreign transnationals. Preventing child labor is a different sort of labor right than the others. It is not concerned with individual rights to join associations or to speak freely and negotiate collectively with employees. The latter represent an understanding of labor rights in which the primary conflict is between workers and employers. If worker rights are protected, they will be able to progress toward a better life. Children need schools, which will afford them the opportunity for a better future. The quality of available education affects the "choice" of child labor. Yet in many countries education is not an attractive option because there are no schools nearby or because the quality of schooling is grossly inadequate to the point of wasting students'

time. Christopher Candland writes, "If one is serious about protecting childhood in Pakistan, one must focus on the improvement of education. Access to education and the quality of
education are poorer in Pakistan than in all other economies at
similar per capita income levels." Nearly 20 million Pakistani
children of primary-school age, which is nearly half of all the
country's primary-school-aged children, do not attend school.
Some of them are prevented from attending school because of
the cost of uniforms, books, and supplies, but most do not attend
school because "the education is useless. Roughly half of the
children who begin school are driven out by the absence of
teachers."[24] Actually, matters are worse than this. The public
education system in most of Pakistan has collapsed and tens of
thousands of boys are being educated in madrasahs, religious
schools funded by Saudi Arabian money for the most part, where
they learn the Koran and not much else along with the
extremist-fundamentalist ideology of hatred of the United States.
Such schools are recruiting grounds for terrorists. Due to decades
of government corruption and to the absence of educational alternatives, these are the only schools to which many parents can
afford to send their children.

When funding for education was obtained from the World
Bank and the Aid to Pakistan Consortium, expenditure on social
development increased but, Candland tells us, the infusion of
cash did not improve the schooling situation. "Elected legislative
assembly members are in charge of provincial education minis-
tries throughout the country. They now sell teaching and administrative positions. Tens of thousands of teachers are 'ghost
teachers' who collect a salary as a political reward but never in-
tend to set foot in a classroom. Newly elected officials also build
new schools without staff or supplies."

In Pakistan, as in many other countries, foreign debt repayment consumes resources, and so it is appropriate to focus con-

cerns about the protection of childhood on the international financial institutions, but it is also true that Third World governments are responsible for much of the problem as well. Both the issues of empowering workers and ending child labor are intimately related to the need for effective participatory democracy and an end to corruption. The North-South focus, while primary, needs to be broadened. Activists need to understand the class dimension of problems within as well as between nations. Labor rights concerns both issues. Empowerment of workers and their collective organizations allows for a change in the balance between class forces as well as for better immediate working conditions and more just compensation.

In this light, one of the more interesting developments of the late 1990s and the early twenty-first century has been the endorsement by the global state economic governance institutions of greater democracy in developing countries. As noted in the last chapter, the World Bank in particular has come to see corrupt Third World regimes as holding back economic growth and wasting resources transferred by foreign donors. The IMF has also recognized the importance of good governance. Its interim committee declaration, *Partnership for Sustained Global Growth* (September 29, 1996), announced that "promoting good governance, including the rule of law, improving efficiency and accountability of the public sector, and tackling corruption" are essential elements if these countries are to develop effectively. Thomas Palley, research director of the AFL-CIO, has suggested that "core labor standards fit neatly within this paradigm, since by granting rights of freedom of association, they promote political competition and independent trade unions. These are exactly the civil society institutions needed to foster good governance so that labor standards may be an important and effective means of accumulating needed institutional capital."[25] It is unlikely that the global state economic governance institutions are willing to go beyond the modernizing of societies so that "money politics" of the sort we enjoy in the United States will prevail in the developing countries. After all, if money can buy electoral outcomes, the corporate elites have the most to gain from replacing venal regimes with representative democracy. Social movements demand much more.

Resistance to labor standards by many employer groups in the developing and developed countries and the governments that reflect their interests have produced a distorted presentation of what labor rights mean. It should be clear that the five generally recognized labor rights are all qualitative and not quantitative. They endorse widely accepted norms. The problem is enforcement. Enforcement has been slowed by the purposeful misrepresentation of just what the core labor standards are and by the exaggeration of the negative effects their adoption would have on developing countries. The failure of any nation to adopt humane conditions for labor is an obstacle for others trying to improve conditions in their country. Solidarity demands that workers of the world support each other. But when workers in the advanced economies who have more influence attempt to push for global labor rights they are accused of being selfish, simply being protectionist. Just as those who a hundred years ago favored factory legislation, child labor laws, and a limit on hours of work were accused of interfering with workers rights to freely contract with employers and with children's and their parents' right to earn a living for their family, so today the call for global standards is portrayed as hurting the workers of the world who have nothing to sell but their labor and so prefer to do so rather than be prevented by those who claim to be their friends in the rich countries. Brink Lindsey of the Cato Institute, for example, writes that "attempts to mix trade and labor policy are just plain ugly. Enforcing international labor standards with trade sanctions will not improve working conditions in poor countries, rather, it will attack those countries at the heart of their comparative advantage."[26] But what the acceptance of these standards does is partially redress the power balance between capital and labor. The standards move toward a more efficient allocation of capital and labor based on free contracting between employers and workers who are represented by organizations of their choice. The outcome of these negotiations are not preordained and certainly are not being imposed by outsiders. Only the process of fair and equitable treatment is required. Universal acceptance of the core labor standards being discussed will not significantly raise labor costs. They should, but the studies made of their likely impact show they will not have the significant impacts either their opponents or their advocates suggest. They will be an important step forward, however, for human rights in a globalized political economy. Authoritarian governments and companies don't like them. But this hardly means they are not needed.

The economic efficiency gains associated with labor standards cannot be realized by competitive markets because firms' profits will be greater if they can discriminate and exploit workers, and so they have incentive to do so. The realization of efficiency and social gains to all is blocked by the difficulty in coming to mutually enforceable agreements. If one company or one country disregards core standards it is harder to reach a voluntary general agreement. That is why standards must be internationally enforced. This does not mean that individual countries cannot act on their own or that consumer boycotts and activists' shaming campaigns are not effective. William Greider has suggested that Congress should enact a law prohibiting entry into the United States of goods made in factories that are not independently certified as employing standard fire protection design and equipment. The safety issue is clear-cut and the human losses in such fires have been dramatic. (The press has featured a number of stories of such disasters.) Greider asks: "Does this sound too burdensome for business or too intrusive on foreign sovereignty? Consider this: The Federal Aviation Administration routinely performs similar safety tasks for aircraft, both at home and abroad. The FAA inspects production of foreign-made components that go into Boeing airplanes, certifies the airworthiness of foreign-made airliners and examines the work done offshore at overseas repair centers. Would you fly on a jetliner that was not certified by the FAA?"[27] Such protection seems reasonable. But what of the accusation that such standards are protectionism on behalf of the workers in the richer countries, and that for that reason are opposed by Third World countries?

Representatives of workers from these countries, at least those where independent trade unions can function, are virtually unanimous in their support for rules mandating enforcement of core labor rights and environmental protection. More than 200 national trade union centers from 143 countries representing more than 124 million workers have endorsed the call for a WTO working group on labor rights as a first step toward enforcing labor rights everywhere.

At the June 1999 World Congress of the International Confederation of Free Trade Unions (ICFTU), the umbrella group representing some 127 million people from 136 countries, the Malaysian Trade Union Congress, over the fierce opposition of its government, urged adoption of the social clause arguing that developing countries had the most to gain, since enforcement of basic labor rights could help prevent a race to the bottom. In similar fashion an Indian delegate voiced concern that China was using more oppressive conditions to lure investment away from other developing countries. ICFTU members with a social movement tradition such as COSATU in South Africa and CUT in Brazil urged the confederation to widen its engagement with the WTO, including activism on environmental issues and participation in the dispute-settlement process.

The issue for labor is certainly not whether all workers are entitled to basic rights but how this is best achieved, and which forms of enforcement are appropriate. The fear is that such rules will be a cover for protectionist tactics by the richer, more powerful, nations. Countervailing measures imposed unilaterally by strong countries on the weaker, even when motivated by moral fervor and not self-interest, can do great harm and fail to achieve their noble goals. Given the long history of colonialism and imperialism, the demands from the West can look like the white man's burden redux. Where rights advocates see a labor-capital conflict, most Third World states see North-South conflict in which an attempt is being made to use the global state economic governance institutions as a vehicle to attack the prospects of developing countries. However, for many repressive Third World governments the real danger may be of a different nature. The adoption of core labor standards could create space for autonomous labor organizations and a new sort of politics that would shake the rule of local elites. Once workers seize the right and gain the ability to organize independently they are not likely to avoid the task of engaging in the political arena. It is the fear of free speech more broadly, and the impact of the right to organize beyond the control of the state, that may pose as much of a problem as the more wage-based threat to the elite's wealth that is derived from the exploitation of its own people, that may be at stake. Organizing in the West against transnational capital's behavior in the South may have larger implications than those initially envisioned by Western labor-rights activists.

As Leroy Trotman, the Barbados trade union leader and president of the International Confederation of Free Trade Unions (the largest worldwide labor federation), has said, "This isn't North against South, or privileged workers against the poor. It is the workers of the world standing together to call on the WTO for justice." Zwelinzima Vavi, general secretary of COSATU, describes the goal: "to link worker rights to trade rules to change the balance of forces for workers in developing countries."[28] It is true that the governments in many developing countries defend the transnationals, who they see as their best hope. But it is also the case that these governments are almost always more representative of local elites than the mass of workers in their countries. Strengthening labor rights would have spillover effects on the governance in these countries. A more confident labor movement would favor the greater democracy and broader participation these elites fear.

Without enforcement of such standards it is more difficult to maintain gains everywhere. Third World working conditions have come to the United States and Europe, and on a wide scale. In Italy, after a sixteen-month undercover investigation, sweatshops in twenty-eight cities from Milan to Rome were raided in April 2000, breaking up a criminal network connecting some two hundred gangsters in China, Russia, and Italy who brought Chinese immigrants to Italy and forced them to work twelve to sixteen hours a day in the construction industry and in textile, apparel, leather, and shoe factories for little or no pay. More and more of our goods and increasingly our services are produced under harsh, frequently slavelike conditions imposed by subcontractors of well-known brands we commonly buy. Many expensive high-end custom retailers are making use of these sweatshop contractors and are selling merchandise produced by slave labor.

The workers in Italy were children as young as eleven, being forced to work twelve to sixteen hours a day. The immigrants were promised all sorts of things and had no idea what the reality would be. Hundreds of thousands of immigrants are ending up in such conditions. As *Business Week* describes matters, "Many of these immigrants become part of a secret underclass of the exploited, which experts are now defining as tantamount to 21st century slavery."[29] The investigators find immigrants locked in rat-infested rooms at night and beaten by thugs hired by their bosses. The U.N. estimates that trafficking in illegal workers is a $9 billion business worldwide. And when traffickers in human laborers are caught, sentences tend to be light.

Gangs from Bangladesh, Chad, and Croatia have been found to be operating large-scale smuggling operations of human cargo. Eastern European women are sold into prostitution in Western Europe. The global assembly line operates in New York and Florence. As the cost of travel drops and with the fall of the Berlin Wall and the formation of the European Union, travel and movement across frontiers have become easier. A *Business Week* report explains: "It's a sick twist on free-market economics: Employers squeezed by global competition are desperate to cut costs, and middlemen—the gangs—are eager to provide illegal workers and slash the price of labor to nearly zero. Europe's rigid labor market regulations and its high labor costs are also fostering a healthy demand for illegal workers just when the world economy is putting competitive pressure on Europe's second-tier companies."[30] That is, the normal workings of the capitalist system produce these problems. The extent of undocumented immigration, the horrors of smuggler practices and the deaths en route, create an awareness of what life is like in the home countries for people willing to take such chances and suffer such abuse in their new homes. The Global Justice Movement is only the start of a maturing journey to international solidarity.

In Prato, outside of Florence, a local economy that has been studied as a "Third Italy" for its concentration of the small, flexible production that is so important to Italy's export performance as the world's leading knitwear industry (with sales above a billion dollars a year), Chinese immigrants live and work in a world of their own, paying no heed to labor or tax laws. More than a thousand Chinese-owned factories and workshops are legally registered in Prato but many more factories are underground.

Experts think that illegal immigrants are responsible for perhaps 70 percent of Italy's underground output. Officials are loath to crack down on this important source of earnings. These sectors do not remain unconnected and other workers feel the pressure to work harder, faster, and for less.

Technology has played an important part in the increased ability of employers to play workers in different places off against each other. Large corporations source from a variety of contractors and plants in different countries so that they have a choice when some workers demand better working conditions and better wages. They will continue in this practice unless there is social regulation to prevent them from attacking the life prospects of workers with little bargaining power. The Internet and the fax allow auction bidding which lowers costs to producers who can buy from unregulated producers all over the world. Air couriers can deliver contracts and products in a timely manner to and from just about anywhere. Information technology allows for the tracking of orders in real time and for supervising worker output down to the number of keystrokes and it enables calls to be answered and orders to be taken incredibly quickly. While particular technological innovations are new, the social relations involved are long familiar. Andrew Ure, writing at the dawn of the first Industrial Revolution of the uses to which the self-acting mule was being put in England's nascent textile industry, declared, "This invention confirms the great doctrine already propounded, that when capital enlists science into her service, the refractory hand of labor will always be taught docility." Karl Marx, commenting on Ure, explained that "capital is reckless of the health or length of life of the laborer, unless under compulsion from society."[31]

Companies as they look to boost their bottom line have also redefined downward pensions and other fringe benefits. Law firms and merchant bankers offer a special "service." They help businesses turn pension surpluses that belong to workers into cash the company can appropriate. Abuse has gotten so bad that the Defense Department and other federal agencies have started to sue companies with government contracts for the return of monies the companies had claimed as required to meet their pension obligations but that they then appropriated for themselves at the expense of the workers. General Electric's pension plan, for example, has been charged in this way, leading the government to demand the return of more than half a billion dollars plus over $400 million in interest.[32]

The failure of any one nation to adopt labor rights affects the workers of the rest of the world. Exploitation of labor is not something that just happens in repressive China or Central America, but in the United States and Western Europe, where the most vulnerable are the recent immigrants, especially the undocumented who do not speak the language and are manipulated and sometimes enslaved by unscrupulous criminal syndicates and immoral employers. This exploitation is functional to capital. It will be changed only when the working-class movement is strong enough to force changes. Reformers and supporters of labor rights have an important role to play in helping to create room for the self-organization of working-class movements. It is easy to mistreat undocumented workers and workers in general. When the middle class becomes involved and a political coalition from the bottom up emerges, significant change is possible. But this is not at all realistic so long as the top-down anti-immigrant ideology dominates. By demonizing the weakest sectors of the working class, immigrants, welfare mothers, and racial minorities, the dividing line in the society is effectively drawn in a way that favors capital. It obscures the extent to which all workers are victimized by the system.

The violation of labor protection is standard practice in the offices and factories of U.S. corporations. Relatively better paid workers are subject to workplace stress, and "desk rage" has become a significant problem. In 2001, Carol Hymowitz and Rachel Emma Silverman, writing in the *Wall Street Journal,* a publication not normally known for its worker-friendly attitude, noted that "a New Economy cocktail of longer hours, increased workloads and stock-market tremors is fueling explosions of temper even in once staid offices. Companies generally do not report instances of worker confrontations, but occupational experts and authorities on workplace stress say the number of incidents is rising, along with their severity."[33] The phrase "going postal" to describe post office workers under intense pressure snapping and becoming violent has become a general phenomenon, with high-profile instances that receive national media attention (as when a worker in a Massachusetts office killed seven people). Most cases involving fistfights and shouting matches do not reach the evening news, but their numbers are growing, representing the underside of the celebrated Information Economy. The *Journal* reporters suggest that "today's stress is, in many ways, about too much information coming from too many sources—and the loss of control it instills. A survey by Pitney-Bowes of some 1,200 workers from receptionists to chief executives at top companies found that employees handle an average of 204 messages a day, counting e-mail, voice mail, snail mail and memos. And all the cool tech tools now available—from credit-card size cellphones to wireless Palm hand-held organizers—have in turn made us reachable anytime, anywhere."[34] Other surveys show half of shift workers report sleeping less than 6.5 hours a night during the workweek. One in five adult workers say they make frequent or occasional errors at work due to sleepiness.[35]

The new economy of 24-7, in which people are connected through fax, cell phone, and the Internet, increases hours worked to the point where the United States, which leads in information technology, now has the workforce that puts in the most hours of any among the advanced economies. As a result nearly a quarter of all American workers have been driven to tears by the stress of work. Nearly half describe their office as a place of "verbal abuse and yelling," and a third admit to yelling themselves. Thirty percent say their work is filled with "unreasonable deadlines," and 52 percent have logged twelve-hour days. Half routinely skip lunch, and a third of us find ourselves too stressed to sleep.[36] Directors of stress management, a job title at some companies, suggest taking deep breaths, using aromatherapy candles in conference rooms, and playing New Age music. Sales are brisk for such books as *Toxic Work: How to Overcome Stress, Overload, Burnout and Revitalize Your Career.*

Companies take advantage of the intensified restructuring, the mergers and acquisitions, to lay off workers and introduce new performance hurdles. Managers face unrealistically demanding expectations from investors for higher returns and they therefore impose impossible targets on their subordinates, who in turn up the quotas for frontline workers. Verizon takes advantage of the changes around its transformation from Bell Atlantic to intensify work to the point where its workers feel they have no alternative but to strike to retain the prior and already outrageously bad terms of employment. At Verizon call centers customer representatives must rattle off the company's numerous products and services, trying to sell them to each caller. The levels of stress in such jobs is incredibly high. Managers routinely "observe" workers, sitting next to them or listening in on calls. The Communications Workers of America, their union, fights such exploitation but only against great odds and overwhelming power. Changes in labor law and workplace regulation would help level the playing field.

There is nothing new in any of this. Companies publicly profess concern for their workers and spend lavishly to advertise their good citizenship, but when they think it is to their advantage and that they can get away with it, they will use their power to take advantage of workers everywhere. Even the most enthusiastic supporters of competition, who also understand the class nature of capitalism, have always known this. Adam Smith, widely regarded as the father of economics, made matters clear more than two hundred years ago when he wrote, "The masters, being fewer in number, can combine much more easily, and the law, besides, authorizes, or at least does not prohibit their combinations, while it prohibits those of the workmen. We have no acts of parliament against combining to lower the price of work; but many against combining to raise it." He wrote that "masters are always and everywhere in a sort of tacit, but constant and uniform combination, both to raise the wages of labor above their natural rate. To violate this combination is everywhere a most unpopular action, and a sort of reproach to a master among his neighbors and equals. We seldom hear of this combination, because it is the usual, and one may say, the natural state of things."[37] And so it is today.

Some analysts of the "new economy" suggest that stocks, bonds, factories, and equipment (what is usually referred to as capital) now compose only a small fraction of our national balance sheet. The vast majority of productive assets by some accounting schema are in human capital, the skills and knowledge embodied in every citizen. Michael Milken, the junk-bond king, having served his time in prison, has been reborn as cofounder and chairman of Knowledge Universe, Inc., a technology and learning company. He suggests that "the days of a sharp division between labor and capital are long past. Today, labor is capital."[38] This sort of analysis is increasingly popular. The idea is that if all workers would get education they each could be dot-com millionaires or at least highly compensated technology and information workers who sell their knowledge for high returns.

Even after the collapse of the technology-stock bubble this perspective is still popular. It ignores the reality that workers sell their labor power and only a small percentage of symbolic analysts, as Robert Reich has called them, do well enough to turn the fruit of their labor into capital. A narrower elite in fact own more of an increasingly concentrated wealth distribution. The information revolution has disempowered more citizens in their roles as workers and consumers than the relatively smaller number, although much celebrated in the media hype, who have done remarkably well in the new economy. Workers are prevented from turning knowledge into capital because large firms routinely force them to sign agreements that they cannot work in the same industry should they leave their job. Such contracts stipulate that they cannot recruit customers or coworkers and must give notice of any future job changes for the next five years thirty days before changing jobs.

Both within core economies and in the less-developed economies, workers' rights are very much on the agenda, in ways that they have not been in years. As such pressures mount even some of the leading transnational corporations are lobbying the Bush administration to accept labor rights in some form as part of new trade agreements. They do not want the United States to be left behind, unable to conclude such agreements because of resistance from labor and its friends in Congress who refuse to grant the president fast-track authorization, without which it is hard to negotiate trade initiatives. They are aware that President Clinton failed to get his fast-track authority renewed in 1994, 1995, and 1997 because of fights over labor-related side agreements. Similarly the proposal for the Free Trade Area of the Americas, agreed upon in principle in 1994 by leaders of thirty-four countries in North and South America, went nowhere because without fast-track authority other countries would not negotiate with a U.S. president, knowing that Congress could amend such an agreement at will and send it back for renegotiation. There will be efforts to buy off labor-rights advocates, as President Clinton did with, as it turned out, the ineffective side agreements to the NAFTA treaty. The strength and sophistication of the Global Justice Movement will be important to how matters turn out in the upcoming rounds of negotiation as President Bush tries to get fast-track authorization to push through the Free Trade Area of the Americas.

The experience with NAFTA's procedure has been that corporations use it not to defend free trade but to challenge the functioning of government. Among cases to date are the Canadian government's being forced to lift its ban on a gasoline additive (which was found to be a health hazzard when it enters the water supply) because the ban was challenged by the manufacturer, which convinced the NAFTA tribunal that this was a restraint on their right to export. Another tribunal ordered Mexico to pay an American company $16 million after it found that its environmental law prohibiting a toxic-waste processing plant was tantamount to expropriation. Such extensions of property rights follow from the definition of free trade and the rights of corporations, which are at the heart of NAFTA. Under the law, the United Parcel Service is complaining that the entire Canadian postal system represents unfair competition and is in violation of NAFTA. It may well be, since the rules are written and interpreted by the international tribunals whose members are unknown, who meet in secret, whose decisions may not be completely disclosed to the public, and who in the name of protecting free trade undermine labor law and environmental regulations established through the democratic processes of member states.

NAFTA of course is just the beginning. In spring 2001 trade ministers and heads of state from all of the countries of the western hemisphere (minus Cuba) met in Quebec City to continue discussion of the formation of a Free Trade Area of the Americas, which had been under negotiation for some time and had a projected completion date of 2005. Activists from the United States, coming to the meeting to protest, were turned back at the border. It seems the right to protest decisions our government makes is null and void if our government goes to another country to make a decision that affects our future. In Canada the security state spent millions of dollars creating a secure zone for the meeting by walling off protesters and mobilizing a huge military presence to do war with any who would exercise the right to peacefully challenge the premises of this effort (which basically amounts to a state-constructed corporate dictatorship over the globalization process).

The revolving-door nature of government-corporate links that allows corporate elites to move to policymaking positions, negotiate such agreements, and then return to the corporations from which they came to then benefit from their "public service" characterizes government policymaking in capitalist society. It defines government participation in structuring economic regulation in corporate interests. Needless to say, labor representatives are excluded from such participation, as are the representatives of civil society who are reduced to protesting outside such meetings as the one in Quebec City. Also excluded are the 95 percent of Americans who do not contribute money to candidates for public office and so have little access to "their" representatives. In the Free Trade Area of the Americas (FTAA) negotiations these government officials consulted regularly with their former colleagues in corporations that would be affected by the negotiations but not of course with those who represent the majority of citizens who have been shut out.

The Global Justice Movement's positive agenda for any hemispheric agreement includes at its core enforceable workers' rights and environmental standards—a rejection of the ineffective side-agreement tokenism of the sort that had allowed the Clinton administration to win the votes of Democrats who otherwise would have prevented NAFTA. In Quebec City hundreds of groups mobilized not only to protest but to put forward the elements they believed essential to international cooperation. These elements included protection under national law and international treaty of the rights of migrant workers throughout the hemisphere regardless of their legal status, along with measures to ensure countries' ability to regulate the flow of speculative capital in order to protect their economies from being destabilized by international finance. Other suggestions and demands included guarantees that investment rules not discipline so-called indirect expropriation, which has become the vehicle for attacks on government regulation under NAFTA. They also included an end to corporations' right to sue governments and overturn economic and social protections of citizens and the environment.[39] President Bush, like his predecessor, faced with the Global Justice Movement demands, tried to find rhetorical concessions that would allow him to get a congressional mandate without yielding on the substance of the corporate globalization agenda.

The labor unions of the hemisphere, represented by ORIT, the western hemisphere federation of trade unions, have united in calling for a process of economic integration that respects internationally recognized core labor standards and allows for legitimate national development policies of the sort FTAA is designed to preempt.[40] Of course these unions are not represented at the trade negotiations, and the AFL-CIO has joined in not only rejecting the current FTAA but demanding an end to the secrecy and exclusivity of the FTAA negotiations. They, and indeed a majority of Americans north and south, reject what the movements of civil society see as the failed NAFTA model of corporate privilege and call for "a new hemispheric model that prioritizes equitable, democratic, and sustained development."[41]

The Bush administration initially made it clear that it is not going to consult labor. Indeed, when AFL-CIO President Sweeney congratulated Bush on his electoral victory and talked about working with the president, his message was not answered because the White House did not recognize the name and confused him with a different Sweeney, who is a fairly obscure representative from upstate New York. Bush went on to sign a repeal of a series of Clinton executive orders on ergonomics standards, intervened in a Northwest Airlines contract dispute (a company Bush administration higher-ups had interests in), and generally did what labor had feared based on their experience with him when he was governor of Texas. After he was elected he then backpedaled on several promises the state labor federation said he had made to them. However, in an unlikely attempt, President Bush's staff tried to find union leaders who would back the FTAA as a job-creation scheme for American workers. They were not very successful in their efforts.

While the Clinton administration had listened to labor views but gave little, the Bush administration refused to discuss trade on labor's terms at all and took as much as it could of labor's past gains. When dealing with a Clinton approach these movements learned that democratizing trade and investment policy means sharing power, not sharing views, yet against a Bush approach they are forced into a different understanding of the struggle that is required. The larger context has also shifted. The international reaction to the Bush administration's shortsighted, unilateral, and narrow interpretation of U.S. interest as coterminous with the most reactionary sectors of capital has aroused resistance not simply from the social movements but from most governments of the world. As we will see in the next chapter the Bush administration rejection of the Kyoto Protocol to slow global warming stunned the world.

The labor movement has become active in new ways since the late Clinton years with the ascendency of John Sweeney to its presidency. The labor federation has launched the ambitious Campaign for Global Fairness, a multiyear, multi-issue campaign to build international solidarity, educate its members, incorporate workers' rights into international trade and investment agreements, and go after corporate criminals. At the beginning of the twenty-first century probably the most important step taken by U.S. labor was to stop the fight against illegal workers coming to take "our" jobs and to adopt a stance of organizing the unorganized, documented or not, and fighting for the rights of immigrant workers and their families. A new internationalism was also evident in the AFL-CIO's efforts to reach out to other unions around the world and to social movements everywhere.

5

Protecting the Planet

At the start of the new millennium there is an odd mix of techno-
optimism and panic abroad in the world. After September 11,
2001, globalization debates were complicated by the threat of
terrorism and the demands for instantaneous punishment, public
safety, and attention to the conditions out of which terrorists
found it easy to recruit. The panic had the effect of pulling attention from other pressing survival issues for people and the
planet. There was dissonance between technological capacities
and the difficulty of bringing resources to bear on problems in a
sensible, constructive manner. This chapter focuses attention on
environmental concerns. Fears surrounding global warming, genetically modified foods, the extinction of species, and the limited ability of the planet to recycle wastes and sustain life coexist
with the celebration of breakthroughs that promise better living
through science. The optimists see economic expansion extending technical capacity to tackle environmental concerns. Ecol-
ogy pessimists see the whole model of growth as problematic.
Matters are complicated because there are so many different areas
of concern. There is not one environmental problem but a complex of interrelated and perhaps unrelated ones, including those
that have an impact in some instances in very local ways and are
controllable at the microlevel and those that, for instance, impli-
cate cross-border externalities and global spillovers requiring

overcoming collective-action problems to coordinate a comprehensive response. There are also intergenerational issues and questions of social justice between the more prosperous and the less developed countries.

It is generally realized in most circles that the impact of industrialization and the resource-intensive lifestyle of consumer society have done great damage to the environment. However, President Bush, in rejecting the treaty to limit global warming negotiated by his predecessor, made known that he would dismiss "anything that will harm our economy and hurt our American workers." His comment was widely interpreted as reflecting the power that business, and especially the energy sector, has over Mr. Bush's policies with regard to global warming. The White House made clear its view that Americans would not have to change their lifestyles to reduce energy use.[1] Most Americans disagreed. In a CBS poll taken at about the same time, 61 percent of respondents said protecting the environment was more important than producing energy. Only 29 percent backed the president in picking energy over the environment. And two-thirds thought the president did in fact elevate energy over the environment compared to only 9 percent who thought the reverse.[2]

As countries that are now poor threaten further ecological damage by mimicking the patterns of the richer countries, there is expanding awareness that everyone cannot use the level of resources consumed unthinkingly by the average North American without destroying the planet. It is not just the longer-term damage to the biosphere, but to the daily lives of people in Mexico City who have to breathe the terribly polluted air, and to the third of the peasants in Gansu Province in western China who are mentally retarded or seriously ill because of the polluted water discharged from the region's fertilizer plant into the river from which they draw their water. In many other places the air is not good to breathe and it is not safe to drink the water. But the wretched of the earth are forced into a bargain: in exchange for work and a small pittance they pay the price by suffering things like perpetual diarrhea and early death from respiratory infections. It is not they but the elites that dominate the world system who calculate the trade-offs to which they are required to submit. Lawrence Summers (he of the infamous memo on optimally polluting the poorest countries) explained the logic that is embraced, if unwillingly, by leaders who see no alternative to the pursuit of the most rapid growth possible. That people are forced to accept the working conditions and the environmental devastations does not of course mean that they are necessary. Nor does pollution stay in one place. Wind carries carbon gases from power plants in Mexico into the Big Bend National Park region of southwest Texas, just as fallout from Chernobyl poisoned crops over much of Europe. It has been a slow process, but awareness has grown that many forms of pollution cannot be isolated, buried, burned, or ignored in one place without being felt elsewhere in time and place.

For the more privileged, who do not feel as intensely the cost of the pattern of accumulation inherent in the way globalization operates, matters do not look quite the same. They and their governments measure growth by stock valuation and the increase in measured gross domestic product (GDP), which does not consider the production of illth, only wealth. Between and within countries costs and benefits of alternative environmental policies have significant distributional impacts on various groups. Amidst the drumbeat that this is the best system imaginable it is easy to forget that it would be possible to regulate transnational capital on a global scale and institute basic protections so that development occurs on a more harmonious basis. We may all be for a clean environment but we worry about the costs we bear, compared to the benefits that can be guaranteed, if we agree to policies that impose costs on us. It is important to be aware of who bears what costs, who receives what benefits, and what alternatives we have, collectively, to corporate globalization's allocations.

Americans get upset when free trade with Mexico produces a two-thousand-mile border that takes on the character of one big Love Canal and when the circle of poison means the pesticides banned here and allowed there come back on the food we import. But many questions arise: Who will pay to clean up? Do U.S. citizens have the right to impose our preferences on the government of Mexico? Do we accept that Mexican sovereignty trumps environmental externalities? Can those who would protect the giant sea turtles, the whales, and the dolphins effectively address corporate globalization and its agents and enforcers on the World Trade Organization dispute settlement panels who put free trade above all else? The environmental movement, with its varied emphases, priorities, and venues, challenges the model of ecologically irresponsible development that corrupt local rulers and transnational capital have encouraged. It confronts the state system and the economic system, demanding basic changes from both.

In the oil-producing region of Nigeria, one of the largest and potentially richest countries in Africa, the transnational energy company Shell has colluded with the murder of activists protesting the despoliation of their lands. In one of the potentially richest countries in the world the people go hungry, oil money has produced a structural corruption that pervades everything, and hope has been a rare commodity. In Nigeria's neighbor, Chad, ExxonMobil works with another dictator and the state security forces, who have also been guilty of murder and torture, beatings and rapes. The World Bank is trying to help the oil company "do it right" in such places. Chad is one of the poorest countries in the world. It is 167 out of 174 on the United Nations Human

Development Index listing. Babies there have half the life expectancy at birth as those born in the United States. A billion barrels of oil lie a mile below its surface.

ExxonMobil knew it could suffer bad publicity, as events in Nigeria showed, and so it "needed insurance against moral culpability. They needed a buffer against both a demanding government and a resentful population."[3] The World Bank was pleased to oblige. Fortunately for ExxonMobil, the World Bank naively offered to broker the deal with Chad's authoritarian President Idriss Deby, who gamely signed an agreement with the World Bank that the oil revenues would be used to help his people. The World Bank even brought its own "representatives of civil society" to meetings. Unfortunately the groups represented "something of a caricature of government propaganda. Its press statement was almost identical to an official press release from the Chad embassy."[4]

The NGOs said Idriss Deby would not honor the agreement but that the money would go to enrich the country's entrenched elite. Indeed, Deby spent some of the money on weapons, in violation of the agreement. The law that required the oil revenues to be used for health education and social services was of course not honored. "It was a major disappointment," said an IMF official. "The first time they got oil money, they did not spend it as promised. It was a bad sign for the future." It sure was. But not unexpected. It was just what the NGOs feared and predicted. Meanwhile ExxonMobil continues business as usual. Chad's action "has not made any change in our plans for the project," said Tom Cirigiano, a company spokesman. "We're still encouraged that the project will benefit the people of Chad."[5] Sure you are. Certainly it benefited the small group of people around the ruler, the elite of the country, and ExxonMobil.

In Ecuador, when Texaco began its search for oil, in one of

the most pristine humid tropical forests in the world, it invaded
the headwaters of an ecosystem that was renowned for biological
richness. Now many of the people of this part of the country,
another of the poorest nations, do not have clean water or
enough food. They suffer malnutrition, memory loss, miscar-
riages, birth defects, and the other familiar symptoms of living
with oil extraction. Texaco, the company's spokesmen say, "uses
internationally accepted practices and complies with all Ecua-
dorian government laws."[6] In another of the poorest regions of
South America another military, this time Colombia's, is guilty
of similar atrocities, but Occidental Petroleum says it is only a
contractor. Like "good Germans" who only built the gas ovens,
these transnationals do not condone what their profit-making
activities produce as their by-product. Seeking justice in the local
courts in such countries is a fool's errand. There must be internationally enforceable standards and the global state economic
governance institutions must stop paying billions to pursue energy extraction projects that generate such damage.

Pipelines that cut through farmland and ecologically sensitive
rain forests and tundra, destroying the homes of indigenous
peoples, are allowed because of collusion between greedy oil
companies and corrupt local rulers. Economic benefits rarely
trickle down to the people whose lives they disrupt. Indeed,
human rights violations frequently accompany such projects.
Repression is a frequent accompaniment to oil extraction in
communities that resist encroachment and destruction of their
living space. Environmentalists and other activists speak of environmental racism. But when they try to sue in court to prevent
such atrocities they find themselves up against a system structured to protect the powerful. Local courts support the powerful
vested interests. Activists are unable to get oil company officials
to appear or to supply records in U.S. courts. The damage is not

being done in the United States, so courts here do not want to accept jurisdiction.

It is of course not only "over there" where oil company greed despoils the environment and where activists resist their power and where solidarity movements demand they stop their activities. The Sierra Club for example has taken up the case of the petrochemical factories surrounding St. James Parish in Louisiana, which is in the heart of the Mississippi Delta and part of what is called "cancer alley," a region that is home to a dense concentration of petrochemical plants and high rates of cancer and cancer-caused death.[7] The Sierra Club is currently drafting formal environmental-justice principles that build on the work of the People of Color Environmental Leadership Summit, which in 1991 established principles of unity and action. Long before Seattle there were such affirmations of the sacredness of Mother Earth, the interdependence of all species, and the right to be free from ecological destruction, as the summit made clear in a seventeen-point document. Groups confronting environmental racism have sprung up all over America as studies show toxic waste disposal concentrated in communities in which high proportions of low-income people of color live. Mainstream economics of course explains that this concentration of high cancer and toxic waste with low-income people of color is not racist. The land in these areas is of low market value. Sites are selected to minimize cost, ergo . . . Besides, hazardous waste creates jobs and revenues that ultimately reduce illiteracy and infant mortality, so how can this be genocide or some sinister plot? It is simple Economics 101. And so it is. We don't expect toxic dumps in Boca Raton or Beverly Hills, not because the rich would never allow it but because of natural market forces. It would be cost-ineffective. There is no such thing as environmental racism. There is only market economics.

These localized environmental problems, as they are called,

can be ignored by the rich and powerful, even as they are caused by them and the corporate pattern of economic growth and profit taking. But the discovery of the ozone hole above the Antarctic in 1985 created awareness of cross-border issues that affect everyone on the planet, even rich people. The U.N.'s Intergovernmental Panel on Climate change, made up of the world's leading climate scientists, has concluded that human activity contributed substantially to observed global warming over the last fifty years and predicts that by 2100 the temperature on the planet may rise by as much as six degrees. Glaciers from Alaska's Columbia Glacier to the Tien Shan Mountain glaciers in Central Asia have lost much of their volume. Greenland's ice sheet has thinned and the South Patagonian ice field in Argentina and Chile has retreated. Global warming will do the most harm in some of the poorest areas of the planet. Bangladesh, which contributes almost nothing to the problem, will be far more affected than the United States, for instance. We can expect the desert to advance across West Africa, the Latin American forests to be ravaged, and a number of Pacific island states to be submerged. One-third of the world's most populous countries would be flooded even with a small rise in sea level. The Netherlands, much of which is below sea level, already copes. Bangladesh cannot afford to pay for such a level of security.

Economists have developed the concept of negative externalities, the costs imposed on third parties, those not directly connected to a transaction but who bear costs as a result of the transaction (if they receive benefits we have a case of positive externalities). Environmentalists have made us aware of how much the cost of externalization imposes. The price system has been fundamentally compromised by the existence of powerful externalities, which allows a major part of the costs of production in a host of areas to be passed on to others in the form of polluted air and water (the by-products of an industrialization that ignores the social costs of avoiding proper treatment of waste by-products). Herman Daly and others have called for "an efficient national policy of full-cost pricing" to address this serious problem at the heart of our economic system.[8]

But there are other problems with the market efficiency argument. One of the most important is the use of discounting to evaluate future costs and benefits, which will be received at different points in time, and reducing them to a common present-dollar-value figure. The mathematics of compound interest here works in reverse so that the present value of benefits and costs that will occur even several decades from now have a present value of a fraction of what they will actually be. The value of the planet a hundred years from now has a tiny present value using any reasonable interest rate to discount the huge future-dollar-value of the planet. Old-growth forests, while irreplaceable, are logged because the present profit from logging in the short run exceeds any benefit that the market can measure in the long run. In the long run environmentalists see greater returns from sustainable usage and urge legal protection of common inheritance natural resources. The market's valuation works differently. Discounting thus builds in an overwhelming bias in favor of consuming now. It grossly favors the generation alive today at the expense of those to come. In some applications this may not be so great a problem because assuming historical rates of growth continue into the extended future, the generations to come will be richer than we are, just as we are wealthier and enjoy higher living standards than our grandparents.

But can such growth continue if we ignore the impacts of resource depletion? We have been using up nature's capital, counting the depletion of natural resources as growth rather than as a using up of irreplaceable resources that will be needed in the future. Economists tend to be an optimistic lot and to believe that technology will save the day. As resources get scarce and

their prices rise they will be conserved and used in relation to
their scarcity value while prompting a search for alternatives that
can substitute for them in satisfying human need. Ecological economics has a different starting point. Rather than seeing natural
resources as part of an economic model it sees the human
economy as part of the global ecosystem, a system that can only
provide limited resources to humans and that can absorb only so
much waste generated by humans without ceasing to function in
the ways we expect it to.

The director general of the sixth largest insurance company in
the world warned The Hague gathering that was charged with
coming up with enforcement mechanisms for the Kyoto Protocol on global warming that if nothing was done, by 2065 the rate
of damage caused by changes in the weather would exceed the
world's wealth. Such extrapolations are of course imprecise, and
besides, before this result occurred the world's wealth would
have diminished substantially, but it gave delegates pause by un-
derlining the seriousness of the problem. Mainstream economists
tend to be less alarmed however. Their method discounts events
that take place in the future in such a way that any cost more than
four or five decades ahead appears to have little measurable impact. For example, suppose the insurance company calculations
are too alarmist and that the world does not come to an end until
the year 2200. The value of the world's output then, if growth
averages 3 percent (a generous estimate), would be eight qua-
drillion dollars (that is a sixteen-figure number). Suppose we use
a long-term discount rate of 7 percent after inflation, as is typical
in cost-benefit calculations. The economic output of the entire
planet two hundred years from now would be worth, using the
standard economic present-value calculation, a mere $10 billion,
which is not very much. And surely not enough to make any of
the costly changes that could save the planet. This is because the
$10 billion could better be invested today in economic growth as

usual. It would be expected, using standard economic calculation, to produce more wealth in two hundred years than if it
were spent to save the world![9]

The economistic argument is that by *not* investing in emissions controls *now,* which would reduce world output growth in
a hundred years, the world would have more resources *then* to
address pollution problems. The gain under such a theory could
be impressive. For example, if such "costly" standards cut world
output growth by a mere one tenth of 1 percent, say from 2.5
percent to 2.4 percent average growth, the world's output after a
hundred years would have been reduced by a sum equal to the
entire current income of the world today. So, the argument goes,
since we can't really afford to do anything today let's do what is
needed a century from now. For people in regions where the
damage over the next century would make human life impossible, this sort of argument is not always terribly convincing.

There are others. Poor countries are too poor to have environmental standards. Given low living standards they cannot afford to be concerned with the environment. Other countries
must compete with such countries, therefore no one can do
much. International agreements are not possible, says George W.
Bush, because the poor won't do their share. It would be unfair
if we did and they didn't. The idea that this is a global issue and
that some form of global progressive taxation should quickly be
adopted to pay for needed changes is both obvious and seemingly
utopian. Indeed, as we'll see in the next chapter, the tax system is
moving in the opposite direction.

The immediate point is that the damage is already occurring.
We do not have to wait until 2065, 2100, or 2200. Drenching
rains brought to the Horn of Africa by a warmed Indian Ocean
in 1997 and 1998 offer a taste of bigger things to come. The
downpour set off epidemics of cholera. Mosquito-borne infections carried malaria and Rift Valley fever, a disease that appears

as a bad flu but can be lethal to people and livestock. Floods in Mozambique and Madagascar killed hundreds and retarded economic growth. Public health disasters of this sort—such as Hurricane Mitch, which killed eleven thousand people in Central America in 1998—while hardly unknown in the past, have become more common, and climatologists expect will become more common still as the planet heats up. Flooding favors waterborne ills as sewage and water supplies intermix, fertilizers are flushed into the water supplies, and, in warm weather, algae proliferate and affect human health.

The projection is that as the world heats up, mosquito-borne diseases such as malaria, yellow fever, and several types of encephalitis will become even more savage killers. Cold temperatures freeze and kill many eggs, larvae, and adult mosquitoes, but warming ends this trend and allows mosquitoes to reproduce and mature faster and more plentifully. Warmer temperatures increase the odds and enlarge the areas facing danger. Weather change is implicated as a possible part of the sequence that brought the West Nile virus to New York City and other urban areas, with their damp basements, gutters, sewers, and polluted pools of water—all of which are natural breeding areas.[10] Globalization even without the added impact of global warming produces new health hazzards.[11]

It may be the case that as nations get richer they are willing to spend more on preserving and restoring the environment. But this so-called "Environmental Kuznets Curve" works for some pollution and not for others. It works best where impacts are local and more easily measurable. Rich countries do not necessarily spend more to address global problems where benefits to themselves are more remote. This is sadly demonstrated in the resistance of the United States to sacrifice in the interests of economic growth for the reducing of global warming, a matter that will be discussed later in this chapter.

The general problem exists on two levels. The first is simply the self-interest of transnational corporations and other powerful actors, including the governments that defend their interests. The second comes from the core approach of mainstream economists. Their means of calculating cost seem totally inadequate to a proper conceptualization of the environmental problems at hand. Their touching faith in the gains from free trade is, for them, so overwhelming that any interventions that introduce other criteria are believed to be the surest path to an inefficient state, making the poor poorer because they will reduce the efficiency with which resources are used. Because "technology will produce solutions before disaster strikes" is a belief of many economists and others, and because trade produces more rapid economic growth and hence the resources to develop the new technological fixes, more growth is the solution, sustainable growth is the problem. Since greater gains are to be expected from free trade, anyone who fights free trade is hurting, not helping. This mantra is repeated over and over again. It is the bludgeon to dismiss protesters at global state economic governance institution gatherings. The demonstrators, it is said, are just ignorant of basic economics. In this chapter we investigate this claim and the issues surrounding the environmentalists' challenge to mainstream economists and policymakers.

The clearest statement of the WTO position is its Secretariat's 1999 Special Study on Trade and Environment.[12] The report attributes environmental problems to market failures and previous government failures. Market failures are situations where the market forces of supply and demand do not deliver an optimal degree of environmental quality to the society as a whole. What is meant by market failure in the context of the environment is that private actors take actions that hurt others because it is cheaper for them to do so than to internalize the negative costs of their activities. They dump toxic sludge in the river and people who drink the water downstream contract diseases, for example. If there are no clear property rights to water or air they can then be used as disposal sites by some to the detriment of others. The market mentality says all assets of value should be owned and so will be rationed efficiently. Most economists favor a property rights approach and stress the prevalence of government failure: counterproductive and ineffective measures taken by government. This market approach can be contrasted to a regulatory perspective in which it is possible to think of the preservation of public property as the need to police the use and abuse of natural resources through government regulation.

The problem with the construct "government failure" is that it presumes some totally separate and isolated entity: government. If our society is organized in such a way that energy policy is set by the oil companies and mining interests, water policy set so as to meet the irrigation needs of agribusiness and those who dump their wastes in the nation's waterways, the public interest is unlikely to be served. The problem is the failure to establish a government of the people, by the people, and for the people. If we have the best government corporate money can buy, we cannot speak of government *versus* private interests, but rather government as in significant measure an agency of corporate interests. This is only an inherent failure of government controlled by capital. It is only an argument for relying on markets if we accept that we cannot design, create, and defend a truly participatory democracy by limiting the power of the corporate rich. For the Global Justice Movement there is the difficult problem of needing to rely on government as a countervailing power to corporate greed while at the same time having to struggle with the reality of really-existing capitalist governments beholden to corporate dominance.

Problems arise as well with the idea of consumer sovereignty when it comes to the environment. We cannot individually buy a clean environment for ourselves. For the most part, either we all have a cleaner environment or we all don't. Many of the most important aspects of environmental preferences are public goods. No one person can enjoy them unless we all do. The exclusion principle cannot be applied. The private market cannot deliver on our individual preference. We also face free-rider problems and the issue of revealed preference. If I say "environmental quality is important to me and I want the river cleaned up" and you say you "don't care and besides are too poor so why don't I pay for the cleanup if I want it so badly," you may secretly be quite happy to enjoy the cleaner river and would have paid part of the cost. But since you can benefit and not pay you enjoy being a free rider. The nature of such public goods, revealed preferences, and the difficulties of collective action are not unique to environmental issues. But they are central to many environmental concerns.

Even in cases where individual consumers could choose to pursue their preferences in the marketplace there may still be reason for regulation. Consider the case of assuring a safe food supply. The WTO report says that "chemical residues in food are not strictly speaking an environmental externality as long as consumers are aware of their existence, are able to evaluate their potential health effects, and have alternatives to choose from." Most people reject such an approach. They believe government should protect the purity of food and drugs. Indeed, against industry opposition they forced the U.S. government nearly a century ago to create the Food and Drug Administration (FDA).

From a free-market perspective it makes no sense to say: "I am not a chemist. I do not want to have to monitor everything I eat. I want the government to monitor imported foods to check for pesticide residues that have been shown to be harmful and whose use is banned in this country." But since the days in the early twentieth century when exposés by radical journalists revealed

the unhealthy practices at slaughterhouses and the dangers in
other foods, forcing the creation of the regulatory agencies, business has weakened these agencies' power where it has been able
to, cut their budgets, and in the present period restricted their
mandates even as public health dangers have appeared to be
growing from untested products. Globalization has made the
problems worse. If the world cannot yet develop common standards, surely we can keep out products without being in violation of the WTO's trade rules. The WTO is willing to accept this
right only if there is overwhelming scientific proof of harm. It
does not accept the precautionary principle. Possibly harmful
products are declared innocent unless proved at a high level of
scientific evidence to be harmful. It has also been unwilling to
recognize trade restraints whose goals involve matters of conscience or social justice (like boycotts of reprehensible regimes).
Thus boycotts on South African products and investment in that
country during the apartheid regime would not be acceptable
today under WTO rules. In the case of a number of health problems there are serious dangers in the approach since such proof
may not be evident for many years, and yet WTO procedures
now prevent strengthening health regulation in individual countries. Such regulations are portrayed as protectionist measures.

There are import restrictions for health purposes because a
country cannot dictate conditions of production in other countries. They have to rely on restrictions at their own border. The
WTO tends to see such "interference with free trade" as protectionism. Because environmental regulation may increase the
cost of production a country which chooses to impose such costs
on producers within its borders may wish to place barriers on the
importation of products that are made elsewhere without such
safeguards. The WTO considers such barriers illegitimate. This
can produce "regulatory chill" as each country must face a potential loss of competitiveness if it imposes costly regulation on its

own industry, no matter how desirable these regulations might otherwise be. Cross-border environmental regulations are considered restraints of trade because the production process outside one's country cannot be a consideration according to the WTO.

In sum, the only organization that now has the power to do something to mandate binding environmental regulations is the World Trade Organization. But "the WTO has proven to be profoundly anti-environmental both procedurally and substantively, handing down environmentally damaging decisions whenever it has had the chance to do so. Fears of a race to a dirty bottom are proving prescient, and optimism that trade rules can be greened from within has waned appreciably." Moreover, as Ken Conca also writes, summarizing their record, "The problem is not just the obvious threat to local environmental quality from the forces of globalizing market pressures. We are also seeing the undermining of global-scale efforts at environmental protection, through the destabilization of several important environmental regimes and the commodification of critical global cycles and ecosystem services."[13]

Environmentalists suggest sustainable development as the criterion for decision making. It incorporates three important principles: integrated decision-making so that social, economic, and environmental goals are considered in a single decision frame; the polluter-pays principle, to avoid cost shifting and externalizing costs on to others; and the precautionary principle, which suggests that unless it is clear that no damage will be done undertakings with potential for grave ecological costs should not be implemented. We are only at the beginning of developing a framework of this sort for policymaking. As Conca writes, "Where progress has been made, it has generally come from isolated individual environmental problems, such as the destruction of the ozone layer or the pollution of the oceans, and negotiating regulatory controls on the proximate causes of environmental damages, such as the phasing out of a particular family of industrial chemicals or the deployment of a particular pollution-control technology. This approach is far from perfect." As he points out, "It produces narrow technical agreements around functionally defined problems rather than broader political bargains that speak to fundamental questions of power, equity and responsibility. The regime approach also tends to reify sovereign territoriality and the authority of states, as though they were neutral parties in the problem regimes seek to contain."[14]

Reducing Greenhouse Gas Emissions

Despite the grave situation when the nations of the world met in The Hague in 2000 to put the 1997 Kyoto Protocol and the 1992 United Nations Climate Change Convention into effect, the meeting broke down over failure of the European Union and the United States to reach a compromise on how emissions would be controlled. The United States, which had, instead of reducing them, increased its carbon emissions by 12 percent between 1990 and 1998, wanted to be allowed to buy its way out of making cuts in its own emissions by planting trees and purchasing unused emissions rights in other countries. The Europeans and most of the rest of the world objected. Muktar Aminu-Kanu, director of the Nigerian Conservation Foundation, said, "We are beginning to think these conventions are no longer a negotiating process, that the west, in particular the U.S., calls the rest of the world to tell them what to do and if they won't do it the whole thing folds."[15]

The Kyoto agreement to cut greenhouse gas emissions between 2008 and 2012 by an average of 5 percent below their 1990 levels was itself insignificant given the magnitude of the problem, but the resistance of American business made this the best goal that could be achieved. The real achievement in Kyoto was that participants agreed to anything at all, and despite that much of corporate America continues to declare that the economic cost of cutting emissions is just too expensive and will bring economic chaos if regulations are enforced. At The Hague, the United States refused to ratify an agreement without the developing countries signing on because of its concerns about competitiveness and the increasing scale of their emissions. The United States continues to demand "meaningful participation" by the poorer countries but balks at offering them financial support to reduce pollution levels by introducing more efficient technologies. Meanwhile, the United States annually pours 5.4 tons of carbon dioxide per capita into the atmosphere, which is three times the amount each Frenchman produces and twenty times what an African produces. The industrialized countries together have a fourth of the world's population but contribute three-quarters of the world's carbon dioxide emissions.[16]

The European Union made some concessions on the use of emissions trading that was demanded by the United States, but not enough to satisfy Clinton negotiators facing a recalcitrant Congress back home. The European Union argued that more concessions would have unduly reduced the pressure on industrialized countries to cut their domestic emissions. The U.S. delegation argued that the proposed cap on emission trading would increase the cost of complying with the Kyoto Protocol and waste scarce capital. To others this showed a lack of any real commitment to achieve what were after all modest, if not totally inadequate, emission reduction goals. The Bush administration simply rejects the Kyoto Protocol and refused to reduce greenhouse emissions (it is too costly and scientific evidence is lacking on the causes of global warming, they say).

Mr. Bush not only did not want to be tied down by any treaty that would lead to a change in American lifestyle, his solution to the short-term gasoline price spike in 2001 was to allow drilling

in the Alaska National Wildlife Refuge, which would not produce any oil for close to a decade and would then yield only 42
million gallons a day. For a comparison, consider that if, instead,
he had backed proposals to increase the mileage of SUVs (sports-
utility vehicles) by three miles a gallon, 49 million gallons a day
would be saved (a plan which Vice President Cheney ridiculed).
In any case the increased price of gasoline in 2001 had nothing to
do with a shortage of crude oil. The constraint was limited capacity in the U.S. refinery industry, the product of years of over-
capacity and an inability to foresee high SUV sales (SUVs, pickup
trucks, and minivans, the so-called light trucks that are exempt
from the more stringent fuel economy targets for cars, account
for half of the U.S. auto market). While in Europe and Japan
high fossil fuel taxation encouraged conservation, this was not
the case in the United States. The SUV loophole kept gas consumption high in part because gas prices had been so low. In
1998, compared to overall consumer prices, gasoline prices were
in real terms 60 percent lower than in 1981, encouraging wasteful consumption and car design in the United States. Refineries
had not been frustrated by government regulation. There had
been excess capacity and low profits. No new capacity had been
added because it had not been profitable to do so and, when
needed, such capacity could not be instantly created—hence the
price spike.[17]

As a presidential candidate, George W. Bush had promised to
regulate carbon dioxide emissions from electricity plants. He
backed away from that promise after the election and started to
dismantle regulations protecting wilderness areas. But what in-
furiated environmentalists around the world most was when
Bush's press secretary made clear that in the view of the administration implementation of the Kyoto agreement would entail
"huge costs . . . disproportionate to benefits." In office, Bush
rejected the Kyoto framework as unworkable. In June 2001 he

said, "For America, complying with those mandates would have a negative economic impact, with layoffs of workers and price increases for consumers." Remarkably, a month later, the rest of the world's meeting in Bonn reached an agreement that formally required industrialized countries to cut emissions of gases linked to global warming. As the *New York Times* headline announced: "178 Nations Reach a Climate Accord; U.S. Only Looks On."[18] The agreement involved major concessions that lowered requirements to levels even below the clearly inadequate Kyoto standards and it accepted an emissions trading scheme (called the "Clean Development Mechanism," under which rich countries could earn credits by providing clean-air technologies to poor countries) and carbon-sink credits (under which Japan was given extra credit for protecting its own forests). It was hoped the United States would sign on later, since these were all proposals it had championed. The response from around the world was unanimous in its condemnations. Kjell Larsson, environmental minister of Sweden, which was highlighting sustainable development as a theme of its European Union presidency, spoke for the world when he declared the U.S. action "sabotages many years of hard work." Chancellor Wolfgang Schüssel of Austria told reporters, "We need to insist that the United States fulfill its duties."[19] It was not immediately clear how they could successfully do this.

While President Bush declared the cost of addressing global warming to be too high for America to consider, a European Union study found that the E.U. should have no problems finding affordable ways to meet its commitments on global climate change. The report by the European Climate Change Program, a coalition of government experts and representatives of industry and environmental groups set up by the European Commission, concluded that there are sufficient potential cost-efficient measures to cut emissions by twice the target set for the fifteen E.U.

countries under the Kyoto Protocol. The report listed more than forty measures that could support the goals, and it estimated that the cost of meeting commitments would be no more than 0.06 percent of total E.U. gross domestic product.[20] A study released by the European Commission shows that European Union industry could cut greenhouse gas emissions by a third between the 1990 baseline and 2010 if it applied all commercially available technologies, and the study also showed that much of the reduction could be achieved at no cost or even at a profit.[21] It was thought by starting such changes sooner rather than later the European companies could develop new markets in energy-efficient technology. There was also a huge potential for solving any energy crisis by finding green solutions to energy problems.

Europe and Japan produce far less of the world's global emissions of carbon dioxide than the United States does. Indeed, for every dollar's worth of goods and services the United States produces, it consumes 40 percent more energy than other industrialized nations. Geographic distances are greater in the United States, but only about 25 percent of American energy usage is for transportation. The heavy European tax on gasoline, which makes it cost three times as much as in the United States, plus investments in quality alternative transportation and strong conservation measures in Europe are all supported by the voters. In the United States, too, more than half of all Americans say the U.S. should abide by the Kyoto accords, and a *New York Times*/CBS News poll also finds that 72 percent of the public believe that it is necessary to take immediate steps to counter global warming.[22] Mr. Bush promised more studies.

If the United States had achieved European levels of efficiency it would have already exceeded its Kyoto target for 2012. (In 1999 emissions would have been about 22 percent below the Kyoto goals.) Many of the more global corporations headquartered in the United States—like DuPont, which operates in more than seventy countries—were troubled by Mr. Bush's attitude. Thomas Jacob, senior adviser to DuPont for global affairs, expressed DuPont's long-term fears about America's isolation from an international deal. The company believes the global warming issue will create fundamental change in energy generation and usage and that if the United States is not subject to significant pressure and incentives to improve, it may not make significant technological progress. "From a competitive standpoint," he said, "the economies that get ahead on that curve will be in a better position to compete in that environment. Since sooner or later we will have to comply, we are losing valuable time and will incur extra costs when we have to catch up."[23]

George W. Bush in his first budget called for billions of dollars in cuts in an array of environmental programs. His 2001 proposed Energy Department budget that cut conservation and research funding and that stressed production expansion of nuclear energy and coal at the expense of energy efficiency incensed environmentalists and was picked apart by scientists and public interest groups. He specifically proposed a cut in the budget for the Environmental Protection Agency (EPA). The budget would prohibit the United States from spending any money to implement the 1997 Kyoto Protocol, although White House budget officials pledged that the United States will "lead other nations" in efforts to reduce environmental risks from climate change and other hazards. Meanwhile he proposed easing clean air rules for coal-fired power plants, loosened federal standards to protect fish, gave refineries relief from tougher state standards, pushed the construction of nuclear plants, and promoted the opening of the Arctic National Wildlife Refuge and other protected areas to oil and gas exploration in the name of a presumed national energy "crisis," which he contends has been created by environmentalists.[24]

The United States alone, with 4 percent of the planet's population, produces 25 percent of greenhouse gases. By 2000 the United States was spewing more than 20 percent more greenhouse gas than it had in 1990, the baseline year for Kyoto calculations. This agreement is itself hopelessly inadequate given the extent of the problem. Even if fully implemented it would fall far short of what is needed to allow the planet's climate to restabilize. The science is pretty much in agreement that restabilization would take a 60 to 70 percent reduction in emissions, according to the Intergovernmental Panel on Climate Change, a group of more than two thousand scientists from a hundred countries reporting to the United Nations.

"Today few scientists doubt the atmosphere is warming. Most also agree that the rate of heating is accelerating and that the consequences of this temperature change could become increasingly disruptive," Paul Epstein has written in *Scientific American*. "Even high school students can reel off some projected outcomes: the oceans will warm, and glaciers will melt, causing sea levels to rise and salt water to inundate settlements along many low-lying coasts. Meanwhile the regions suitable for farming will shift. Weather patterns should also become more erratic and storms more severe."[25] If the good news is that climate science can no longer be denied, the bad news is that greedy corporations and politicians in their orbit continue to do so. There is however a widening fissure among corporate leaders.

In January 2000, just as the Bush administration with its anti-environmentalist team was moving in, at the World Economic Forum in Davos climate change was voted the most pressing problem facing humankind. At her confirmation hearing Interior Secretary Gale Norton testified that "there is beginning to be more of a consensus" that global warming is under way but there is "still disagreement as to the causes and the long-term future" of global warming.[26] This was taken as an effort at partial reconciliation with ecologically minded Democrats who would vote on her confirmation. That she was not challenged offers some indication of the laxity on this issue in official Washington. Of course once in office it was clear she intended to continue her work of dismantling environmental regulations to which her corporate clients and ideological community had objection. Since a majority of voters had not chosen Bush, and certainly not endorsed the environmental policies he implemented, it can hardly be said that this is democracy's finest moment. The situation, however, better than most lays bare the nature of capitalism and its perverted form of democracy, which continues to allow capital's domination under Democrat and Republican administrations. If that seems harsh, consider the public opinion polls showing overwhelming support for stricter environmental regulations.

Polls show a large majority of U.S. citizens want the government to take measures even if this increases taxes. More than one in four U.S. citizens strongly agree to a willingness to pay 10 percent more for gasoline to reduce air pollution. A third of Germans would, so would two out of five Mexicans and about half of Chinese.[27] They see climate change as a serious threat. However, many elected government officials are afraid that the backlash from corporate contributors and a reputation for being against growth and for "big government" will hurt them politically, and so they buckle under. The power of the energy companies (for whom Secretary Norton worked before coming to the Bush administration) and others who resist regulation is of course enormous. This is evident in any national election. Indeed at George W. Bush's inauguration, events were sponsored with private money thanks to the large contributions from Texas oil men and transnational oil companies, including BP Amoco, Enron, and Texaco. The energy companies are not alone in paying for candidates seeking office and then events celebrating their victories. As Leslie Wayne has written, of those contributing the

$45 million for the Bush inauguration, "Most of the money has come from corporations with business pressing in Washington: energy companies seeking favorable drilling policies; pharmaceutical companies concerned about a Medicare drug program; sports teams wanting to protect subsidies for sports arenas; and individual companies like American Airlines, America Online and Microsoft with special issues before regulators."[28] These companies can buy many channels to make their views heard. On the same day that the *New York Times* detailed the political contributions of the oil companies and others to the Bush inaugural, ExxonMobil paid for an opinion piece in the paper, as they very often do, on the op-ed page giving its advice to the new president. ("Regarding climate change, the unrealistic and economically damaging Kyoto process needs to be rethought," it said in part.[29])

It is perhaps useful to say more about Exxon itself. It "earns" more revenue currently than any other corporation in America and has the power to match. It abuses power on this scale as well. Since the Exxon *Valdez* oil spill it has been a poster corporation for the environmental movement. In the legal cases that ensued and in its litigation generally, the company, as one opposing litigator said, consistently refuses to concede the obvious. It shows little or no respect for the civil justice system. This usually works for them. However, in December 2000 a jury in Alabama awarded $3.4 billion in punitive damages against the company, a large amount even for Exxon. The company had tried to cheat the state out of oil royalties due to it. The award was way out of proportion to the amount of ExxonMobil's attempted theft. The jury found the company had cheated the state of only $88 million, but they were outraged by internal corporate documents indicating that Exxon was well aware that it was shortchanging the state and thought it had enough muscle to get away with it. Exxon knew exactly what it was doing.[30]

Anthony Bianco ends a long discussion of the company in a leading business publication: "There is no question that Exxon's insistence on doing things its way breeds conflict most everywhere it goes. But this is one American company capable of a continuity of approach and a tenacity of purpose that makes even the institutions of government seem transitory by comparison."[31] Exxon is used to manipulating governments around the world on matters large and small. To take an example of the small, when a shareholders' resolution was introduced at their annual meeting that accused the company of misleading shareholders by minimizing the risks of global warming, the company tried to get the Securities and Exchange Commission (SEC) to disallow such shareholder action. Nothing unique in this. Exxon failed but went right back to the SEC to try again the next year, despite the fact that SEC rules allow resolutions with 3 percent support to be put on the agenda for the following year. Resolutions for the company to promote nonfossil energy won the backing of more than 6 percent of shareholders, and another linking the level of top executive pay to the company's environmental and social performance received 7 percent.[32] The men who run the company don't like this sort of challenge and they expect the SEC and any other agency of government to comply with their demands.

Most large corporations are aware of the public relations damage such crude tactics can produce. Exxon it seems doesn't care. It is in this, the attitude toward possible public relations impacts, that they may be different, not in their attitude toward doing whatever makes the most money. More enlightened corporations see the inevitability of environment-compatible and safer energy and see the money to be made in getting there first. They also look for market mechanisms that will allow them to continue to pollute while appearing to be cooperating. At the November 2000 climate change conference at The Hague the

United States insisted on extensive use of what its negotiators called the "Clean Development Mechanism," which would allow it and other rich countries to purchase emissions-reduction credits from poorer countries instead of reducing greenhouse gas emissions at home. Under such a program it could buy its way out of compliance without changing its wasteful lifestyle or interfering with corporate business-as-usual and its wasteful and destructive resource use. As the *Guardian* wrote from London, "Such initiatives undoubtedly have a place, but they are no substitute for government action to curb U.S. profligacy, including the ludicrously cheap price of gasoline, which encourages the use of large, energy-guzzling cars. If Americans can't be persuaded to curb their excesses, then what moral authority will they have to dissuade the world's most populous country, China, from following the same path of conspicuous consumption."[33]

The corporate presence behind the scenes in The Hague, where the countries of the world were meeting to find ways to implement the Kyoto agreement, was an important factor. In the back room was the Emissions Marketing Development Group, an organization launched by Arthur Andersen (the consulting firm), Credit Lyonnais (the bank), and Natsource (the broker). These "champions of the emerging emissions trading market," "a group of bankers, brokers, executives and consultants . . . eyeing a market that is potentially worth billions of dollars a year," pushed for the U.S. plan for unrestricted use of emissions-trading rights.[34] Others were not buying it. The European Union was concerned that the crumbling Russian and Ukrainian economies, among others, would sell emission rights from outmoded plants, which would soon have been closed anyway, to prevent the United States from having to make improvements in its own emissions.

The emissions-trading Clean Development Mechanism pushed by the Emissions Marketing Development Group and others, they said, is an approach that can work within nations but is not a workable way to achieve this goal internationally. There are simply too many sources of emissions and enforcement, and verification of pollution trades are not possible to the degree required for such a scheme to work.

Instead, a serious energy tax on polluting sources of energy and the expansion of the renewable energy sectors becomes, in their view, at this point in world history the most workable solution. The taxes could be distributed to pay for the transition. Rather than undermining economies the switch would create jobs and spur sustainable development. Many of the large transnationals have gotten on board to some extent, since they could make money in solar and wind generation and in designing and selling cars that run on alternative fuels. Endorsing such an approach, Ross Gelbspan explains, "While emission trading is, at bottom, no more than a grab bag of loopholes to be exploited by carbon interests and recalcitrant governments, the incorporation of fossil fuel energy standards into the Kyoto Protocol would create an immediate worldwide market for renewable energy technologies—wind farms, photovoltaic generators, small-scale hydropower, and fuel cells—since all are virtually 100 percent fossil fuel efficient, using no or minimal carbon fuel and producing no or minimal carbon emissions."[35]

The developing countries do not want to accept a lower living standard to make up for the damage to the environment produced by the rich nations. Yet for a country like India to reach European living standards would bring a tenfold increase in its already high carbon dioxide emissions. The Global Commons Institute in London has proposed a concept known as "contraction and convergence," which begins with the assumption that every country has an equal right to use fuels that emit carbon and that huge cuts in emissions from the developed nations are necessary to allow a corresponding emissions increase for still-

developing countries. The goal is to contract total emissions
while seeing that entitlements to emit become proportional to
population.

One of the most prominent reasons Mr. Bush gave for rejecting the Kyoto Protocol was in fact that the developing nations
were not required to make cuts in greenhouse emissions. This he
said was unfair, ignoring that it is the rich countries that created
almost all of this man-made part of the problem to date and that
the long-term consensus strategy has been to incorporate them
in the process at a later stage. As the *Economist* notes, Mr. Bush's
"revelation that the poor are getting off scot-free rings hollow,
for the notion of 'common but differentiated' responsibilities is
enshrined in the Rio treaty which Mr. Bush's father signed and
which passed the American Senate unanimously."[36] His second
rationale, that compliance would cost too much, is equally questionable. A 2000 study by five national energy laboratories operating under the U.S. Department of Energy found that
incentives, including for fuel-efficient vehicles, could reduce the
growth of energy demand in this country by a third through
2010. David Nemtzow of the Alliance to Save Energy says that
energy-efficiency regulations promulgated at the end of the
Clinton term, most importantly for air conditioners, could reduce the total projected demand for future energy by an eighth
through 2020. The Bush administration is reevaluating this and a
host of other regulations the Clinton people imposed in the closing days of their administration. President Bush's first budget
proposal cut funding for energy efficiency and renewable energy
by 30 percent.[37]

The United States's negotiating position for a long time has
been dominated by the Global Climate Coalition, a business-
backed group that has tried to prevent costly changes in its
pollution-producing production methods by attempting to
create doubt about the scientific basis of global-warming predic-

tions and the need to reduce greenhouse gas emissions, even though an overwhelming majority of scientists conclude that there is such evidence. The financial press, most especially the *Wall Street Journal*, has attacked the global-warming findings as unscientific and sought to discredit particular researchers as a way of scaring off others. Some conservatives (although that is probably not the best word to describe such people) have joined in defending the view that scientific evidence on global warming is lacking.

About three thousand scientists signed a Scientists' Statement on Global Climatic Disruption in 1997 that called for action to reduce emissions. Later in the year a second statement, the World's Scientists' Call to Action, urging all government leaders to demonstrate a new commitment to protecting the global environment for future generations, was signed by more than a hundred Nobel laureates and sixty U.S. National Medal of Science winners. These overwhelming responses were met by a Global Climate Coalition press release criticizing the signers of the Scientists' Statement on Global Climate Disruption, who "want to believe the worst case scenario predictions made by imperfect computer models," and saying that their own more optimistic conclusions were supported by "peer reviewed science" and "spoke for itself." The business-sponsored public relations offensive continue, attempting to stall as long as possible global action to reduce greenhouse emissions, a project that was seen as seriously cutting into their profits and calling for a dangerously different model (for them at least) of economic development.

In January 2001, in Shanghai, China, scientists from 150 nations met to try to agree on what evidence should be used as the basis of setting global environmental policies. They had before them the Intergovernmental Panel on Climate Change draft report, which increased the estimate of the upper range for possible global warming over the next century to eleven degrees, twice what it had estimated a mere five years earlier based on new data. It estimated the sea level rose in the last century at a rate ten times the average of the last three thousand years. Political attention focused on China's rejection of references (which were then omitted from the draft report) stating that greenhouse gases and associated warming stemmed primarily from human activities, a contention seen as bearing directly on the use of its own coal-dependent power-generating plants. China now generates as much emissions as the European Union, and India produces almost as much as Germany. China is not the only country that says it is not going to be locked into an inferior position and give up the possibility of development to cut emissions. The Chinese accuse the United States of hypocrisy and they refuse to do anything about global warming, pointing to their own poverty and to U.S. practice and its policy stance. The International Energy Agency predicts that developing nations will become the leading generators of greenhouse gases by 2020. China will increase its production by 3.3 billion tons, compared to an increase of 2.8 billion tons for all of the Organization for Economic Cooperation and Development (OECD).

While most developed nations have accepted the need to take action, even in the absence of commitments by the poorer countries, the United States almost alone rejected the plan others were willing to accept at the 2000 Hague and the 2001 Bonn conferences to establish enforceable promises to meet the Kyoto target. The failure of The Hague talks delighted the Global Climate Coalition, since they saw the demands of the rest of the world as too costly. But a more common reaction from business was dismay about the uncertainty over future regulation.[38] Businesses having to plan their investments over years preferred to know what the rules would be so they could cost them in to their forecasts. Nonetheless, politics, especially in the United States, will not now allow greater progress to be made. James Matas

Palau, Spain's environment minister, while acknowledging that there were many reasons an agreement had not been reached at The Hague, saw one dominant factor behind the failure. "For many leaders who went to The Hague, it was not only tolerable but cost-free to stand up in their countries and explain that, in defense of their economic interests, they have succeeded in avoiding commitments that might involve harming their current standard of living." He said, "It is more acceptable to say that the country's competitiveness is preserved better by opposing the measures foreseen in the Kyoto Protocol than by acting seriously against the polluting emissions."[39] The point he was making, that until society applies enough pressure on its politicians to put preservation of the planet ahead of other more pecuniary interests not much real progress can be made, directs environmentalists to examine the nature of corporate power over the molding of public opinion and political outcomes. The watered-down standards accepted in Bonn in 2001, while a start, should be seen in such a perspective.

A group of environmental specialists working out of the Center for Health and the Global Environment at Harvard University have offered an approach for achieving a worldwide transition from oil and coal to renewable energy sources, one that would produce no climate-changing emissions. Such an alternative is necessary, since, they say, "the science is unambiguous: stabilization of the earth's climate requires emission reductions of about 70 percent."[40] Such sensible solutions seem further away under the Bush administration, with its close ties to the oil companies. Many observers believe participants at The Hague conference would have done better to reach an agreement, even a weak one granting even greater concessions to the United States, given the expected position on global warming measures that were to be forthcoming from the incoming Bush administration. The president's statements and his appointments to fill key environmental positions reinforced this view. Even before Bush was inaugurated the thirty-eight-member advisory group on Interior Department issues read like a Who's Who of representatives of affected industries. When President Bush weeks into his administration declared the agreement dead, the world, as we have noted, reacted. The prospects for U.S. compliance with a meaningful global-warming treaty are minimal unless the environmental movement is able to very seriously ratchet up its pressure and political organizing. The world can only proceed at a pace acceptable to its one superpower. U.S. environmentalists have their work cut out for them.

A number of transnationals have broken ranks with the Global Climate Coalition. Some of these firms see the campaign as a losing strategy and one that will bring on an anticorporate backlash. Others see money to be made in selling antipollution technology. While ExxonMobil puts substantial resources into undermining the Kyoto Protocol, other oil companies are investing significant monies in clean renewable energy alternatives. British Petroleum now advertises that BP stands for "Beyond Petroleum." The auto industry is investing a billion dollars in fuel-cell-powered cars, and at the 2000 World Economic Forum in Davos the CEOs of the planet's largest corporations voted climate change the most urgent issue facing humanity today.

There should be celebration when wind and solar energy, which are now attracting serious, widespread attention and significant financial investment from such firms as Siemens in Germany, Sharp in Japan, and BP in the UK, succeed commercially. General Electric is looking at fuel cells as a possible replacement to the conventional power stations it sells. The most prominent effort is perhaps by the Swiss-Swedish engineering company ABB, which is working on wind power and high-efficiency gas-driven microturbines. When these succeed it will be said, "see, the market can solve such problems." However, without social pressure to act that is erected by environmental groups and civil society more generally, there would have been little interest in developing alternatives. Moreover, efforts to push things along in these directions through regulation and incentives that would speed up such changes were resisted, and are resisted, by the likes of ExxonMobil in well-financed political campaigns. Individual companies will act under pressure where it is in their bottom-line interests to do so. This requires continued pressure, which has become the life's work of many global citizens. I will comment on some success stories along these lines. But it should be remembered that when problems require collective action, solutions are far, far more difficult.

NGOs, Regulation, Consumer Activism, and the Precautionary Principle

In particular industries that have garnered criticism in the past for their particular environmental practices, there have been changes in strategy. Chiquita Brands, for example, once famous for their notorious dominion over the people of Central America, the "banana republics" as these countries lacking real sovereignty were disparagingly called, has gotten religion. They have received environmental certification from the Better Banana Project, which was started by the Rainforest Alliance and its partners in 1991 as an international certification program for both environmental and working standards on banana farms. The company says all its 127 Latin American farms (they are not called plantations anymore) are certified, as well as about a third of its contractors, with the rest under orders to comply. These guidelines involve control of pollution, use of toxic chemicals, soil and water conservation, and the health and safety of workers. After protests and boycotts got the industry's attention, the

Rainforest Alliance moved to offer a "green label" seal of approval for companies who make progress in these areas. There have been benefits for workers in the form of better housing, shower facilities, and reduced use of damaging herbicides.[41]

A similar program, in the timber industry, involves a third-party certification group called the Forest Stewardship Council (FSC). It has gained endorsement, from such companies as Home Depot, after protracted campaigns by environmentalists. (These included such tactics as commandeering a store's public address system to make announcements such as "Attention shoppers, in isle seven you'll find mahogany ripped from the heart of the Amazon." Such tactics continued for months.) Home Depot officials claim that protests did not affect their change of heart but as a strict business decision they promised when possible to stock products certified by the Forest Stewardship Council. Such certification means that the organization has found that the trees have not been harvested in a way that threatens the health of the forests or of endangered plants and animals, in a way that employs too much herbicide, or that leaves hillsides exposed to erosion, and that the rights of workers and indigenous peoples have been respected.[42] A number of other large retailers have joined the FSC.

Timber companies have set up a competing certification organization, the Sustainable Forest Initiative. They complain that the environmentalists are unrealistic and that industry has more credibility as the real expert. Environmentalists see such "fox guarding the henhouse" organizations that rely on self-policing and less stringent standards as an attempt to mislead the public. So far the FSC has been winning the public relations battle and has gotten participation from the likes of the IKEA furniture chain and funding from both the European Commission and the World Wildlife Federation. It has had substantial impact on the way the industry does business. This may change. In 2001, the industry trade group, American Forest and Paper Association, announced a major campaign on behalf of its logo and its Sustainable Forest Initiative. It hired True North Communications, creator of the effective "Got Milk" ads, and devoted $25 million to making the public believe in its "green label," as opposed to the less well financed Rainforest Action one, in what environmentalists saw as a hideous example of "green washing." The industry's environmental rules put no constraint on the use of poisonous chemicals such as herbicides and allow clear-cutting up to three times the amount of land the Rainforest maximum standard would allow, 120 acres, the size of 116 football fields.

A second challenge comes from a group called Frontiers of Freedom, a conservative nonprofit group which is attempting with a major court challenge to get the Internal Revenue Service to disallow the Rainforest Action Network's tax exempt status. Frontiers of Freedom, which calls itself the "antithesis" of the environmental movement, says that it will challenge other environmental groups if it succeeds in its effort. Frontiers biggest contributors include ExxonMobil (the largest oil company in the world, which leads the attack on the regulation of greenhouse emissions, claiming the environmentalists use bad science and have not sufficiently proved we need to do anything), Philip Morris (the folks who explained to the Czech Republic's government how cigarette smoking was good economics because it kills off people prematurely and saves on medical and pension expenses), and RJ Reynolds Tobacco Holdings. Even if they do not win with the IRS the attack will force the Rainforest Action Network "to spend resources and sleepless nights," which will, it is thought, weaken the organization and perhaps scare off potential contributors. It is perhaps no coincidence that the corporate-backed attack group is starting with the Rainforest Action Network. RAN not only is sending nonviolent protesters to the gatherings of global state economic governance, but is increasingly focusing its protest actions on companies like Citigroup, Boise Cascade, and ExxonMobil. As Mike Brune, its campaign director declares, "Corporate campaigns are the next frontier. . . . We're going after the root of the problem."[43]

When vibrant movements from below are in motion the powerful above are persuaded to say the appropriate words as a sign of commitment to higher values and decent behavior. If the movement pounds them hard enough, the rules that supposedly could not be changed are modified, often in direct proportion to the pressure from below and the degree of popular consciousness and commitment. If people settle for less the response is correspondingly less adequate. It is not really what the powerful can afford to give in some precisely measurable sense but rather what they must give, what they can be forced to concede.[44] Still, as Bernie Sanders, Vermont's independent socialist congressman, says, quoting a friend, "Important change nearly always begins in hypocrisy."

The reality is that it takes a powerful popular movement to force such changes, even while those who fought the changes for so long usually want the credit for being "leaders in corporate responsibility." Because corporate globalization does damage in so many areas, the social movements can easily call attention to other areas of corporate abuse, and the process starts all over again. Global civil society has to continue to monitor compliance, and the extent of real change depends on the level of public consciousness and indeed suspicion of the hypocrisy of the corporations. The same issues arise for environmentalists and others "sitting down at the table" with the global state economic governance institutions. For example, they have been frustrated by the Committee on Trade and the Environment, established in January 1995 by the WTO General Council, which they have seen as a tool of free-trade advocates to defuse environmental concerns (rather than as an organization that should be usefully addressing them). Part of the problem is that mainstream economics rather than ecological economics guides the organization's policymaking.

Countries, including the United States, do not consistently follow pro- or antienvironmental priorities. They pursue their self-interests as their leaders are led to perceive them. Thus the government of the United States, which has also backed the oil transnationals in very questionable activities, has been in the forefront of saving the dolphins from Japanese whalers and the sea turtles from South Asian shrimpers. Our government's action is understandable because the political benefits accrue to them and the cost of adjusting to the policies we impose would be paid by foreign producers who were in noncompliance with our safeguards. The environmentalists who have effectively organized around such issues have gotten laws through Congress only to come in conflict with WTO rulings that the protections imposed by the United States restrain free trade.

Some of the same incentives and politics are seen in the lead often taken by U.S. presidents who have to be accountable to a powerful proenvironmental voting bloc whom they would like to count on for support, and in the reality that at the congressional level a narrow-minded antienvironmentalism prevails when business lobbying groups contend that the agreements will be too costly. As the environmental movement gets stronger it becomes easier to get agreements on banning particularly harmful chemicals even where there are economic interests who stand to lose money but where the harm is shown to be severe. On this basis some of the worst pesticides and toxic chemicals, the so-called dirty dozen, were phased out in 2000 by agreement of 120 countries meeting in Johannesburg.[45] These discussions began when researchers reported exceptionally high concentrations found in the bloodstream of residents of northern nations. Unfortunately, each year thousands of new and harmful products may hit the market.

The United States and some other countries opposed a European Union initiative that would have made it easier to ban harmful substances based on the precautionary principle. To go one by one and demand overwhelming scientific evidence (a high pile of dead bodies) when there are thousands of new potentially harmful compounds coming on the market each year is to make for limited progress. As Joe Thornton, a scientist at the Columbia Earth Institute, says, "We know nothing about most of the chemicals produced, and right now they are considered harmless until proven dangerous. We are being killed by our own ignorance."[46] The traditional requirement has been that companies introducing a new drug must prove that it is safe and effective under the U.S. Federal Food, Drug and Cosmetic Act before it can be marketed. The WTO places the burden on the nation with prohealth food-safety policies to prove that in any particular case a product they wish to restrict is *not* safe. The government must prove a negative. Science cannot always provide this information in a timely fashion and irreversible effects may occur. The precautionary principle, which has been the internationally recognized standard that requires proof of safety before a product that poses potential threat is marketed, is reversed under the new neoliberal constitutionalism. This is a political choice to accept a far higher level of risk and requires all governments not to legislate a higher standard than the WTO will allow. Only if a country can prove harm to a WTO panel's satisfaction can governments take action.

One of the most high-profile disputes in the area of whether the precautionary principle should be applied is with regard to genetically modified foods and the proliferation of hybrid seeds. A handful of companies have been selling seed varieties in conjunction with giant food processors who buy the crops and demand that they are produced with such seeds. With such tight corporate control Monsanto is able to insist that farmers who use their seeds also use their pesticides and allow inspection of their fields. It has been able to rush genetically engineered seeds to market and get their wide adoption without proper testing. The company, "long a political power with deep connections in Washington," got the government to regulate it in just the way it preferred so that the rules governing genetically modified foods were not designed to limit the company, but rather to protect it from environmentalists and other public-interest groups. Government regulation was demanded by Monsanto to "reassure a public that was growing skittish about the safety of this radical new science," as the *New York Times* reported. "Even longtime Washington hands said the control this nascent industry exerted over its own regulatory destiny—through the Environmental Protection Agency, the Agricultural Department and ultimately the Food and Drug Administration—was astonishing."[47] The government did exactly what the industry told it to do. Yet the days when government telling people something is safe and good for them without anyone asking questions are gone, if there ever were such days. Corporate influence and control over government has eroded government's credibility.

While the industry denies there is any problem with genetically modified foods, a January 2001 poll by the Pew Charities Trusts found most people (58 percent) opposed such ingredients and three-quarters of respondents wanted to know in any case about the presence of genetically modified ingredients in food. Unfortunately it has gotten harder for even the most scrupulous farmers and manufacturers of food products to keep bioengineered crops from contaminating their products even with elaborate security systems. Banned products that are not permitted in the United States for human consumption—such as StarLink, a brand of corn genetically modified to produce its own pesticide, and found in EPA tests to cause allergic reactions in some people, and that was thus not approved for human consumption—has been turning up in 10 percent of the corn at some of the nation's big grain processors. It was found in Kraft taco shells, meatless corndogs produced by a unit of Kellogg, and in Kroeger's corn tortillas. Samples of foods with GMO-free labels sent to independent labs return very disturbing results.[48]

Toward the end of 1999 a lawsuit was filed against Monsanto by a group of farmers who contend that the company is at the center of an international conspiracy to control a large part of the world's corn and soybean seed supply. Monsanto spent $8 billion to buy up large seed companies with the goal of inflating prices, forcing small farmers to pay excessive technology fees and to agree to restrictive planting contracts. The suit charges that they initiated efforts to neutralize competition through licensing agreements and the misuse of intellectual property rights. Named as coconspirators were DuPont and Novartis, among others.[49] The suit is important because if these companies were allowed to continue to accumulate power over the world's food supply a monopoly would be created and because the implications of genetic engineering of foods are not well understood. Behind the suit are environmental groups who see the company's seeds as possibly leading to "genetic pollution" and capable of creating "superweeds," which will drastically alter the environment. An environmental "dream team" has been assembled from a group of ten leading law firms who contend that Monsanto has gained a monopoly position by intimidation, deceptive business practices, and restrictive technology deals imposed with bully tactics. The lead lawyer is Michael Hausfeld (the Washington lawyer who won the price-fixing suit against the vitamin makers). Also on the team is David Boies, who led the Department of Justice's prosecution of Microsoft. The suit is likely to raise the profile of the issue in the United States if it goes to trial.

In Europe, Monsanto is under attack for "playing God" with

the world's food supply by introducing genetically modified seeds that the Europeans refuse to allow. The United States has challenged this use of the precautionary principle as an illegitimate violation of free trade under WTO rules. The WTO panel has found for the United States, seeing no definitive evidence that genetically modified foods present a health hazard. Transnational corporations working through Trans-Atlantic Business Dialogue have ardently supported regulatory harmonization through binding international agreements to establish a single global regulatory standard, which has usually meant acceptance of the weakest standard that can gain universal agreement. Such a procedure blocks evolution to tougher regulation, since any nation wanting to raise the standard is held back by such agreements from doing so unilaterally. Just as in the United States some state governments pioneered the establishment of standards and others followed, so too some countries that have been more sensitive on an issue and moved first have been the model for others to follow. Under premature harmonization more serious regulatory standards become much more difficult to achieve.

There is also the issue of the promiscuous granting of patents by the United States government. The European Patent Convention of 1975 states that patents cannot be granted for plant varieties. Biotechnology corporations have gotten around this by patenting genes in plants. They are claiming a monopoly on human cells, traditional rice varieties long used by farmers in India, painkillers developed by the ancient Chinese, and a host of other resources that have been common knowledge and in wide use in traditional societies around the world, where it would never occur to people to patent the common inheritance of humankind. The United States government has pushed for laws that legalize such biopiracy.[50] If the first to patent seeds, genes, and cells get monopoly ownership, the rules of the game of life will be changed dramatically. The assignment of property rights in this way extends commodification and corporate ownership to life itself.

Washington has fought to prevent any biosafety or biodiversity treaties from taking precedence over WTO intellectual property rules. It thus defends the interests of genetically modified organism producers who see unlimited market potential in controlling life-forms. It has also almost single-handedly fought against acceptance of the precautionary principle in negotiations in the 2000 global biosafety talks in Montreal and in other venues.[51] The Clinton administration finally agreed to some compromise on the applicability of the precautionary principle in the Biosafety Protocol, in part because U.S. consumers have shown increasing wariness.[52] The issue is not at all yet settled. It will be difficult for the United States to get access to European markets for its genetically modified foods even if they are successful in beating down European and other governments. Consumers there will not buy them and want warning labels. The United States refuses on behalf of its agribusiness giants.

Internal Food and Drug Administration documents that have been made public as a result of a lawsuit filed against the agency by the Alliance for Bio-Integrity have exposed internal criticism of the simpleminded proindustry way the agency handled decisions about genetically modified foods. Early decisions on how to regulate genetically altered foods were made in the George Herbert Bush White House and announced by Vice President Dan Quayle, who in offering the details of the streamlined guidelines declared, the United States "was the world leader in bio-technology" and the "government wanted to keep it that way." Any doubts its own scientists had were to be kept to themselves so the products could be rushed to market.[53]

"So are genetically engineered crops safe—both to people and the environment?" *Business Week* joins us in asking and it answers, "The truth is we just don't know for certain." The publication quotes DuPont's chief executive, Charles O. Holliday, Jr., as saying that "to brush off concern as unfounded, is to be arrogant and reckless," and yet the WTO would put the burden on critics to prove "frankenfoods" dangerous rather than on the industry to show they are safe. A "frightening leap into the unknown" is justified by free-trade advocates prompted by agribusiness transnationals as the new rules of globalism. Interestingly, some food producers, Gerber and H. J Heinz among them, do not allow genetically modified ingredients in some or all of their products. Many independent researchers argue we cannot say that products containing genetically modified organisms are safe.[54]

Transnational agribusiness has also changed the lives of farmers the world over in other ways. The Global Justice Movement has come to pay attention to how economic "modernization" actually works, how when agribusiness invades an area fewer farmers are needed but more capital is required for the insecticide-intensive and energy-intensive mechanized production for the export market. After centuries of exploitation by the elites who dominate their economies and systematically rob them, the poor become the victims of a modern-day Enclosure Movement, which forces them off the land and into the cities, where they become the marginalized dwellers of the makeshift hovels that surround the cities of the Third World. The wealthy owners of capital-intensive agribusiness spend their earnings outside of the country, and so this export industry adds little to local well-being. Because less rice, beans, and other locally consumed crops are produced (because there is less profit in doing so), malnutrition increases. Local farmers who do produce for local markets are driven off the land, unemployment grows, and the population of ill-serviced and nonserviced residents of the gigantic cities of the South swells. The pattern of economic growth considered a manifestation of success by World Bank economists breeds poverty and marginalization of the majority of the human beings who inhabit the planet. The hope is that in enough time they will eventually all be incorporated into the modern sectors of the local economy. In that long run, as Keynes might have said, they will be dead.

In the United States farmers have pretty much lost independence and are contractors to huge agribusiness firms who tell them when to plant, what seed to use, and so on. If times are bad the farmers suffer, not the transnational who buys from them. If times are good the farmer is squeezed as well. Four firms control more than three-quarters of beef packing and hogs and sheep, and half of chickens sold. In close to a hundred cities four super-market chains control three-quarters of the market and new mergers are announced seemingly every week or so. Contract poultry growers, those who raise hogs, and other livestock farmers who work under a risk-shifting system must purchase their own highly automated single-purpose expensive equipment and buildings constructed to exacting specifications, use the feed and drugs specified, and deliver product to meet precise requirements on penalty of not having them accepted and not having their contract renewed after they have made this single-purpose investment. They sell to a very few huge corporations that dominate distribution channels and take no responsibility for what happens to these independent contractors or their workers. It is a system rank with abuse and brings the realities of corporate globalization home. Old McDonald's farm is gone. Now we just have McDonald's (registered trademark for assembly-line standardized food to go) employing more than a million people in tens of thousands of restaurants in 111 countries. And we have nutritionists telling us the kind of high-fat low-fiber diet McDonald's offers is linked to cancer, diabetes, heart disease, and obesity, the diseases that are responsible for three-quarters of all premature deaths in the West. Activists ask, shouldn't their throwaway packaging carry warning labels. Should they be allowed to sponsor sports events, or to operate restaurants in hospitals and schools?

The food factory where the beef is processed and where the chickens live in little boxes all their lives and where the crops are grown in chemical-intense ways are more invisible to us these days. The family who once worked the land has been replaced by hired immigrant labor at the lowest possible wages. So too in the slaughterhouses, where such superexploited people do the dangerous, dirty work. Agricultural communities become rural slums, with bad public services and little community life. New pockets of poverty surround farms and factories using the most advanced technologies.[55] This factory agriculture is being challenged by a new awareness of what is in our food and by the growth of organic farming. The problem is that the big companies are now calling their stuff organic and have prevailed on the Department of Agriculture to set standards of what can legally be called organic in a way that has led to loud protest by the real organic farmers and food advocates who unfortunately have far less influence in Washington than the big agribusiness corporations.

Once we start to think about whether our food is healthy, perhaps we wonder as well about the workers who are in the fields and the reprocessing plants and the conditions under which it is produced. When we buy fresh flowers we may ask with Kirsten Appendini, "From Where Have All the Flowers Come?"[56] And how is it that we are able to buy beautifully shaped, bright red tomatoes year-round? Leonardo Llamas has called the globally produced tomatoes "fruits of injustice." Lauren Baker suggests that while some may think that the demand to be able to buy organic tomatoes and other products is an elitist special privilege, organic farming helps farm workers who are the major victims of the pesticides and fertilizers that are dumped on our foods. Customers can demand food that is grown in an ecologically sound and nonexploitative manner. As consumers become more critical and knowledgeable shoppers they can help reshape the food system and create the public consciousness that will demand regulations to help protect their own health and that of the workers who produce their food.[57] Perhaps they will begin to look with new eyes at what they eat and consider the social relations that lie behind the facade of franchised foods, which seductively taste good but poison our bodies and the planet, and which destroy tropical forests to make way for cattle ranching on the scale necessary to supply billions of Big Macs.

The Global Justice Movement is in part about the action of individuals taking responsibility by questioning powerful features of the world as it is. One case that should be better known involves Helen Steel and David Morris, two young working-class activists of North London who when they look at McDonald's see a company promoting unhealthy food, exploiting children and their parents, damaging the environment, and inhumanely treating animals and other living things. They produced and distributed a pamphlet entitled "What's Wrong with McDonald's" in front of one of its restaurants. McDonald's took them to court for libel under the very strict British libel laws. It turned out to be the longest trial in that country's history. Steel and Morris, "the McDonald's two," defended themselves against a battery of very high priced legal talent the company bought to attack them. The defense was to call expert witnesses who testified that what they had written was the truth. They did well in marshaling evidence. McDonald's was embarrassed in the media to the point where they no doubt wished they had never gone to trial. It was perhaps the most disastrous public relations debacle ever by a transnational corportion. You can go to the web site that has the McDonald's material for which Helen and Dave were tried and for material on the trial.[58]

Beyond considering the health implications of fast food we might spend a minute considering the labor relations involved in their model of assembly-line production. The company has pioneered a model for the casualization of its just-in-time marginally compensated—a casualized workforce that can be sent home when customers are scarce and called in when the need arises. Their labor practices of regimentation and minimal compensation have spread to other workplaces, forced down wages in the restaurant trade, and forced out of business competitors who pay a more livable wage and offer benefits to employees.[59] McDonald's Happy Meal is the smiley face of corporate globalization.

The question of health standards and food extends well beyond genetic-modification issues. Many other foods widely marketed would not pass the sort of tests consumer and health advocates are suggesting. If health risks were studied and publicized more and easily understood labeling was required, not just at the supermarket but at fast food chains like McDonald's, eating and buying habits might change. Regulatory agencies are for the most part captives of industry and don't ask obvious questions about ecological impacts, as recent independent research on the harm caused by genetically engineered changes in corn (done to produce a natural pesticide but also killing Monarch butterflies) demonstrates. Questions of how easily added genes can spread via pollination to related plants and with what consequences raise still other disturbing questions. Industry always says the risks are small. One can almost hear the nuclear industry in the 1950s telling us about the peaceful atom and how by the time they have to get rid of spent uranium, "science" will know what to do. We still don't know what to do with nuclear wastes and reactor safety is an ongoing problem.

The environmental category gets larger and larger. The outbreak of foot-and-mouth and mad cow diseases first reported in
Britain and spreading widely are another aspect of the global
environment's interconnectedness. Viruses, bacteria, and para-
sites, microscopic agents of disease that threaten our food supply
and animal and human health, are carried by the wind and water
and by birds and other living creatures who know no borders and
by humans who travel more than ever before and in larger and
larger numbers. As standardization and inbreeding reduce diversity and as the promiscuous use of drugs, including antibiotics,
increases vulnerabilities, reduces resistance, and promotes stronger strains of diseases, new and more dangerous epidemics become more likely. The corporate greed that denies regulation as
protectionism leads to closing borders as panic spreads from phenomena caused by the corporate avarice that resists application of
the precautionary principle as an impediment to the profit system. Insisting on minimal standards has a health cost even if it
fattens the bottom line.

As this is written Sweden holds the presidency of the European Union and that country's agricultural minister is working
with a green alliance that includes the agricultural minister of
Germany, who is a member of the Green Party there, and Den-
mark's agricultural minister, who is an organic farmer. These
three women and the movements from which they spring represent a potential for shaking up corporate agriculture in Europe.
It is clear that the safe food and environmental movement more
broadly had serious impact on policy debate and may be close to
having important victories thanks to their impact on public consciousness concerning these issues.

Companies who do business with the public worry about bad
publicity and the threat of boycotts and education efforts by activists, which show their activities in an unfavorable light. For
example, McDonald's in the summer of 2000 sent a letter to the

producers of the nearly 2 billion eggs it buys each year ordering them to comply with new guidelines for the humane treatment of hens or risk losing the company's business. Scientists and animal rights activists had expressed vocal concerns, the company was worried, and so it acted. The egg industry warned the campaign could drive up prices. This had little or no effect. McDonald's also took actions to audit animal-welfare practices of its beef and chicken producers. Enough? No. But most companies are responding to social pressures. It will be up to the activists to monitor the results of such announced changes in policy. What will be much harder is to effectively question the whole McDonald's model of fast food of dubious nutritional value and to create guidelines for how much fat goes into the typical American diet, or obtaining a livable wage for the company's employees. Beyond this sort of closer examination of the normalcy of consumer society the issues of sustainability and establishing the harmony of ecological relationships needed for the long-term survival of the planet and its living creatures, including us humans, remains central to the constituencies of the Global Justice Movement.

We can expect corporations, especially those whose brands have become their most valuable assets, to make changes when put under enough pressure. Given the nature of capitalism (that is the name of our economic system, although it seems startling to see it called that in print), this will always be a defensive-after-the-damage-is-done process, or at least it will be until the precautionary principle is truly embraced in the context of placing people and planet before profit as the guiding principle of economic decision making. The Global Justice Movement, while it has made great strides, is up against popular faith and trust in brands as a source of status and satisfaction. In our time as never before belief in consumer brands has replaced religious faith as the inspiration that gives purpose to people's lives. "Brands are

the new religion. People turn to them for meaning," declares
Young & Rubicam, the transnational advertising agency. It explains that successful brands are more than just products. They
represent a set of beliefs, and the people who push them on the
world are much like missionaries spreading religion. Indeed, the
advertising agency thinks that the decline of religion in people's
lives has created a void which is now filled by consumerism. The
cross and the crescent are out, and the brand logo replaces them
at the center of personal identity formation as emotional life
force, although not without a strong backlash in some circles.
(Many see the growth of fundamentalism—whether among
American Christians or Middle Eastern Moslems—as a response
to the onslaught of stylized violence and the depersonalized sex
that are flaunted in popular entertainment.)

"The brands that are succeeding are those with strong beliefs
and original ideas. They are also the ones that have the passion
and energy to change the world, and to convert people to their
way of thinking through outstanding communications."[60] That,
and spending billions upon billions of dollars advertising through
the good offices of firms like Young & Rubicam. Many people
see their brands as a way of expressing their personality, indeed it
becomes their personality to a significant degree. It signals what
social group they identify with and where they see themselves
belonging. With people going to Walt Disney World to be mar-
ried and being buried in Harley-Davidson–brand coffins, traditional religion is a hard sell these days against the competition of
materialism, consumer culture, and the fetishism of commodities. Surely this is not new, but as with much else corporate
globalization colonizes the mind in new and powerful ways.

It's about the money of course. The trouble with facing capitalism as a total system, in thinking of governments and advertising agencies as the agents of a system based on endless
accumulation at the expense of authentic life choices made by

freely actualizing individuals, is that it can be overwhelming. The human self-protective mechanisms kick in so that we close off such a way of understanding our world. As a result it is more difficult to change it. Greed is, at the level of understanding within an individualistic framework of the sort mainstream economics teaches and market ideologies inculcate into every aspect of our socialization, finally quite banal. It is obvious and attributed to the human condition. There is no hope of escaping it. TINA—"there is no alternative"—works on many levels to encourage fatalism and passivity. Its justifications are structurally reinforced and driven home continuously by media and mass culture. The power of capital in all its forms makes change hard.

And yet, at the start of the new millennium, a grassroots counterhegemonic way of thinking about the world—about food, the environment, labor rights, and the destructive activities of transnational capital—*is* changing the way millions think about the system under which we live and what it is doing to our minds as well as our bodies.

Taxation, Public Provisioning,
and the Good Global Society

Removing barriers to the penetration by American corporate interests into other nations has been a consistent U.S. foreign policy since the era of dollar diplomacy at the beginning of the twentieth century, through post–World War II efforts to encourage currency convertibility and end capital controls in Europe, to the pushing of loans on Third World countries to recycle petrodollars in the 1970s, and into the contemporary era of IMF conditionality. The United States and the United Kingdom have been the aggressive liberalizers forcing other states to follow or see their banks and other financial institutions lose market shares. Speculative capital flows have grown apace. The volume of financial market activity is such that only 10 percent of foreign-exchange transactions are related to trade, official government transactions, or direct investment. The other 90 percent involves very short-term movements by speculators and to a lesser extent central bank activities aimed at defending exchange rates. Daily activity is vastly greater than the total reserves of all the central banks in the world. It is therefore not difficult for speculators acting in concert to create large movements in a currency's value. Seeing weakness they can attack a currency and set in motion a profitable change in expectation as others follow their lead, contributing to the profit made from such attacks.

The hardship that is the aftermath of financial liberalization is often seen in the creation of a sequence of asset bubble, panic, capital flight, and economic collapse, followed by austerity. An attack on a currency is like a run on a bank. As more people who still have their money in the bank panic and rush to obtain their money, the bank, having committed most of its funds and thus in an illiquid position, can be driven to bankruptcy unless it can borrow to make good on its obligations. Central banks act as lenders of last resort, making funds available to restore consumer confidence. Deposit insurance has the same effect, assuring depositors that even if the bank doesn't have the money, the insurance fund will meet the bank's commitments to the depositors. Without a lender of last resort banking would suffer periodic panics, as U.S. banks did on an average of about once a decade through the nineteenth century. When government promises are not credible, panic and capital flight result. A country faces the same problem as a bank. If people lose confidence in it, they move their money out. Investors fearing that the economic outlook has deteriorated, which will mean lower returns, take their capital elsewhere. To do this they sell assets denominated in the local currency and put their money into other currencies to buy stocks and other assets in a country whose economy has, they think, stronger prospects. When many people sell the currency it goes down in value. This leads others to conclude that they will get higher returns in another currency and to sell as well. As the currency declines in value, imports cost more to local people, who have to spend more to purchase imported goods that have to be purchased in now more expensive foreign currencies. Hence there is rising inflation, which is to say the local currency buys even less. There is less reason to hold it and more reason to move wealth into stronger currencies to avoid loss. Once a country enters such a situation there may be panic selling of the local currency, like a run on a bank. The government desperately needs more hard foreign currency to pay those who want it. If they cannot buy their own currency, paying with a currency people want more, like dollars, real panic strikes, and the value of the country's currency drops dramatically. Since its debts are denominated in foreign currencies (usually dollars), the burden of the debt for local borrowers increases dramatically. They cannot get new loans except at much higher interest rates or perhaps not at all (given the perception of extreme risk). This is the point at which the government goes to the International Monetary Fund for an emergency loan. It is desperate. No other sources of funds are available. It must accept any conditionality the Fund chooses to impose, thus creating and reinforcing the sort of problems we have already discussed.

While countries have always faced problems of the credibility of their exchange rates the vast increase in money moving quickly around the world seeking higher returns means that national currencies can fluctuate dramatically with agonizing implications for the countries' businesses and for ordinary citizens. When prospects look bright money pours in, asset values go up and up, and more money comes in until a bubble inflates. But so long as speculators think they will be able to sell for more than they pay, the buying spree continues. At some point the bubble bursts, money goes out faster than it came in, and crisis results. Most countries have experienced these cycles. The surges and hard landings can be extreme, with harsh consequences for those with the least resources to last through them. This is why reregulation of finance is needed and why the forced liberalization pushed by international agencies and financial institutions has been so roundly criticized. There is a need to insulate local economies, to avoid these destructive cycles. The costs they impose suggest that ways must be found to allow for real foreign direct investment in which foreign funds are used to build factories and make other tangible investments (under terms acceptable to host governments), which help develop an economy but at the same time limit short-term speculative capital flows that are so destructive.

There is another problem that is intensified by financial liberalization in an era of rapid and easy capital mobility. This is the ability to hide wealth from the tax collector and the law. As well-publicized episodes involving deposed dictators and drug cartels who move funds through U.S. banks and involving vast sums of monies flowing to offshore tax havens in the Caribbean and elsewhere demonstrate, it has become all too easy to evade norms that had in the past held money laundering and tax evasion within some bounds. Today the ability to avoid regulation and for criminal activities to thrive is undermining the ability of governments to collect tax revenues. While social-movement activists have not yet demonstrated against the lack of regulation of capital flows, this is an issue that is exceedingly important for the quality of life and for the future of the public sector and that of the welfare state. The problem has not appeared as dramatic as the debt crises and their aftermath in forced structural adjustments, declining living standards, cuts in public services, takeover of the local economies by the global state economic governance institutions, and the appropriation of the nation's resources at bargain-basement prices by foreign investors, but it is cancerous nonetheless.

Money laundering is the conversion of illicit cash to another asset to conceal the true source of ownership and create the perception of legitimate ownership. The point is to take illegal funds and make them indistinguishable from other monies. Bank secrecy laws in various countries make money laundering a great deal easier. Many jurisdictions in fact sell this service and resist implementation of policies to establish the true identity of their customers and the real ownership of accounts. There have been a number of efforts to deal with drug-money laundering. For example, the Council of Europe in 1990 adopted the Convention on Laundering, Search, Seizure and Confiscation of the Proceeds from Crime. The problem has been that efforts to crack down on what governments see as criminal activity associated with drug cartels and organized crime interfere with what they accept as the legitimate behavior of other financial actors, for example transnational corporations and banks. It is however the activities of the latter, the legitimate corporations and financial institutions, rather than the criminal syndicates, who do the most damage to the treasuries of countries around the world. It is undetected "normal" procedures of tax avoidance that should be the center of scrutiny.

Globalization has increased tax competition, produced wide-spread fiscal crises, and changed dramatically the way the tax burden is allocated. The corporate rich pay less. The ordinary citizen pays more and gets fewer of the services than they would be receiving if tax avoidance was not being practiced on such a scale. The developed countries have effectively ended tax with-holding. In 1984 the United States first abolished its withholding tax on interest paid to foreigners. This action meant that no other country could continue such withholding without losing busi-ness to the U.S. financial markets. As a result hardly anyone with real money pays taxes on such income when with a little trouble they can avoid it. When Germany tried to impose a tax on in-terest income in 1988, monies in huge quantity moved to neigh-boring Luxembourg. The tax was quickly repealed. The Germans have tried to get a European Union–wide withholding tax on all interest paid to E.U. residents, but Luxembourg and more importantly the United Kingdom have successfully fought the effort. London is the center of finance not only for Europe but for much of the rest of the world and is not about to give up any of its advantage.

Liechtenstein, a tiny country in the Alps, comes into the news occasionally when it is discovered that some prominent figure, former German chancellor Helmut Kohl being a good example, has kept hundreds of millions of dollars, in his case from secret campaign contributions, conveniently parked in that country's accommodating banks. Prince Hans Adam II, whose ancestors bought the country from Austria three centuries ago, from his 130-room palace, defends hiding people's money for them. The country of thirty thousand people has grown quite wealthy on the family business. Its richest citizens, in addition to the prince, are the lawyers and the bankers who set up mailbox corporations for the Sicilian mafia and Latin American drug cartels, as well as leading European political and business figures.[1]

Rolf Breuer, the chairman of Deutsche Bank, the world's largest bank, was accused by German prosecutors of abetting tax evasion after four hundred clients of the bank admitted investing money in tax havens such as Luxembourg and Switzerland. Breuer is one of the most prominent bankers in Europe, and that he and his bank were thought to be involved in this practice suggests that the extent of the corruption is on a grand scale indeed.[2] It also highlights the degree to which it is not those we think of as the criminal element in society but rather its most respected members, leading bankers, chief financial officers, and billionaire hedge-fund operators, who are laundering the most money. Many other countries are involved. Israel, established as a safe haven for Jews, with a tradition of welcoming immigrants and their money with no questions asked, encourages foreign racketeers to deposit funds, in local banks, made out in the name of fictitious people and corporations. Reporting requirements are minimal and foreign tax evasion is not considered a crime. An Israeli passport is easily arranged. Even if the money is shown to be from fraud, theft, or narcotics, it is not seized and the person is prosecuted only if they have committed a crime within Israel. Secrecy laws make it difficult for foreign governments to gain access to records.

Effective regulation will eventually have to apply globally, since there are so many countries willing to set up corporations, to hold investor monies and move it in and out of bonds and other interest-earning investments made in higher-tax jurisdictions. They exempt earnings from taxes under so-called portfolio interest exemptions and do not tax the income of the offshore corporation they set up. In the Bahamas there are more than four hundred foreign banks and trust companies that exist merely to facilitate such activities. The island imposes no taxes on corporate profits, capital gains, or income from inheritance. The Channel Islands off the coast of France, Mauritius off Africa's southeast coast, and the Cook Islands in the Pacific, a collection of rocks sticking out of the ocean eighteen hundred miles northeast of New Zealand, are a few of the jurisdictions where one can hire a lawyer or see a banker and arrange to hide money from one's creditors, government, and business partners. An offshore company can be your vehicle for making money invisible without anyone knowing it is yours or coming to collect taxes.

One does not have to go to such obscure places to launder money. A congressional inquiry reports that it is "relatively easy" for foreigners to hide their identities, form shell companies, and to launder money through American banks. In a nine-month inquiry that subpoenaed bank records it was discovered, for example, that one enterprising recent Russian immigrant had set up more than two thousand corporations in Delaware for Russians back home and then opened accounts for them. Hundreds of millions of dollars were sent to these accounts from Russia by corrupt officials and other criminals of all sorts.[3] Neither New York nor Delaware demand that the owners and officers be listed on incorporation filings. Where company directors are supposed to be listed, lawyers name themselves or leave forms blank. No one seems to care. The banks like the business. Politicians like to please the bankers and their lawyer-lobbyists who reciprocate with campaign contributions.

Federal investigators followed the activities of a customer of one major New York bank, a powerful Russian organized-crime leader in the United States (whether Russians are more clever at this sort of thing having been trained to avoid regulations under communism, or not as good at it as others and so get caught more and are in the news, is hard to say) who was running money in from the Cayman Islands, the Isle of Man, and other havens through thousands of accounts. Officials tapped his fax and found four thousand phony corporate fronts in New York, a thousand in Delaware, and a few hundred in Pennsylvania, Massachusetts, Ohio, and other states.[4] Thousands of U.S. visas are issued each year to individuals connected to nonexistent businesses. But investigators have a hard time. State records do not allow computer searches to locate corporations by filer. New York State Police agents had to search by hand the papers of every corporation filed with the state to identify those with recognizable names of particular suspects.

Most of the dramatic stories in the popular press convey the impression that money laundering and tax evasion are by mafia types and other uniquely corrupt individuals. In reality the greatest loss to the public treasury comes from the systematic tax avoidance by our richest business leaders. Even more importantly large transnational corporations routinely avoid taxes by booking their profits in low-tax jurisdictions. In 1966, for example, corporate income taxes accounted for 23 percent of U.S. government receipts. In fiscal 1999 they were only 10 percent of the total. The difference, since total taxes have surely not gone down, is paid for by you and me. Money laundering, while a severe and growing problem, is a small one compared to tax avoidance using corporate-accounting gimmicks, and many of these scams originate in the headquarters of the country's most prestigious financial and accounting firms.

There are many ploys. Consider one case. "Financial engineers," as they are called in the trade, at Merrill Lynch saved Allied Signal $180 million in taxes owed on the sale of an oil business, in a scheme that transferred the taxable profits from the sale to a newly created partnership with a foreign company, and that company then returned the money to Allied Signal in a way that was not taxable. For their efforts Merrill Lynch received $25 million. By creating such paper transactions, whose only purpose is to deprive the government of legitimate taxes, both the businesses and individuals involved get rich at the expense of public health and education, which are starved of funds. Merrill Lynch is not alone in the practice, of course. Goldman, Sachs does it. So does Bear, Stearns. The Big Five accounting firms, all of them, PricewaterhouseCoopers, Ernst & Young, Deloitte & Touche, KPMG, and Arthur Andersen, charge corporations a fee based on a percentage on the tax savings using these shelters. Whether courts find such shelters illegal, as they should since the shelters serve no business purpose, indeed no purpose other than tax avoidance, depends on who the judges are, how good the lawyers are, and the climate in the country as to how far corporate thieves can push the envelope of allowable criminality. While Allied Signal lost the case in 1990, the scheme declared a sham and illegal, the company in its contemporary identity (Allied Signal is now Honeywell and as such is soon to be merged with General Electric) is still appealing the case. It would not do to have such a precedent on corporate accountability established.

As David Cay Johnston writes at the start of this new century, "Few tax shelters are uncovered by the Internal Revenue Service, whose resources have been significantly reduced in recent years. And even if one is discovered, penalties are rare. Criminal prosecution is almost unheard of. And, as in the Allied Signal case, the Treasury is still without the money while the appeals drag on for years."[5]

The effect of these actions by the IRS has been that Congress has cut the IRS budget and limited its powers so that it now goes after primarily the lowest income-tax bracket individuals and not the rich, and certainly not the corporations. It would really be abolished, by the best Congress money can buy, if it tried to enforce the tax law, as inadequate as it now is, without fear or favor. As a result, corporations, or rather the people who run them, make a calculation: What are my chances of getting caught? Small, bordering on nonexistent. What happens if I do get caught? Probably nothing. What if I am after much delay and appeals found guilty? I will pay a fraction of what I should. The odds are such that perpetual, systemic corporate dishonesty is the logical choice for any profit maximizer. As one former chair of the American Bar Association explains of those who engage in such practices, "Once I got past 'I know I am doing something wrong here,' the arithmetic settles it for me."[6]

Money laundering and tax avoidance are so routinized, and legal ways of cheating so common, that hundreds of thousands of rich individuals and corporations (many of which are shells to hide individual wealth) are sheltering huge amounts of money. As the World Bank delicately concludes, "A large portion of the trade these networks generate happens within firms that are able to realize profits in countries with low tax rates. Countries with high corporate tax rates may attract foreign direct investment but will realize lower profits than they expected. . . . The benefits of these networks to the economy are then partially offset by a smaller national corporate tax base increasing the pressure to raise taxes on incomes that are less internationally mobile, such as labor. Multinational corporations appear to be the primary beneficiaries of liberalization, while contributing little to the infrastructure that encourages production networks in the first place."[7]

The governments of the rich countries have taken action as the publicity over drug-money laundering, and over the capital flight of billions of dollars that were stolen by Third World dictators and looted by oligarchs and terrorist networks, has been spread over newspaper pages to the edification and alarm of readers. The trick for the major governments wishing to protect the tax-avoidance capacity for those well-connected nationals who show their gratitude in ways appreciated by officials is to control these flows coming from places like Nigeria and Colombia and moved through islands like Dominica and Antigua without cutting into the profitable activities of Western transnational corporations and international banks headquartered in the countries of the core. Because the issue of money laundering is now so prominent that it can't be ignored, major governments are working to protect the main culprits, who are the corporate rich and who are closely watching reform efforts to see that their interests remain unaffected. Thus U.S. Treasury officials have been concerned that they do not put "an undue burden" on the private sector.[8] Yet they may have to limit their excesses. The social cost imposed by the hemorrhaging of revenue is simply too great. A General Accounting Office (GAO) study reports that from 1989 to 1995 a majority of both U.S.- and foreign-controlled companies paid zero U.S. corporation income taxes. They were able to do this using tax-avoidance methods, many of which were legal. Transfer pricing shifts income (at least as a matter of the way they do the accounting) so that it appears as earned in jurisdictions where low or no taxes are required of the companies. Some free marketeers celebrate the way such tax avoidance starves the public sector, saying such competition among governments to better meet the demands of the market are what capitalism should be about.

The fear, as Dan Mitchell of the Heritage Foundation points out, is that the ultimate target of an anti-tax-regime competition campaign is likely to be the world's biggest tax haven—the United States. Monies from around the world have found their way into the U.S. economy, fueling to a significant extent the stock market and bond market booms of the 1980s and 1990s. The ability to move money to the United States puts limits on the ability of other countries to raise taxes from their own wealthier citizens. But lower tax rates do not stop avoidance. The sixty offshore tax havens with about 1 percent of the world's population hold more than a quarter of the world's financial assets, and according to Merrill Lynch and Gemini Consulting's "World Wealth Report," a third of the wealth of the world's wealthy individuals may be held offshore, about $6 trillion. Offshore havens hold more than 30 percent of the profits of U.S.-based transnationals. Robert M. Morganthau, the Manhattan district attorney, citing previously secret Federal Reserve Bank data, told a senate committee that more than $80 billion of American money is on deposit in just one tax haven, the Cayman Islands. That sum is equal to one-fifth of all bank deposits in the United States. It is too large, said Morganthau, to be primarily the fruits of organized criminal activities such as drug dealing. Rather it is the product of huge and growing tax evasion by wealthy Americans who have little fear of prosecution. The hearing at which he testified was held in response to Secretary O'Neill's refusal to cooperate with a plan by the Organization for Economic Cooperation and Development to pressure the Cayman Islands and other tax havens into cooperating with investigations of tax evasion and money laundering. Secretary O'Neill had declared the project "not in line with this administration's priorities." The secretary had said "we should not presume to interfere with the internal tax policies of sovereign nations."[9] Secretary O'Neill says such laws impose "significant

costs on society" and has questioned the value the U.S. government gets from the money it spends fighting money laundering.
Senator Carl Levin, on the other hand, points out that the $70
billion in taxes the United States government loses annually from
such evasion is so huge that if even half of it were collected it
would pay for a Medicare prescription drug program without
raising anyone's taxes or cutting anyone's budget. Perhaps the
best part of this interchange was Secretary O'Neill's response
to a letter that seven former Internal Revenue Service com-
missioners sent to him in June 2001, questioning his stance on
the OECD effort to make foreign tax havens cooperate with
investigations of tax crimes. Mr. O'Neill said he was "frankly
thunderstruck when I got the letter; they responded to misinter-
pretations in the press." Actually the letter came in response to an
article in the May 10 *Washington Times,* which appeared under
Mr. O'Neill's own byline.[10]

The struggle for equitable taxation is an important part of the
larger battle to win back the public sector; the idea that society as
a whole should be responsible for public goods requires that the
wealth corporations accumulate be taxed fairly. That capital
avoids taxes means not only that working people's burdens go up
but also that the public sector must rely on charity from these
very same companies who engage in both tax avoidance (arrang-
ing things so that they do not incur tax obligations within the
jurisdiction of the IRS) and tax evasion, escaping payment of
taxes due, such that, for example, when kids in the St. Louis zoo
want to study bugs it needs to be at a Monsanto Insectarium
because the city has had to go hat in hand to corporations to
underwrite public space. If corporations are properly taxed and a
well-funded public sector is able to provide, then the city could
pay for its Insectarium as well as for schools, teachers, and even
books so as not to have to rely on "Kellogg's Froot Loops!
Counting Fun Book" and such corporate beneficence, tax-

deductible advertising vehicles the students are forced to be indoctrinated with by the very teachers they should be able to trust to teach them about nutrition and other important life-shaping things that matter.

Today, at the Hasbro Children's Hospital in Rhode Island, a facility for which that company's employees reviewed the architectural plans to ensure the hospital had "a fun, aesthetically pleasing atmosphere" in harmony with the company's preferred image, the children's menu features bowls of cereal named for Mr. Potato Head, the Hasbro toy. Is this a cynical attempt to increase company profits? No. The company just wants to "bring a smile to a child." All this cost the company only $2.5 million, not much for corporate America, but apparently beyond the capacities of the tax base of the city. In Philadelphia, the children's museum has "a virtual partner in McDonald's without whose help the building might not bear the company's name and its food served on site." The museum couldn't get the $5 million McDonald's gave it from taxes. In Chicago, a historic Ferris wheel has a McDonald's logo on every chair. At the city's Field Museum of Natural History, a corporate consortium, including McDonald's and Walt Disney, donated half the cost to acquire Sue, the most complete fossil extant of a *Tyrannosaurus rex*, and McDonald's finances two cast models of the dinosaur for a traveling exhibit and an educational kit that contains proper recognition of its munificence. The withdrawal of public funds from municipalities who have to give subsidies to attract jobs from the companies which then turn around and "generously" get a further tax writeoff from a well-publicized investment in perpetual publicity through association with a worthy cause is the new shame of the cities. If Detroit wants a high-quality display of African American art, General Motors is happy for the chance to garner some positive publicity by underwriting it after the automaker has shuttered plants in the city and laid off many city residents, blacks and whites.[11]

While corporate culture continues to invade every nook and cranny of public space in an effort to sell more and more and commodify everything from public schools to prisons, accepting no limits to its expansion, tax avoidance has grown to such a point that it threatens the viability of the social order. Globalization intensifies the erosion of a minimally adequate level of public funding due to the mobility of capital. Technology allows further opportunities for tax avoidance, as we have noted. Treasury officials express concern over electronic commerce. Web sites are set up by companies in jurisdictions unwilling to share taxpayer information with U.S. officials. This allows selling products globally without paying taxes. Encryption technologies allow for further concealment of money and its rapid movement using the Internet. This kind of activity has become the ultimate tax haven and creates massive erosion of the tax base, and governments cannot allow this to continue without dire consequences.[12] Business rejects proposals to tax their Internet earnings. Even milder tax reform proposals are resisted in the United States and by businesses elsewhere.

In Britain, the Confederation of British Industry (CBI), the country's principal employers' organization, launched a campaign in the spring of 2000 to sabotage measures their government proposed taking to clamp down on tax evasion by multinationals. As Michael Peel reported in the *Financial Times*: "The CBI assault shows how the issue has made a mockery of talk of a consensual approach between the private sector and government. The battle has revealed divisions over the definition of tax avoidance." The clash demonstrated the importance and the extent of such strategies used by multinationals to minimize the extra tax paid on profits repatriated from countries with low corporation tax rates. Companies avoid this by channeling profits through mixer companies, overseas subsidiaries that offset earnings. And of course business says that abolition of mixers would cause them to invest more of their profits abroad or even to relocate their headquarters out of the country.[13]

Individual governments are routinely blackmailed in this way when they try to establish a fair rate of taxation on corporations, which enjoy both great political influence in their own countries and the ability to move if governments desperate for tax revenues grow insistent. Yet officials have become so scared of the consequence of dramatic tax erosion that they are willing to some extent to challenge the corporations on these issues. At the end of the Clinton years the Treasury Department was alarmed at the proliferation of abusive corporate tax shelters, which had become so widespread as to be normal operating procedure. It proposed new regulations aimed at such practices. The new regulations would require corporations to disclose shelters on their tax returns under certain specified conditions (such as that they paid more than $100,000 to an outside firm for help in creating such shelters, and that the firms who arrange such shelters disclose them to the IRS as soon as they begin offering them—one can foresee more of the work being done in-house by the large corporations). The Treasury's actual steps taken were to be cautious ones.[14] Clinton administration proposals aimed at money-laundering abuses received tepid responses from bankers. "My overall perspective on this is we don't believe any new legislation is warranted," says John Byrne, senior counsel at the American Bankers Association.[15] The banking industry was particularly concerned that they might be forced to identify the true owners of U.S. accounts held through their so-called brass-plate banks in offshore jurisdictions. These are banks which exist as a brass plate in front of a building on some far-off island, in a small room with a telex machine, and which establish the right for the bank to do business there and thus avoid regulation.

As it was leaving office, the Clinton administration suggested voluntary guidelines as a result of what is described as "a delicate compromise" between leading banks and law enforcement officials. The bankers had objected to a binding anti-money-laundering initiative. Some banks protested even the voluntary guidelines, revealing how eager they were to continue managing money for these wealthy individuals. At this point the U.S. banks have far more lax practices than the Swiss bankers. Citigroup led the effort to water down even the voluntary regulations.[16] It would be interesting to see if they would favor making robbing banks at gunpoint legal, then simply asking for voluntary guidelines that people should please not rob banks. Far more is stolen through private banking's good offices than at the point of a gun at the local branch offices. Citigroup makes a great deal of money laundering the ill-gotten gains of the families it gives its personal-banker attention: the sons of Nigerian dictator General Sani Abacha; the daughters of Indonesia's former president General Suharto; the brother of Mexico's former president Raul Salinas; Asif Ali Zardari, the husband of the former prime minister of Pakistan; and others. Each time Citigroup says it is putting new controls in place, but the beat goes on. In February 2001 Citigroup was caught yet again in a corruption investigation surrounding one of its wealthiest customers, Joseph Estrada, the ousted president of the Philippines. The amounts stolen by such leaders and their friends and families frequently run into the tens of billions of dollars, comparable in size to the foreign debt the citizens of such countries continue to owe to the banks. Ironically, the banks making loans to dishonest leaders of poor countries get the money back as private banker deposits from these rulers, and then they get it back again from the people of the countries involved, who are saddled with the debt repayment.

A report that was critical of money laundering and published by the Financial Action Task Force, which is linked to the Organization for Economic Cooperation and Development (OECD), a report that detailed the extent of abuses and led to a blacklist of tax havens, jurisdictions that were told to clean up their acts or they would not be allowed to do business with OECD member banks, may have some impact.[17] The well-heeled bankers in Switzerland were forced after decades of stone-walling to account for Holocaust victims' monies. But they are clear that they do not expect to give up their top-drawer customers.[18] The Swiss Banking Commission named some of the country's most respected banks as having failed to check adequately before accepting the ill-gotten gains of General Sani Abacha, for instance.[19] The new Nigerian government's efforts to reclaim these monies has put the spotlight on the largest Swiss banks in a repeat of the reaction to efforts by the Philippines government to recover the late Ferdinand Marcos's wealth that was appropriated from that country's people (and one presumes a new round will take place as they try and recover Estrada's ill-gotten monies). Switzerland, which accounts for an estimated third of the world's offshore private banking industry, claims it already fully complies with the recommendations of the OECD's proposed tighter banking standards for cracking down on tax evasion. At the same time, the Swiss Bankers Association pledges "in no way" will it weaken the protection of the privacy of bank customers.[20] Indeed, the French parliament's task force on money laundering has denounced both Switzerland's "predator world of finance" and its government's "sham war" against the problem.[21] As the *Economist* wrote, "Any further tightening up on money laundering faces big obstacles. Banks understandably want to protect the privacy of their customers, and they face fierce competitive pressures not to ask too many questions."[22] It will be hard to change their "don't ask, don't tell" policies given the priorities of the Bush administration, whose willingness to use all methods to track terrorists' funding ignores this issue.

The measures so far which have been taken against the respectable tax avoiders are only the mildest steps. They are more to assuage popular outrage than to ensure any meaningful change. What needs to be done is much bolder. It should not be a surprise that as inadequate as these efforts have been shortly after President Bush took office the *Wall Street Journal* reported that the administration considered backing away from an international campaign to crack down on tax havens like Panama, Monaco, and the Bahamas. In internal discussions, Treasury Secretary Paul O'Neill (who at the time raised a minor tempest by refusing to sell his hundred and whatever million dollars of stock in Alcoa, the company he had worked for, while in public office) had expressed skepticism, as we have noted, about OECD efforts, saying, "It was important to respect the integrity of the various tax systems."[23] Treasury officials offered such explanations with straight faces in a collection of remarkable performances from a government that has never hesitated to dictate policies to other smaller governments when it suits its purposes.

OECD officials have been hampered in their efforts by the opposition of the Bush administration and congressional leaders such as Dick Armey, who says the OECD initiative would create "a global network of tax police," which he as a good freedom-loving American opposes. Mark Weinberger, the Bush Treasury Department's assistant secretary for tax policy, says the United States is not interested in any effort to curb tax competition among jurisdictions. OECD officials also identified lobbying in the United States by a coalition of free-market advocates, the Center for Freedom and Prosperity, financed by unnamed wealthy individuals, who would be hurt by any such regulations.[24]

Action does need to be taken to restore tax equity and proper law enforcement on a global basis. What meaningful measures should be considered? One is a unitary tax. Transnational companies, defined as any firm that does business above some modest level in more than one country, would be taxed on its total global business activities. No matter where they produced and how they sold their products on diverse markets, all of these corporations would be taxed on the same basis. The revenues would be distributed to countries based on business done by the firm in their jurisdiction. Such a unitary tax would make avoidance harder. It would be more difficult for countries to offer tax-haven services. A global tax on interest income and a stock-transfer tax would raise huge amounts of revenue.

The corporations have been enthusiastic about the establishment of the World Trade Organization and in using it, the International Monetary Fund, and the other global state economic governance institutions for their own ends. It is unlikely that they would like to see a World Tax Organization or a World Environmental Organization, or an International Labor Organization with enforcement powers. But these are developments that will have to come at the global level if there is to be fairness in place of the unilateral rule by corporate capitalism. The challenge will be to see that they are democratic in their operation and progressive in their policies. If tax competition were to be limited in these ways all countries would gain, or at least the majority of their citizens would. Investors could continue to invest based on expected profitability. They would simply pay what most people consider their fair share of the tax burden.

The benefits of international coordination of a tax on speculative financial transactions, the so-called Tobin Tax, named after Nobel laureate James Tobin of Yale University, have been widely recognized. Even at rates so low as not to impact on long-term direct foreign investment, such a tax would discourage short-term capital movements of a day or two which now dominate and are directed at speculative profits. Nine-tenths of foreign exchange transactions are reversed within a week, 40 percent within a day. Very little of the vast movement of monies sloshing around the world represents a net transfer of resources from investors in one country to actual investments in economy building in another. These huge gross movements are destabilizing and socially costly. A small Tobin Tax would raise in excess of a trillion dollars a year, which, if earmarked for Third World development could produce relatively painless funding to finance sustainable improvements in the lives of the world's poor. Strong support for the Tobin Tax led French premier Lionel Jospen to endorse such a tax on speculative foreign exchange transfers. He was joined by Helmut Schröder who has, as one financial writer notes, "sharp political antennae." Horst Köhler, the IMF's managing director, also jumped aboard. While acknowledging that he remained "very skeptical," he said that "if it is necessary to look again at the Tobin tax and related issues, we should certainly do so."[25] While these politicians were certainly not themselves supportive of a such a tax on capital, they were in part responding to organized pressures. "Like them or not, anti-globablization protesters have succeeded in altering political debate at the top."[26]

"Altering" may be putting it a bit strong, as there has been no real conversion. Governments continue to avoid the social regulation of capital. However, what is called the anti–globilization movement has at least become a potent political force that can no longer be ignored. In response to the Franco-German decision in the fall of 2001 to set up a high-level group to examine better ways of controlling international financial markets, lip service had to be given. As the *Financial Times* reported, "one monetary official argued it would be counterproductive to reject the Tobin tax idea without giving the impression it had been given serious thought."[27]

These are not new ideas. The Brandt Commission in the 1970s proposed a global armaments tax, the proceeds of which were to go to development of the poorer countries. The Brundtland Commission endorsed the idea and added another tax on pollution to protect the environment with the same redistributive use of revenues. Indeed, the idea of the world community pursuing progressive goals of development and meeting basic needs in an inclusive global community has been the core of the United Nations purpose since its inception. Its various gatherings to support the rights of women, to protect the environment, to deal with the problems of displaced persons, to address the root causes of war, and other noble undertakings, whatever the cynical manipulations and maneuvering we have seen, speak to an alternative vision well worth pursuing. That the powerful choose, at best, only rhetorical support while moving functions of economics and finance to the parallel governmental institutions over which they exercise more direct control, namely, the global state economic governance institutions, has precluded progress in these areas while imposing new burdens on the world's people.

Fair taxation of transnationals will be a major struggle. It will need to be followed or accompanied by a global antitrust effort and other social and economic regulation that addresses the implications of growing concentration and centralization of corporate power. Given the close relationship between elected officials and the corporations that fund their election, many in global civil society are skeptical that such regulation would be very meaningful. It is likely to be only symbolic, should there be enough pressure to force governments to act. Such pessimism points to the need for even more basic changes, that could make democracy itself more than a ceremonial anointing of candidates preselected by an essentially compromised process.

As mergers occur in the airline, auto, energy, and telecom

industries and planet-spanning monopolies and oligopolies are created, such questions will be inevitably on the agenda for global civil society. Challenging the market power of transnational capital, their labor and environmental practices could lead to a still deeper critique of other elements of market society. U.S. corporations spend about $200 billion a year in advertising to train people to demand instant gratification through consumption, touting possessions as the means of dealing with insecurity and gaining personal status. By changing one's toothpaste you get more kisses, a new shampoo promises orgasms in the shower, taking the grandchildren to McDonald's guarantees the kids will pay more loving attention to you, and so on.

If many Americans have not been much interested in the rest of the world and the future of the environment, it is in part because they have been kept too busy by the thousands of commercials that pander to an individualistic outlook in which one exists only in the role of consumer in a commercially driven society. Having begun with a critique of the global state economic governance institutions, social movements come to challenge the priorities of the U.S. hegemonic state and then the international banks and the drive of transnational corporations. Once critique begins, capitalist social relations are understood to be about more than the exploitation of powerless workers and their families in the poorest countries, but about work life in this country. Oppression extends as well to ideological and cultural domination. It is easy to see why defenders of corporate globalization try to cut short criticism as early in the process as they can.

Is a healthier society possible?

The United Nations Declaration on Human Rights more than half a century ago enshrined such principles into promises signed onto by the nations of the world. More recently, the Copenhagen Declaration on Social Development called for equitable sharing of debt burdens, placing a priority on meeting human needs, ensuring democratic representation in decision making, and guaranteeing fair rewards for labor. World leaders seem capable of endorsing admirable values and enumerating the requirements for the good global society. The problem has been when it comes to changing the real world they have not done a very good job of following through. They have deferred to other values, the values of the market, an acceptance of existing power relations, and a grossly unequal wealth distribution.

The need for alternative investment priorities is clear enough. The United Nations Children's Fund (UNICEF) tells us 11 million children die every year from mostly preventable diseases, 170 million are malnourished, and 100 million children do not attend school.[28] The United Nations World Food Program details the plight of the 830 million persons around the world who, because of natural disasters, armed conflict, and grinding poverty are consigned to chronic malnutrition. "From generation to generation, people don't have enough food to eat," Catherine Bertini, the agency's executive director, tells us. "The combination of poverty and disaster causes people to have even less possibility to build resources to end their hunger."[29] Such conditions have bred hatred of the United States, which many see as responsible for the perpetuation of unnecessary suffering.

From behind John Rawl's veil of ignorance, the presumption that we will be born into the world not knowing what position we shall have, it would behoove us to see that the desperate plight of such people is attended to and that all of the people of the world are helped to the resources that give them the capacities to make a better life for themselves. If we can absorb the message of the religions of the world that we are all sisters and brothers and that we are judged by how we treat the least of those among us then we would do well to embrace the priors of the models of philosophers, such as Rawls and his Harvard University colleague and Nobel laureate in economics, Amartya Sen, that the importance of human capabilities as primary goods that are required for substantive freedom need to replace neoliberal assumptions of procedural freedom. As Sen has argued, the need is not primarily for more goods, as the mainstream economics model presumes, but rather for enhancing the capacities of people.

Neoliberalism is a version of trickle-down economics. The presumption is that if there is growth, it will eventually reach those at the bottom. This has not happened in most parts of the world. Where it has happened it has been the result of deliberate social intervention in the form of redistributional programs and government-provided services enhancing the capacities of people, empowering them, and allowing them to some extent to break out of their structural position of unequal opportunity and exploitative relation to the larger social and economic order. As Vinod Thomas, a vice president of the World Bank and the head of its education arm, the World Bank Institute, has written, "Experience in developing as well as industrial countries shows that it is not merely more growth but also better growth that determines how much welfare improves—and whose welfare."[30]

In its discussion of the pursuit of basic human rights the United Nations Development Program's (UNDP) *Human Development Report 2000* calls attention to the need for more than the rhetoric of good intentions on the part of governments. It points out that: "Global corporations can have enormous impact on human rights, in their employment practices, in their environmental impacts, in their support for corrupt regimes or in their advocacy for policy changes. Yet international laws hold states accountable, not corporations." As has been noted, many corporations have adopted codes of conduct and policies of social responsibility in response to public pressure. But, as the UNDP reports, "many fail to meet human rights standards, or lack implementation measures and independent audits."[31] Such conclusions suggest that it is time to take on corporate power.

Throughout this book we have detailed the reality of this assertion and have explained how state power is used to protect corporate interests and advance their agenda. Those who criticize demonstrators protesting the actions of global state economic governance institutions blame the messenger and typically repeat the mantra that free trade is the only way to help the poor and that efforts to ensure labor rights and environmental protection slow growth and so hurt the poor. This is not a convincing argument, as we have seen. Rather, the real issue is how shall the rules of interdependence be decided and enforced? Can this be done in a democratic fashion that gives pride of place to the needs of the least advantaged instead of the most privileged? Can we talk sensibly about income distribution and the provision of public services, deemphasize ecologically damaging patterns of growth, and instead design sustainable growth with equity? Are we not allowed to say that in a democratic society what those who control markets declare as efficient can be judged undesirable? Can we not instead start with the principle of the subsidiarity of economic life to values of community, security, equity, and social solidarity?

There are different possible paths forward. Those who prefer the corporate-controlled version of neoliberal globalization do not want us to take any of those paths seriously except the one true path they declare best for us. In a sense such people are the easiest for those promoting a globalization from below, peoples' alternatives of a different sort, to deal with. More difficult is the issue of what to do when World Bank President James Wolfensohn invites "reasonable NGOs" who are "interested in serious debate" in for discussion. There have been efforts to present new and more realistic NGO representatives who welcome such invitations as the more effective successors of the Seattle protesters.

Roger Cohen in the Sunday *New York Times,* for example, in-
troduces readers to Annie-Christine Habbard, thirty-one, who
with "her Danish mother, her Syrian father, her French passport,
and her Oxford education seems every inch the global citizen
equipped to succeed in a shrinking world. Yet here she is, chic in
black, articulate in several tongues," at the annual meeting of the
World Bank and the International Monetary Fund, protesting
the state of the globe. Ms. Habbard, with her "cool features and
articulate aplomb," wants social justice and is "determined to
change the world through international human-rights law where
her predecessors deployed Marxist revolution or flower power.
She is intensely pragmatic. . . . Nothing dreamy here: this fight
to shape globalization has all the romance of a corporate takeover
battle."[32]

Now, I do not know Ms. Habbard (or Mr. Cohen) and I am
not sure what we are to take from such an article. Are the powers
to be to feel better that at last there are persons with whom to
negotiate who have the proper behavior and clothes, the education and the pragmatism that will enable the game to now be
played indoors in a grown-up fashion? We can handle such
people, no problem. If the crowds stay home we can talk to these
"chic in black" protesters until the cameras are gone, and then
we can stonewall them for years in court. Thank goodness the
specter of violence and, worse, of mass activism and nonviolent
civil disobedience by tens of thousands supported by public
opinion is over and we can deal with all this in a civilized manner
on our terms. Walden Bello calls the strategy "disarmament by
dialogue."[33]

It is not that we do not need legal challenges and the talents
Oxford-educated people may bring to the struggle. There is a
need for pragmatic folks working the inside. But social movements that demobilize and leave things to experts may watch the
concern for their issues dwindle and see less, rather than more,

willingness on the part of the powerful to make real concessions. At this post-Seattle moment, there will be efforts to divide and, in the shadow of fears of renewed terrorist attacks, subdue social justice activism. We need to remember that the currency of the movement's power is a mix of moral authority, size, and credible analysis. The three are related.

There are NGOs that act as think tanks for global civil society. Some mobilize activists. Some deliver concrete assistance through local presence in arenas of suffering where the need for outside help is great. One of the most successful NGOs, Oxfam International, offers a model of how social movements can be effectively institutionalized, can focus global awareness, and can hold governments accountable. By balancing an implicit denunciation of hypocrisy with surmounting a particular issue, appealing to moral decency, and offering moderate yet meaningful steps to resolution, Oxfam walks the line between opposition and helping governments regain legitimacy by actually making a difference. I want to say something about how Oxfam's strategy works to combine solid research and clarity in presenting issues with concrete actions that speak truth to power. It is one model. The large aggregation of approaches that compose the broad Global Justice Movement include others, such as mass protests against institutional injustice and anticapitalist foci that do not ask for reform but demand revolution as the only possibility of a better society. There are civil disobedience activities and puppet-making. The imagination of the movement, the range of its issues, and the tactics it embraces are wide indeed, as we have seen. Nonetheless I want to single out Oxfam's Global Action Plan for education as one model of combining consciousness-building with proposals to governments for programmatic alternatives and the employment of tactics for building effective support to achieve a goal supplementing and enforcing mass mobilization.

In an August 2000 briefing paper on the topic of education,

Oxfam begins with the facts, allowing them "to speak for themselves." One hundred twenty-five million children never attend school. Another 150 million children start primary school but drop out before they learn to read or write. Two-thirds of children who are out of school are girls. One in 4 adults in the developing world is illiterate—some 880 million people, and so on. Its briefing paper was circulated just four months after world leaders had gathered in Dakar, Senegal, to review progress and to affirm education as a fundamental human right. The gathering had set goals of free and compulsory education for all and the halving of adult illiteracy by 2015, the elimination of gender disparities in school by 2005, and other worthy targets. Oxfam expressed "grave concern that the high-flown promises of Dakar might come to nothing."[34] It remembered the failure after the 1990 World Conference on Education for All to back similar encouraging words with decisive action.

The donor community has a scandalous record of neglect with regard to basic education. Overall, amounts going to education have fallen. Aid to education, it turns out, overwhelmingly favors higher education, which benefits the richest groups in countries whose children attend advanced institutions. Less than one-tenth of aid goes to basic education. Aid to basic education, they point out, does loom large in speeches, just not in real spending. Most money for basic education is delivered as technical assistance, although "delivered" is hardly the right word, since most of the money never leaves the rich countries. It is spent on technical assistance, plans, research, and that sort of thing. There is little recipient involvement and participation. Oxfam reviews the state of education aid, looks at the role aid could play, focuses on particular areas of concern, such as the educational needs of girls, and outlines reforms. It points out that repayment of debt has made matters worse. Such well-researched campaigns can be the basis for mass mobilizations in support of the right of all children to an education. The impediments to the achievement of such a basic entitlement include debt peonage and the larger economic relations of unequal exchange structured by capitalism on a global scale and enforced by the global state economic governance institutions.

In Zambia, where debt repayment required the adoption of an IMF stabilization program, the reduction in government education spending resulted in a disastrous education cut, by a quarter in just three years. As the largest item of government spending it was the first to be reduced. Other cuts insisted upon by the IMF meant small farmers in remote areas did not get help with continued crop purchases and so had no money for school fees for their kids. Zambia is now a country where children are more likely to be illiterate than their parents. Debt repayment first. Education and other social programs that should come first are instead cut first under IMF structural adjustment. Oxfam makes connections between limiting capital market liberalization in developing countries that have been the catalysts for financial collapse to what happens to education. It sees an effective transaction tax in currency markets as a disincentive to speculative activities as well as something that is not unconnected to the financing of primary education.

Oxfam's report points out that although the linkage between education and democracy may be complex, education reform was, for example in Britain, the catalyst for the extension of voting rights and the social legislation of child labor. Finally, the report suggests that the distribution of education is the driving force behind growing income inequalities in much of the world and it cites the United States experience as a taste of things to come. It points to our educational system in which the poor get a poor education and young adults from the poorest 20 percent of wage-earning families are eleven times more likely to drop out of high school.

Of course, from an elitist perspective this is fine. The rich would not want the children of the poor adding to competition for the good slots in society. Lack of education ensures a supply of cheap hands, people who blame themselves for their failure. The Oxfam analysis carefully avoids class as a category and so appeals to the morality of people who may be somewhat challenged in this area. This Oxfam approach is not ineffective, but it does not ask about the content of education, the uses to which literacy is put in a capitalist society, problems that have come up repeatedly in our discussions throughout this book. By pursuing the goal of more funding for effective basic education, Oxfam reflects an effective approach to moving the broader policy debate forward.

After its analysis, Oxfam then asked what the criteria are for an effective global initiative, it offered estimates on realistic costs of meeting the targets, and it then proposed the concrete resource-mobilizing that would be required of the international community. It suggested a mechanism for funding. The Global Alliance for Vaccines and Immunization (GAVI), a successful initiative, might, Oxfam thought, provide a possible model. GAVI is a broad-based global partnership that uses money raised from a private foundation, that is dedicated to closing the disparity of access to vaccines, and it invests in vaccine research in areas important to the poor of the world. The program is overseen by a board and its chair rotates. For the last two years it has been chaired by the World Health Organization followed by UNICEF. Oxfam suggests a similar partnership for education, with resources allocated by a board chaired by the same sort of groups and open to participation from prominent political figures, people who could help raise the organization's profile and raise money as well. The key would be that no viable action plan should be denied the financial support needed for successful implementation. Once reviewed and approved, the plan would get automatic entitlement to enhanced funding.

Such a plan might make some difference if it caught on. The chances of it being endorsed by the powerful, however, depend not on the logic, the data, the careful analysis of the situation, but on the street heat the establishment feels. Meaningful reform will come about because people want and struggle to obtain revolutionary change. They may perhaps settle for reform in any particular instance, given the political forces arrayed, but they don't get even that unless they have a vision and a commitment to far more radical change. It is the unity of such a vision and the outrage at the structural injustice of the system that brings any meaningful change. We badly need the Oxfam researchers and campaigners, Ms. Habbard, and other skilled, well-educated, and committed progressive intellectual activists, and we also need those willing to face the water cannon and the rubber bullets, people who are determined to express their right to protest injustice in the face of unleashed police power.

When activists say, "If you want real change you have to abolish the capitalistic mode of development," the powerful really get upset and start to talk about what reasonable people they are and how we can talk things out. They are the soft cops. The hard cops are the ones who come to beat people over the head, shoot the pepper spray and tear gas, and jail people who don't want to be reasonable. For establishment types, getting the balance between commitment to dialogue and repression is not a clear process, because elites are divided on tactics just as the movements for social change are. I myself suspect even the seemingly most militant demands of the popular movements aren't enough. The cold-eyed defenders of capitalism as we know it (and as they would like it to continue to be) at the *Wall Street Journal* and the other pundits are right to fear that if enough people get to hear the criticisms of the ways contemporary capitalism works to oppress, exploit, and divide working people, and if they see how the growth of consumer society is destroying the planet, they may well become anticapitalist. They will not be satisfied with token marginal changes. They will want a new and better system. I could be wrong. But we will see. Let us detail the consequences of corporate greed and the sellout cooptation of politicians who represent the interests of those who bankroll their campaigns. Let us propose sensible controls and alternative strategies and let us see whether the powerful willingly and reasonably and promptly accept such necessary and desirable changes. If so, fine. But if not let us get rid of the structures that enable them to make the decisions that affect our lives. Let us strive to establish democratic rights to an economic system that provides for the development of the capacities of each for the benefit of all.

To get from here to there so that the world can deal more effectively with the ecological dangers and the social injustices that characterize the present world system and its corporate-dominated version of globalization, more people need to educate themselves as to the nature of the issues, be able to evaluate the self-serving justifications and rationales offered by those who would deflect the movements for a progressive globalization from below, and understand the reasons for the different positions, thence making up their minds to act responsibly and become active shapers of our collective future. The Global Justice Movement has done a great deal to encourage such developments.

The scope of the protest movement under way in global civil society is hard to grasp, to place into a holistic understanding of what it may mean in a longer historical context. A useful parallel may be to the Fugitive Slave Law of 1850, which said that slaves' owners had a right to have their fugitive slaves returned to them. In the North, vigilance committees were established to identify and make things difficult for the slave catchers, who hunted escaped blacks on the grounds that the slaves were engaged in immoral acts and violating the Fugitive Slave Law and that their own resistance was to act justly. The slave owners made such laws and established mechanisms to achieve their objectives. But from the point of view of a higher ideal of justice, the claim of legal justice under such laws was seen by many people as illegitimate. A hundred and fifty years later, the anti-debt coalition—in proclaiming the illegitimacy of the debt-slavery it saw as being imposed on the poor of the underdeveloped world—made a similar claim. In an era of globalization the IMF and other global state economic governance institutions could be seen as the slave catchers, taking away liberties and claiming a right to property legally demanded to be returned to its "rightful" owners—the banks and bondholders. To critics this appears no more just, obligations that should no more be honored, rules that should no more be enforcible than the right to return human beings to chattel status. To make the poor suffer death and a hopeless future to pay debt others have incurred and over which they have had no say is widely seen as wrong.

Whether in a century and a half this parallel will be accepted we shall see. We know that 150 years ago the slave owners believed in the right to own other human beings and that they were actually helping their slaves to live better than they would have otherwise. They therefore thought it reasonable to have Northerners cooperate in imposing slavery as a system and enforcing its rules, such as returning runaways as the law required them to do. Defenders of debt collection sound little different today. Samuel Brittan writes, "Whatever one thinks of particular institutions and governments, the fact remains the form of capitalism that has developed in the fifty-plus years since the Second World War has brought a bigger rise in worldwide living standards than anything before in the history of mankind. The first part of the period saw the freeing of trade and payments. The second part saw the rise of world capital markets." He thinks that while one can argue about the timing of some policies, "the main thrust of the opponents of globalization is to say that the whole development has been wrong."[35]

I suspect this sort of defense will sound, in retrospect a hundred years from now, very much like that of the defenders of slavery who condemned the bad treatment of slaves but pointed out that slavery is in the Bible. It is natural. Or a century before that the defenders of the divine right of kings who declared it not only God's will but the only workable system of governance. I hope it does not take a hundred years for people to understand capitalism in similar terms. At this point we can criticize slavery because, of course, "everyone" knows it is wrong. At some point everyone will know that the control over the lives of the many by a small number of transnational corporations and by the governments who do their bidding is a wrong way to organize a society. But it will be a long haul. It will come about by forcing them step by step to submit to social control so they do not pollute the environment, poison the food, or pay wages too low for people to live in dignity, and by forcing them to share the surplus created by all of us and built on the contributions of the generations who have gone before to meet the health, education, and other public needs of the entire human family.

If we were to transpose the sort of arguments we hear in the defense of corporate power, or as it is called, "free markets," it might sound like this: "The backward blacks have benefited by being made our slaves and they are happy. Those who say they should be able to choose their own form of government and live free of obligation to their masters just do not see how much we have done for them." If living standards are falling, if people are poorer now than before the banks were so kind as to create this debt-peonage and the IMF to enforce the squeezing of blood money, isn't there something wrong with the rules of the international economic system? The idea that the poor countries should be exempt from regulations on workers' rights and the environment, and that the social contract is unimportant because growth will happen faster in a freer market, and the argument that when these poorer countries are wealthier they will choose to introduce social protections, are suspect to say the least. Following Jeff Faux we may ask, "Suppose, for example, that the state of Mississippi argued it should be exempt from all federal laws concerning child labor, antidiscrimination, the minimum wage, clean air standards, and even the Bill of Rights, on the grounds that the resulting increase in economic growth would eventually enable a more prosperous Mississippi to fashion a social contract of its own. It does not even pass the laugh test."[36]

Just as "free" markets are never free but always have rules that prevent other more important goals such as fair treatment of workers and protection of the environment to come first, so too "free trade" is a misnomer. If the trade agreements we have been seeing, the North American Free Trade Agreement or the trade agreement between the United States and China, were aimed at establishing free trade, as Faux points out, "they could have been written on one page—a simple treaty to eliminate tariffs. Instead, they add up to hundreds of pages largely devoted to strengthening protections of international corporate investors' rights and weakening protections of human rights as well as worker and environmental standards. As these documents make clear," he reminds us, "the agreements' primary purpose is not free trade, but to dismantle social protections and financial regulations in order to allow capital to invest across borders." Transnational capital does not voluntarily accept that democracies have a right to legislate restrictions of their freedom.

Where formal democracy is without mass popular movements, active democracy atrophies. Those who can afford to spend time and money seeking favors from government that will enrich them still further at the expense of others come to dominate the process. If we follow Aristotle's definition of democracy (in his *Politics* Book IV, section 4), "a democracy is a state where the freemen and the poor, being the majority, are invested with the power of the state," it can hardly be said we yet live in a democracy. If the people being invested with power only means that they can choose between the best candidates money can produce, then freedom to vote for representatives is the only requirement of living in a democratic society. However, in a society with sharp inequality of wealth and income representative democracy is inadequate, because while there may be free speech and freedom of the press, in mass society speech is effectively limited to those who are rich enough to own a chain of newspapers or a TV network. From this second perspective Noam Chomsky defines democracy as "a system of governance in which elite elements based in the business community control the state by virtue of their dominance of the private sector while the population observes quietly."[37] The state gets upset when citizens demonstrate and protest policy. That they use police violence to keep crowds down (and do not distinguish between the very small number of protesters who carry out property damage and the vast majority who do not) is the method of closing down the possibility of the articulation of alternative views, even when they are endorsed by large numbers of citizens.

Raymond Williams tells us that "with only occasional exceptions, democracy, in the records that we have, was until C19 [the 19th century] a strongly unfavorable term."[38] It was not until the late nineteenth and early twentieth centuries, with the rise of working-class movements that could be neither ignored nor successfully repressed, that a "majority of political parties and tendencies have united in declaring their belief in it. This is the most striking historical fact."[39] Democracy was taken to be uncontrolled popular power. For this reason those without property were often denied the right to participate. There were countless other formal and informal restrictions, so that only the better-quality folks could take part in government. In every age there are efforts by the powerful to discourage participatory democracy.

We will not know what lasting significance the events in Seattle in November–December, 1999, will hold in historical perspective. The high-profile alliance of turtles and teamsters celebrated in some accounts obscures the importance of the breadth of participants, which included the United Students Against Sweatshops; the Women's Resource Center, from Pakistan; the Human Rights Clinic and Education Center, from Cameroon; the Indigenous People's Biodiversity Network of Peru; the United Peasant Association, from Mindanao in the Philippines; Pax Christi, of Florence, Italy; Pax Romana, from Thailand; the Hawaii Pesticide Project, from Honolulu; Green Action, of Tel Aviv, Israel; the Memphis Audubon Society, from Tennessee; and hundreds of other groups. As nongovernmental organizations continue to gain the respect of the world's people and governments that are unwilling to stand up to corporate greed become discredited, new forms of democracy will become even more important actors. We cannot know the consequences of the destruction of the World Trade Center and the attack on the Pentagon on September 11, 2001, nor can we know the full results of the U.S. response to those terrorist attacks and the climate of fear and violence produced. The hypocrisy of Washington policy makers who think the only injustice in the world is what is done when America and American interests are attacked—and which mimics the terrorists' certainty that any actions they themselves take are justified by the righteousness of their cause—became a profound challenge for the Global Justice Movement.

This book begins by describing the hegemonic understanding of globalization, which is that, in the post–cold war era, a new polarity is asserted, not between right and left, but between those who accept global change and those who resist it. This is yet another end of ideology, creating a rationale for accepting existing power relations. It suggests there is only one possible form globalization can take, and that unless this version is accepted we go back to a world of national barriers, protectionism, economic nationalism, constant fear, massive destruction, and endless conflict. This formulation has been rejected. The task has been to articulate an alternative understanding of contemporary corporate globalization and to suggest that an alternative model is necessary. It has been argued with reference to labor and other human rights, the protection of the environment, and a more equitable system of taxation and public expenditure that corporate globalization needs to be rejected in favor of the sort of globalization from below demanded by the Global Justice Movement. It has been further argued that there are important differences between parties of the center-left and the center-right, but that for those who identify themselves with the progressive social movements of global civil society neither of the two mainstream electoral coalitions shares its critique of corporate globalization or its commitment to participatory democracy. Social movements whose causes range from AIDS education and treatment to battered-women's shelters, safe food, and world peace have found that governments pay more attention to increasing profit rates for corporate capital, even at the price of public-sector austerity, than they do to the felt needs of communities of conscience. They find separately, and then examine the need to better understand collectively, that they must be prepared to challenge the overriding priorities of the corporate version of globalization and to define an alternative vision of the good global society. This generation has its work cut out for it. They have made an impressive start.

Appendix: Internet Resources

Inevitably a book like this is in some ways obsolete by the time it is published. There are new events, information, analyses, and activism that I would like to have incorporated from just the time I sent it off to the wonderful folks at The New Press to be copy-edited and put into production, to when you get to read it. The best way to update is through the Internet. In this appendix I will discuss some sites that I find helpful.

Just about every group that is concerned about globalization's impacts on the environment and labor, about the activities of the global state economic governance institutions, and about campaigns to bring greater social justice maintains a web site. For example, for April 18–22, 2001 (when leaders of the western hemisphere met in Quebec City to pursue a Free Trade Area for the Americas), an "International Day of Action—Stop the FTAA" web site was planned. At this web site, www.a20.org, there were statements from a variety of groups, such as Long-shoremen Saying No to FTAA, and links to "Stop FTAA Resource Library" and "Stop FTAA Media Tools for Activists" web sites as well as a place to insert your e-mail address for update bulletins. There were requests for help in bringing pressure against Nike on behalf of workers at the Kukdong factory in Mexico, where there was a work stoppage, and lots of other links to planned teach-ins and to an International Calendar with an invitation to "add your event." There were details for potential protesters and other interested parties, from local activists offering accommodations to law collectives who were standing by to help those arrested. This sort of decentralized, inclusive model of activism and information is typical of what we have called the Global Justice Movement. Such a format allows, for instance, rights activists from Honduras, Guatemala, and Chiapas to get a sidebar with their announcements and web address (www.rights action.org).

Because the commercial mainstream media cannot be expected to cover such demonstrations the way the movement might like, the Independent Media Center (www.indymedia. org) offers an alternative source of information and makes the movement's material available to mainstream outlets that wish a more complete coverage, coverage that includes the activists' views. The mainstream media are subjected to careful, insightful critique by Fairness and Accuracy in Reporting (FAIR), and their web site (www.fair.org) is a constant source of solid analysis. FAIR covers such stories as the takeover of Pacifica by an unelected board and the dangers to free-speech radio this tactic represents. Such sites are typically "hotlinked," meaning that you simply click on the highlighted URL, and the site that interests you pops up on your screen. By "surfing" this way you can follow your interests. FAIR covers meetings of the National Association of Broadcasters and how the corporate media try to squelch the independent outlets and what you can do about it. From Indymedia you could, for example, click on "CIA Boasts of Manipulating News" to link to Indymedia Italia and learn of protests at the G-8 Environmental Ministers meeting in Trieste, or to a "background" link to "in-depth analysis of capitalism and global economics" from znet. Znet is a community of people concerned about social change. On their site you can find a major strategic essay by the thoughtful Walden Bello, and a report

from Prague by Julie Light, who is a Corporate Watch corre-
spondent on the scene. You might then want to click on their site
(www.corporatewatch.org) for analyses and information on all
manner of corporate misdeeds. On the other hand you can link
to web sites about crises in Kosovo, East Timor, or Colombia, or
to sites dedicated to freeing Mumia Abu Jumal. Mumia, and all
sorts of groups—from the Chicana/Chicano Studies Foundation to the members of the British Parliament, who filed an
amicus brief on his behalf—explain why he is being unjustly
threatened with execution. There are links to all of this, so much
that you could navigate from znet (www.lbbs.org/weluser.htm)
for days, finding new information that is not available from the
mainstream media.

Confining ourselves to English-language sites around the
world we may call attention to two of the more useful ones out
of South Africa and Thailand. The Alternative Information and
Development Centre (www.aidc.irg.za/mail.html) is an alternative information center (or "centre," as they spell it) doing research, education, and training, as well as campaigning and
lobbying on issues affecting the development process in South
Africa. Currently the Jubilee 2000 South Africa campaign, "Stop
the Killing," directed against the transnational pharmaceuticals
and AIDS drugs manufacturers, is prominently featured, but
there is also inspiring coverage of struggles by churches and the
People's Housing Network Forum, the New Women's Movement, and Youth for Work, giving a sense of the vibrancy of civil
society in South Africa. There are links to SAPSN, the South
African People's Solidarity Network, and from there links to
reports on "Relations between Africa and the European Union
in the 21st Century" and to the "Dakar Declaration for the Total
and Unconditional Cancellation of African and Third World
Debt," along with articles covering activism in South Korea
and Brazil, among other places. Focus on the Global South

(www.focusweb.org) is located in Thailand and does research linked to advocacy work in the Asia Pacific region especially, but it is global in its interests. It has useful publications and links as well. Another useful site is www.twnside.org.sg, where the Third World Network covers issues from biotechnology and biodiversity to trade rules and global financial crises. Its publications and seminars are also listed, on topics ranging from current developments to the WTO to negotiations on agricultural services. Similar centers exist in all parts of the world. One useful European one is the Transnational Institute in Amsterdam (www.tni.org).

What I have written about Oxfam's work comes from mainstream media coverage of its activities, but these articles alone were hardly enough to understand the organization's strategy and achievements. For this I referred to material on Oxfam's extensive Internet site (oxfam.org). There you can read about their strategic plan and educational campaigns and learn how to get in touch with them to support their work. Global Exchange (www.globalexchange.org) is a human rights organization dedicated to promoting environmental, political, and social justice around the world. It is involved in many campaigns. It offers "reality tours" and online fair-trade shopping. There is also a site called www.oneworld.org, with pages and pages of information and links to other sites that offer a sense of the breadth of the activities of many of the global civil society groups' activities. There is Food First (www.foodfirst.org) and the World Watch Institute (www.worldwatch.org), which contain important original research you are unlikely to find elsewhere and whose work is well worth supporting.

Public Citizen's Global Trade Watch site (www.tradewatch. org) has alerts and action notifications as well as useful reports and links. It is one of the centers for strategic thinking and activism. Other "watch" sites include WTOWatch (www.wto

watch.org), a center concerned with the World Trade Organization, trade, and sustainable development. It has news updates and links to 50 Years Is Enough (www.50years.org) and other important sites as well as action steps for safer food and NGO vision alternatives. On the more technical side there is a Global Trade Negotiations Home Page, a project of the Center for International Development at Harvard University (www. cid.harvard.edu), which links research on trade and globalization. There are sites that are more militantly antisystem, such as DestroyIMF (www.destroyimf.org), a web resource "for all those mobilizing to end the poverty and injustice inflicted by global capitalism." It is an exceedingly useful site, with links to the United Kingdom's "No Sweat" interactive web site for sweatshop busters, reports from Turkey, Palestine, and the Ukraine, coverage of other specific activities, and background analyses of struggles around the world. The Bank Information Center (www.biusa.org/policy/globalization.htm) carries links to the Overseas Development Council Taskforce of NGOs (with members from academia and people who formerly worked at the World Bank and the IMF), which criticizes the IMF and makes recommendations. It has links to Mobilization for Global Justice's web site (www.a16.org). It has policy-debate links and tool kits for activists. One of the most interesting sites dedicated to particular corporate campaigns is www.mcspotlight.org, which has information about McDonald's and covers everything from information on McDonald's Workers Resistance to animal rights activists, and generally takes on what this fast food giant is guilty of, with discussions of its deceptive advertising, its health issues, and the famous libel trial.

The environmental groups all have web sites, and these all have links and updates to campaigns and new research findings. For example Greenpeace (www.greenpeace.org) offers a Greenpeace Americas Toxic Tour and links to such stories as Multinational Unilever being told to "clean up" rather than "cover up" mercury pollution in India. The Sierra Club site (www.sierraclub.org) has headline news, such as "Bush's Global Warming Flip Flop," and its Environmental Justice Home Page is excellent at www.sierraclub.org/toxics/ejhome.asp. By clicking on this item you can learn how "President Bush Bows to Corporate Polluters and Decides Not to Limit Carbon Dioxide Pollution," a limitation he had promised during the campaign. The National Wildlife Federation (www.nwf.org) and other groups are accessible via the Internet. Among perhaps less well known groups that are doing good work are Earthjustice (www.earthjustice.org), which is suing the U.S. trade representative on behalf of the Center for International Environmental Law to disclose written proposals the Bush administration is secretly making to other governments as part of the FTAA negotiations, proposals affecting the environment and human health. You might also want to look at www.presidentbushwatch.org. The Intergovernmental Panel on Climate Change (the United Nations group) has a web site (www.ipcc.ch) posts its climate-change reports and other assessments of vulnerability, emissions, land use, and policy debates. In many areas regional community-based movements for environmental health involve collaboration among neighborhood activists, progressive foundations, and local colleges. For example, see the Occidental College Environmental Justice page at www.oxy.edu/departments/ess. Many colleges and universities have made major contributions to the cause. Check out the University of Michigan's Environmental Justice Program at www.personal.umich.edu/~jrajzer/nre/index/html, and for terrific (and fun) annotated Environmental Justice/Environmental Racism links see www.hensonscales.com/erlinks.htm. I cannot leave out my friends at the University of Connecticut, whose site expertly explains the long history of colonialism and social inequality in the Arctic, which has left northern indigenous peoples highly vulnerable to environmental damage: www.arcticcircle.unconn/SEEJ/menu/html.

The antisweatshop campaigns are well represented on the Internet. The place to start is the National Labor Committee site (www.nlcnet.org), which has reports on how the U.S. government provides unlimited access to apparel made in sweatshops that are run by the brutal Burmese military regime, and other coverage of such issues as Vietnamese "guest workers held in indentured servitude for nearly two years at a Daewoo factory in American Samoa, a U.S. territory, sewing clothes for J. C. Penney, Sears, and Target." They were beaten, sexually harassed, starved, and forced to work twelve to eighteen hours a day, seven days a week, and made to live in crowded, rat-infested dormitories. The site reports other such cases and the progress of solidarity campaigns. Other sites include Alliance for Responsible Trade (www.igc.org/dgap), the Interhemispheric Regional Workers Organization, representing the unions of the western hemisphere that are active in calling for a different model of integration for these economies (www.ictfu.org). The International Labor Rights Fund site (www.laborrights.org) features factory reports and updates on important cases, along with urgent action alerts and news reports. UNITE!, the union that organizes garment workers (www.uniteunion.org), carries news of "Sweatshops Behind the Swoosh: Nike's Global Sweatshop" and news of activist campaigns. The Academic Consortium on International Trade (www.spp.umich.edu/acit) promotes free trade and counters antisweatshop activists analyses with their own.

There are some other web sites containing opinion and information that may be of interest, such as Tom Paine (www.tom paine.com). It lists opinion and news pieces related to all manner of current events and includes "TOMPAINE.COM INDEX: Bush's Record on the Environment." There is the progressive

think tank the Economic Policy Institute (www.epinet.org/
epihome.html), which has analyses on trade and globalization,
labor standards, and sustainable economics, among other topics.
Other think tanks have sites. I find the material at the Carnegie
Endowment for International Peace (www.ceip.org) particularly
useful. But don't forget the free-market right and libertarian
sources, such as the Cato Institute. "Foreign Policy in Focus,"
edited by Tom Barry and Martha Honey, offers brief but sophisticated policy-relevant essays, most of which relate to topics
covered in this book and written by knowledgeable people
(www.foreignpolicy-infocus.org). Search engines such as
Yahoo! turn up valuable links. Look, for example, at dir/yahoo.
com/Business_and_Economy/Global_Economy. The catego-
ries under this designation will keep you clicking away usefully
for some time. Student groups are active across the spectrum.
Look, for example, at the Alliance for Democracy, in Madison,
Wisconsin (www.sit.wisc.edu/~democrac/front.html), to be reminded that "the university is not a factory." This group, supported by student, labor, and community organizations, is
dedicated to transforming the University of Wisconsin into a
fully democratic place and suggests the sort of education needed
to make the world a better place. As an old Badger myself, I am
happy to see this group making connections to the progressive
traditions of the university. Finally, there are lots of good books
to read. If you order online you might think about doing so
through the web site of ILWU Local 5, the home of Powell's
Bookstore Workers ("No Decisions About Us Without Us") in
Portland, Oregon (powellsunion.com). By visiting the site you
will learn about unionism and save money on your purchases,
and 10 percent of the proceeds goes directly to the employees.

In the aftermath of the destruction of the World Trade Center
and the attack on the Pentagon on September 11, 2001, the site
www.peacefuljustice.cjb.net was set up to make known the ac-

tivities of groups united in their desire for a solution that does not target innocent civilian populations, and with an understanding that there can be no peace without justice.

The Internet grows by the minute, and I surely cannot list all of the important sites, but fortunately most sites contain a "Links" feature that will alert you to kindred sites. For those who are not yet using the Internet, take it out for a spin. For those who want to share sites with me, I can be reached at wkt$econ@qc1.qc.edu.

Notes

CHAPTER 1

1. Darryl Lerous, "World Beaters, Global Trade Baton Passes from U.S. Forces to Canada's Mounties," *CovertAction,* April–June 2001, 15.
2. Mary Kaldor, "'Civilizing' Globalization? The Implications of the 'Battle in Seattle,'" *Millennium: Journal of International Studies* 29, no. 1 (2000): 106.
3. See Pierre Bourdieu, "Neo-liberalism, the Utopia (Becoming a Reality) of Unlimited Exploitation," in *Acts of Resistance: Against the Tyranny of the Market,* trans. Richard Nice (New York: The New Press, 1998).
4. Peter Engardio with Catherine Belton, "Special Report on Global Capitalism," *Business Week,* 27 November 2000, 75.
5. Joseph Stiglitz, "What I Learned at the World Economic Crisis," *The New Republic,* 17 April 2000, at http://www.thenewrepublic.com.
6. "Global Business," *Financial Times,* 31 January 2001, 14.
7. Hugh Carnegy, "Guild Drives West to Adopt Lofty Ideals," *Financial Times,* 30 January 2001, 9.
8. Nanette Byrnes, "The Boss in the Web Age," *Business Week,* 28 August 2000, 106.
9. Patrick Heller, "Moving the State: The Politics of Democratic Decentralization in Kerela, South Africa, and Porto Alegre," *Politics and Society,* March 2001.
10. John Lloyd, "To Have and Have Not," *Financial Times,* 28 January 2001, 9.
11. Raymond Williams, *Keywords: A Vocabulary of Culture and Society,* rev. ed. (London: Oxford University Press, 1983), 11.

12. Richard Tompkins, "Laundry, with a Minor in Linguistics," *Financial Times,* 11 June 2000, 9.

13. Williams, *Keywords,* 144–45.

14. Henry A. Kissinger, "American Politics and American Foreign Policy," *Trilateral Commission Tokyo 2000,* 82.

15. Christopher Hitchens, "The Case Against Henry Kissinger," *Harper's,* February 2001, 33.

16. "Quotes of the Year," *Financial Times,* 30 December 2000, and 1 January 2001.

17. Bruce Cummings, "The American Ascendancy: Imposing a New World Order," *The Nation,* May 2000, 20.

18. Thomas L. Friedman, *The Lexus and the Olive Tree* (New York: Farrar, Straus & Giroux, 1999).

19. "World Law and World Power," *The Economist,* 5 December 1998, 16.

20. "Does Anybody Love the IMF or World Bank?" *Business Week,* 24 April 2000, 40.

21. C. Fred Bergsten, in *Trilateral Commission,* 45.

22. Robert L. Borosage, "Who Speaks for the Third World?" *The American Prospect,* 17 January 2000, 20.

23. Nicola Bullard, "The World Bank and Globalization," Focus on the Global South, n.d., at http://www.bicusa.org/ptoc/htm/bullard_global.htm.

24. Michael M. Phillips, "IMF, Weary of Criticism, Braces for Protests at Its Annual Meeting," *Wall Street Journal,* 22 September 2000, A2.

25. Kaldor, "'Civilizing' Globalization," 109.

26. Stephen Gill, "Globalization, Market Civilization, and Disciplinary Neoliberalism," *Millennium: Journal of International Studies* (Winter 1995).

27. "Will Hutton and Anthony Giddens in Conversation: Is Globalization Americanization?" *Dissent* (Summer 2000): 58.

28. Pierre Bordieu, "For a Scholarship with Commitment," *Profession 2000:* 43–4.

CHAPTER 2

1. "Protesters for Poverty," *Financial Times,* 28 September 2000, 18.

2. Ibid.

3. "The Non-governmental Order: Will NGOs Democratize, or Merely Disrupt Global Governance?" *The Economist,* 11 December 1999, 20.

4. Jim Vallette, "Larry Summers's War Against the Earth," *Counter Punch,* at http://www.counterpunch.org/summers.html.

5. Gordon Fairclough, "Philip Morris Says It's Sorry for Death Report," *Wall Street Journal,* 26 July 2001, B1.

6. Mohan Rao, "Equity in a Global Public Goods Framework," in *Global Public Goods: International Cooperation in the 21st Century,* edited by Inge Kaul, Isabelle Grunberg, and Marc A. Stein (New York: Oxford University Press, 1999).

7. "Anthony Giddens and Will Hutton in Conversation," in *Global Capitalism,* edited by Will Hutton and Anthony Giddens (New York: The New Press, 2000), 43–44.

8. Emily S. Rosenberg, *Financial Missionaries to the World: The Politics and Culture of Dollar Diplomacy, 1900–1930* (Cambridge: Harvard University Press, 1999), 1.

9. Ibid.

10. Ibid.

11. John Gallagher and Ronald Robinson, "The Imperialism of Free Trade," *Economic History Review,* 2d ser., 6, no. 1 (1953).

12. Jeff Gerth and Elaine Sciolino, "I.M.F. Head: He Speaks, and Money Talks," *The New York Times,* 2 April 1996, 1.

13. Joseph Stiglitz, "What I Learned."

14. Ibid.

15. Jeffery Sachs, "The Charade of Debt Sustainability," *Financial Times,* 26 September 2000, 17.

16. Nicholas D. Kristof and David E. Sanger, "How U.S. Wooed Asia to Let Cash Flow In," *The New York Times,* 16 February 1999, A1.

17. Ilene Grabel, "The Political Economy of 'Policy Credibility': The New-Classical Macroeconomics and the Remaking of Emerging Economies," *Cambridge Journal of Economics,* January 2000, 13.

18. Alan Meltzer, "A Better Way to Help the World," *Financial Times,* 28 April 2000, 19.

19. Amity Shlaes, "A Convenient Punchbag for America's Leaders," *Financial Times,* 27 June 2000, 15.

20. "Anti-Capitalist Protests Angry and Effective," *The Economist,* 23 September 2000, 87.

21. Alan Beattie, "Independent Watchdog Plan for IMF," *Financial Times,* 10 April 2000.

22. David Ferranti, Guillermo Perry, Indermit Gill, and Luis Servén, *Opportunity and Risk in a Globalized Latin America and the Caribbean* (Washington: World Bank, 2000); see Richard Lapper, "World Bank Calls for Stronger Social Policy," *Financial Times,* 20 June 2000, 5.

23. John Thornhill, "ADB Adds Battle with Poverty to Profit and Loss Account," *Financial Times,* 5 January 2001.

24. Ibid.

25. Joseph Kahn, "World Bank Chief to Unveil an Ambitious Educational Program," *The New York Times,* 27 April 2000, A11.

26. Martin Wolf, "Banking for the World's Poor," *Financial Times,* 21 June 2000, 19.

27. "Quantity and Quality," *The Economist,* 30 September 2000, 82.

28. Alan Beattie, "Protesters Warn of 'Seattle East' in Washington," *Financial Times,* 18 June 2000, 6.

29. John Saul, interviewed February 26, 1999, by Aurora, 2000, 8. http://auroracaap.org/talks/jsaul.html. Accessed October 22, 2000.

30. Robert Wade, "The World Bank Is for Borrowers," *Financial Times,* 15 February 2001, 15.

31. Bruce Stokes, "Preparing to Bypass the WTO," *Financial Times,* 29 March 2000, 13.

32. Robert E. Lightizer, "Conceding Free Trade's Flaws," *The New York Times,* 3 December 1999, 22.

33. Ibid.

34. Jeanne Cummings and John Harwood, "Arsenic Issue May Poison Bush's Compassionate Conservatism," *Wall Street Journal,* 20 April 2001, A16.

35. Helene Cooper, "Firms Rethink Hostility to Linking Trade, Labor Rights," *Wall Street Journal,* 2 February 2001, A12.

36. Ibid.

CHAPTER 3

1. Ignacio Ramonet, "The Year 2000," *Le Monde Diplomatique,* December 1999.

2. Charles Onyango-Obbo, "Only a Madman Would Colonize Africa Today," reprinted in *World Press Review,* September 2000, 48.

3. Barbara Crossette, "What It Takes to Stop Slavery," *The New York Times,* 22 April 2001, 5.

4. Sarah Coleman, "Pfiser Scandal," *World Press Review,* April 2001, 25.

5. See the most recent *Human Development Report* published by the United Nations Development Programme and the International Labor Organization's *World Labour Report.*

6. Oxfam, *Missing the Target: The Price of Empty Promises* (London: Oxfam, 2000).

7. Nicholas Stern, "A Fairer Deal for the World's Poor," *Financial Times,* 11 December 2000, 15.

8. Guy de Jonquìres, "Brussels' Trade plan for World's Poor Countries May Change," *Financial Times,* 11 December 2000.

9. Michael M. Phillips, "Mozambique Faces Sugar-Industry Debate," *Wall Street Journal,* 20 July 2000, A2.

10. Mattias Lundberg and Branko Milanovic, "The Truth about Global Inequality," *Financial Times,* 25 February 2000.

11. Richard Lapper, "Policy Makers Focus on Region's Poor," *Financial Times,* 24 March 2000, 4.

12. Larry Rohter, "Brazil Collides with I.M.F. Over a Plan to Aid the Poor," *The New York Times,* 21 February 2000, A9.

13. Robert Naiman, Marc Meally, Jim Cason, and Bill Martin, "Discussion Note on Debt Cancellation, Africa, and the Structural Adjustment Institutions," *Bulletin of the Association of Concerned Africa Scholars,* Spring/Summer, 20–1.

14. "Do You Believe in Fairies?" *The Economist,* 23 December 1999, 3.

15. Robert Naiman, "A Plea to the IMF: Stop Collecting Debts," *Financial Times,* 12 January 2001, 16.

16. Alan Beattie, "The Listening Approach to Development," *Financial Times,* 12 January 2001, 17.

17. The editorial appeared 11 December 1998 and is reprinted in *World Press Review,* May 1999, 48.

18. Anne O. Krueger and T. N. Srinivasan, "The Harsh Consequences of Forgiveness," *Financial Times,* 9 August 2001, 11.

19. Michael Dobbs, "The Politics of Foreign Aid," *Washington Post National Weekly Edition,* 5–6 February 2001, 6.

20. Ibid.

21. Mark Turner, "Breathtaking Challenge for Africa," *Financial Times,* 22 September 2000.

22. Donald G. McNeil, Jr., "AIDS Stalking Africa's Struggling Economies," *The New York Times,* 15 November 1998, A1.

23. "South Africa's President and the Plague," *The Economist,* 27 May 2000, 45.

24. Barton Gellman, "Disease That Could Destroy Nations," *Washington Post National Weekly Edition,* 8–14 May 2000, 15.

25. Miriam Jordan, "Brazil May Flout Trade Laws to Keep AIDS Drugs Free for Patients," *Wall Street Journal,* 12 February 2001, B4.

26. Jagdish Bhagwati, "Patent Protection Does Not Belong with WTO," *Financial Times,* 20 February 2001, 15.

27. Donald G. McNeil, Jr., "Oxfam Joins Campaign to Cut Drug Prices for Poor Countries," *The New York Times,* 13 February 2001, A5.

28. David Pilling, "GSK Facing Crusade over Drugs for Poor," *Financial Times,* 12 February 2001, 19.

29. Meredeth Turshen, "Access to Drugs: A Universal Issue," *ACAS Bulletin,* Winter 2000, 21. The ACAS is the Association of Concerned Africa Scholars.

30. Merrill Goozner, "The Price Isn't Right," *The American Prospect,* 11 September 2000, 24–5.

31. Ibid.

32. Michael A. Heller and Rebecca Eisenberg, "Can Patents Deter Innovation? The Anticommons in Biomedical Research," *Science,* May 1, 1998.

33. Donald G. NcNeil, Jr., "Drug Makers and Third World: Study in Neglect," *The New York Times,* 21 May 2000, 6.

34. Melody Petersen, "Lifting the Curtain on the Real Cost of Making AIDS Drugs," *The New York Times,* 24 April 2001, C10.

35. Eileen Stillwaggon, "AIDS and Poverty in Africa," *The Nation,* 21 May 2001, 23.

36. Charles Geshekter and Meredeth Turshen, "Health, Drugs, and AIDS, Background Paper: Reconstructing the Health/AIDS? Drug Debate," *Bulletin of the Association of Concerned Africa Scholars* (Summer/Spring).

37. Jeffrey Sachs, "The Best Possible Investment in Africa," *The New York Times,* 10 February 2001, A15.

38. David Barboza, "Six Big Vitamin Makers Are Said to Agree to Pay $1.1 Billion to Settle Pricing Lawsuit," *The New York Times,* 8 September 1999, C2.

39. Dean Baker, "Patent Medicine," *The American Prospect,* 29 January 2001.

40. Shailagh Murray, "Drug Companies Are Spending Record Amounts on Lobbying and Campaign Contributions," *Wall Street Journal,* 7 July 2000, A14.

41. Deborah McGregor, "Study Details Vast Outlays in Congress Election Race," *Financial Times,* 6 February 2001.

42. Jeff Gerth and Sheryl Gay Stolberg, "With Quiet Unseen Ties, Drug Makers Swat Debate," *The New York Times,* 5 October 2000, A28.

43. Debbie Field, "Putting Food First: Women's Role in Creating a Grass-roots Food System Outside the Marketplace," in *Women Working the NAFTA Food Chain: Women, Food & Globalization,* edited by Deborah Barndt (Toronto: Second Story Press, 1999), 200.

44. Salih Booker, "Bush Medicine for Africa," *The Nation,* 26 February 2001, 6.

CHAPTER 4

1. Aaron Bernstein with Michael Shari and Elizabeth Malkin, "A World of Sweatshops," *Business Week,* 27 November 2000, 86.

2. Richard Freeman and Joel Rogers, *What Workers Want* (Ithaca: Cornell University Press, 1999), 88.

3. James M. Poterba and Andrew A. Samwick, *Brookings Papers on Economic Activity* 2 (1995): 328.

4. Roy J. Adams, "Choice or Voice? Rethinking American Labor Policy in Light of International Human Rights Consensus" (Hamilton, Canada: McMaster University), 8.

5. Human Rights Watch, *Unfair Advantage: Workers' Freedom of Association in the United States Under International Human Rights Standards* (New York: Human Rights Watch, 2000), 73.

6. Human Rights Watch, "Workers' Freedom of Association Under International Human Rights Law," 2000, at http://www.hrw.org/reports/2000/uslabor.

7. Kate Bronfenbrenner, "We'll Close! Plant Closings, Plant-Closing Threats, Union Organizing and NAFTA," *Multinational Monitor,* March 1997.

8. Tom Juravich, "The New Face of Organized Labor," *Washington Post National Weekly Edition,* 11–17 September 2000, 23.

9. Sam Dillon, "Profits Raise Pressures On U.S.-Owned Factories in Mexican Border Zone," *The New York Times,* 15 February 2001, A16.

10. Andrew Bounds, "Nicaragua's Textile Workers Turn Free-Trade Zone to Battle Zone," *Financial Times,* 29 November 2000, 4.

11. Steven Greenhouse, "Rights Group Scores Success with Nike," *The New York Times,* 25 January 2001, C2.

12. "Ethical Shopping: Human Rights," *The Economist,* 3 June 1995, 58.

13. Yunya Yimprasert and Christopher Candland, "Can Corporate Codes of Conduct Promote Labor Standards? Evidence from the Thai Footwear and Apparel Industries" (Hong Kong: Asia Monitor Research Center, 1999).

14. Dexter Roberts, "A Life of Fines and Beatings," *Business Week,* 2 October 2000, 124.

15. National Labor Committee, *Made in China,* at www.nlcnet.org.

16. Roberts, "A Life of Fines and Beatings."

17. James Pereira, "Apparel Makers Back New Labor Inspection Group," *Wall Street Journal,* 10 April 2001, B1.

18. Liza Featherstone, "The New Student Movement," *The Nation,* 15 May 2000.

19. Leslie Kaufman, "As Biggest Business, Wal-Mart Propels Changes Elsewhere," *The New York Times,* 22 October 2000.

20. Wendy Zellner with Aaron Bernstein, "Up Against the Wal-Mart," *Business Week,* 13 March 2000, 76.

21. "A Stitch in Time," *The Economist,* 6 June 1992, 27.

22. Robert L. Borosage, "Who Speaks for the Third World?" *The American Prospect,* 17 January 2000, 20.

23. Dennis Bernstein and Leslie Kean, "WTO and Forced Labor," *The San Franscisco Bay Guardian,* 22–28 December 1999.

24. Christopher Candland, "Enriching the Human Rights Debate: The Debate Over Child Labor in Pakistan," *Human Rights Review,* Fall 2001.

25. Thomas Palley, "The Case for Labor Standards" (Washington, D.C.: AFL-CIO, 1999), Research Paper E036.

26. Brink Lindsey, "Free Trade from the Bottom Up," *Cato Journal* (Winter 2000): 368.

27. William Greider, "Global Agenda," *The Nation,* 31 January 2000, 14.

28. Borosage, "Who Speaks for the Third World?" 19.

29. "Modern Slave Trade," *Business Week,* 27 November 2000, 148.

30. *Business Week,* 27 November 2000, 149–50.

31. Karl Marx, *Capital* (New York: International Publishers, 1967), 270.
32. Ellen E. Schultz, "Raw Deals: Companies Quietly Use Mergers and Spinoffs to Cut Worker Benefits," *Wall Street Journal,* 27 December 2000, A4.
33. Carol Hymowitz and Rachel Emma Silverman, "Can Workplace Stress Get *Worse*?" *Wall Street Journal,* 16 January 2001, B1.
34. Ibid.
35. Kathleen O'Brien, "Fighting Sleep on the Job? Join the Crowd," *The New York Times,* 7 February 2001, G1.
36. Lisa Belkin, "If Chocolate Doesn't Work . . . ," *The New York Times,* 31 January 2001, G1.
37. Adam Smith, "On the Wages of Labour," *Wealth of Nations,* bk. 1, chap. 7.
38. Michael Milken, "Amidst Plenty, the Wage Gap Widens," *Wall Street Journal,* 5 September 2000.
39. See Lance Compa, "Democratizing the Trade Debate," *Foreign Policy in Focus* 3 (August 1998), at http://www.foreignpolicy-infocus.org/briefs/vol3/v3n23trad_body.html.
40. See the Joint Declaration of Unions and NGOs from Around the Western Hemisphere on the Free Trade Area of the Americas, which was issued by a parallel meeting to the Third Trade Ministerial Meeting in Belo Horizonte, Brazil, May 1997, at http://www.corpwatch.org/feature/humanrts/resistance/latinam.html.
41. The complete AFL-CIO statement on the FTAA can be accessed from their web site or as part of the menu choice at http://www.stopftaa.org/organize/org_aflcio.html.

CHAPTER 5

1. Nancy Dunne, "Bush Dismisses 'Green' Changes to US Lifestyle," *Financial Times,* 8 May 2001, 4.
2. Jeanne Cummings and John Harwood, "Arsenic Issue May Poison Bush's 'Compassionate Conservatism,'" *Wall Street Journal,* 20 April 2001, A16.
3. Peter Rosenblum, "Pipeline Politics in Chad," *Current History* (May 2000): 197.
4. Ibid., 199.

5. Paul Raeburn, "This Clean Oil Deal Is Already Tainted," *Business Week,* 7 May 2001, 92.

6. Paul Raeburn, "Legal Wrangling Won't Restore the Rain Forest," *Business Week,* 11 October 1999, 97.

7. See the Sierra Club web site at http://www.sierraclub.org/toxics/ejhome.asp.

8. Herman Daly, "The Perils of Free Trade," *Scientific American,* November 1993.

9. "Deep Discount," *The Economist,* 26 June 1999, 90.

10. Paul R. Epstein, "Is Global Warming Harmful to Health?" *Scientific American,* August 2000.

11. Richard Levins et al., "The Emergence of New Disease," *American Scientist,* January/February 1994.

12. http://www.wto.org/wto/environ/environment.pdf.

13. Ken Conca, "The WTO and the Undermining of Global Environmental Governance," *Review of International Political Economy* (Autumn 2000): 484.

14. Ibid., 487.

15. Vanessa Houlder, "Accord at The Hague Would Boost Market in Emissions Trading," *Financial Times,* 23 November 2000, 6.

16. William Wallis, Andrew Bounds, Canute James, Richard MacGregor, and Carola Hoyos, "Poor Nations Bear Heat of Climate Conference Failure," *Financial Times,* 30 November 2000, 6.

17. Paul Krugman, "The Unrefined Truth," *The New York Times,* 9 May 2001, A31.

18. Andrew C. Revkin, "178 Nations Reach a Climate Accord; U.S. Only Looks On," *The New York Times,* 24 July 2001, A1.

19. Edward Alden and Nancy Dunne, "US Casts Pall over Kyoto Pact on Climate," *Financial Times,* 29 March 2001; Paul Mellor, "European Union Voices Concern for Climate Pact," *The New York Times,* 29 March 2001, A22.

20. Michael Mann, "EU 'Can Afford' to Exceed Kyoto Goals," *Financial Times,* 12 June 2001, 6.

21. Vanessa Houlder, "Economics of Kyoto under Scrutiny," *Financial Times,* 5 April 2001, 7.

22. Edmund C. Andrews, "Frustrated Europeans Set to Battle U.S. on Climate," *The New York Times,* 16 July 2001, A3.

23. Vanessa Houlder, "Winners and Losers Wait for Fog to Clear Around Kyoto," *Financial Times,* 25 July 2001, 6.

24. Joseph Kahn, "A New Role for Greens: Public Enemy," *The New York Times,* 25 March 2001, 3.

25. Paul R. Epstein, "Is Global Warming Harmful to Health?" *Scientific American,* August 2000.

26. Quoted in David Corn, "Democrats Play Softball," *The Nation,* 12 February 2001, 4.

27. "Gasping," *The Economist,* 27 January 2001, 77.

28. Leslie Wayne, "Big Companies Picking Up Tab in Inauguration," *The New York Times,* 18 January 2001, A1.

29. ExxonMobil, "An Energy Policy for the New Administration," *The New York Times,* 18 January 2001, A23.

30. Mike France, "When Big Oil Gets Too Slick," *Business Week,* 9 April 2001, 70.

31. Anthony Bianco, "Exxon Unleashed," *Business Week,* 9 April 2001, 70.

32. David Buchan, "Green Vote Puts Pressure on Oil Groups," *Financial Times,* 30 March 2001, 6.

33. "Sins of Emission," *The Guardian,* 27 November 2000, reprinted in *World Press Review,* February 2001, 16.

34. Vanessa Houlder, "Accord at The Hague," *Financial Times.*

35. Ross Gelbspan, "Rx for a Planetary Fever," *The American Prospect,* 8 May 2000, 30.

36. "Oh No, Kyoto," *The Economist,* 7 April 2001, 74.

37. Kahn, "A New Role."

38. Vanessa Houlder, "Talks' Failure Clouds the Picture on Climate," *Financial Times,* 27 November 2001, 3.

39. Jaume Matas Palau, "Why The Hague Failed," *El Mundo,* 26 November 2000, reprinted in *World Press Review,* February 2001, 17.

40. Gelbspan, "Rx for a Planetary Fever."

41. Jim Carlton, "Chiquita to Take Part in Environmental Program," *Wall Street Journal,* 16 November 2001, A3.

42. Jim Carlton, "How Home Depot and Activists Joined to Cut Logging Abuses," *Wall Street Journal,* 26 September 2000, A1.

43. Yaroslav Trofimov and Helene Cooper, "Globalization Protesters Plan to Target Companies," *Wall Street Journal,* 23 July 2001, A16.

44. Bernie Sanders, "Waking Up the Global Elite: Activism in the Streets Has

Led to an Outpouring of Platitudes in the Suites," *The Nation*, 2 October 2000.

45. Vanessa Houlder, "Deal in Sight over Toxic Chemical Treaty," *Financial Times*, 7 December 2000, 3.

46. Hannah Fairfield, "Negotiators Focus on 'Dirty Dozen,'" *The New York Times*, 28 November 2000, F3.

47. Kurt Eichenwald, Gina Kolata, and Melody Petersen, "Biotechnology Food: From the Lab to the Debacle," *The New York Times*, 25 January 2001, A1, C6.

48. Patricia Callahan and Scott Kilman, "Some Ingredients Are Genetically Modified, Despite Label's Claims," *Wall Street Journal*, 5 April 2001, A1, A14.

49. David Barboza, "Monsanto Sued over Use of Biotechnology in Developing Seeds," *The New York Times*, 15 December 1999, C1.

50. Janet Bell, "Patenting Our Food System," Genetic Resources Action International, at http://www.grain.org/publications/reports/piracy.htm.

51. Andrew Pollack, "Talks on Biotech Food Turn on a Safety Principle," *The New York Times*, 28 January 2000.

52. "Caution Needed," *The Economist*, 5 February 2000, 69.

53. Marian Burrows, "Documents Show Officials Disagreed on Altered Food," *The New York Times*, 1 December 1999.

54. John Carey with Ellen Licking and Amy Barrett, "Are Bio-Foods Safe?" *Business Week*, 20 December 1999, 70.

55. Kaldor, "'Civilizing' Globalization," 109.

56. Kirsten Appendini, "From Where Have All the Flowers Come? Women Workers in Mexico's Non-Traditional Markets," in Barndt.

57. Lauren Baker, "A Different Tomato: Creating Vernacular Foodscapes," in Barndt, 258; Harriet Friedmann, "The International Political Economy of Food: A Global Crisis," *International Journal of Health Services* (1995).

58. Http://www.mcspotlight.org. Also see John Vidal, *McLibel: Burger Culture on Trial* (New York: The New Press, 1997).

59. Ann Egerman, "Serving Up Service, Fast-Food and Office Women Workers; Doing It with a Smile," in Barndt.

60. Richard Tompkins, "Brands Are the New Religion, Says Ad Agency," *Financial Times*, 1 March 2001, 14.

CHAPTER 6

1. John Tagliabue, "The Prince and His Black Sheep: This Is No Liechtenstein Fairy Tale," *The New York Times*, 8 April 2000, A4.

2. Tony Barber, "Deutsche Bank Executives Hit by Tax Evasion Inquiry," *Financial Times,* 17 June 1999, 1.

3. Samuel Brittan, "Protest Against the Protesters," *Financial Times,* 28 September 2000, 19.

4. Jeff Faux, "Whose Rules for Globalism?" *The American Prospect,* 5 June 2000, 14.

5. David Cay Johnston, "Sham Shelters for Business Flourish as Scrutiny Fades," *The New York Times,* 19 December 2000, A1.

6. Ibid.

7. World Bank, *World Development Report,* 2000, 66.

8. Joseph Kahn, "Money Laundering Prompts US Drive for a Tougher Law," *The New York Times,* 1 March 2000, A1.

9. David Cay Johnston, "Treasury Chief: Tax Evasion Is on the Rise," *The New York Times,* 19 July 2001, C1.

10. Ibid., C13.

11. Julie Edelson Halpert, "Dr Pepper Hospital? Perhaps, for a Price," *The New York Times,* 18 February 2001, Bu1, 21.

12. Peter Spiegel, "US to Stop Net Becoming an Offshore Tax Haven," *Financial Times,* 11 July 2001, 10.

13. Michael Peel, "Business Battle Lines are Drawn for Showdown on Taxing Multinationals," *Financial Times,* 29–30 April 2000, 5.

14. David Cay Johnston, "US Takes Aim at Tax Shelters for Companies," *The New York Times,* 29 February 2000, C10.

15. Michael Allen, "Clinton Proposal to Curb Laundering Receives Tepid Response from Bankers," *Wall Street Journal,* 3 March 2000, A8.

16. Joseph Kahn, "Clinton Seeks to Keep Foreigners from Hiding Wealth in U.S.," *The New York Times,* 16 January 2001, A11.

17. Richard Lapper, "OECD Scrutiny Latest in String of Challenges," *Financial Times,* 22 February 2000.

18. Markus Affentranger and Philip Marcovici, "Co-operation? Yes, But with Limitations," *Financial Times,* 16 November 2000.

19. William Hall, "Swiss Fear Tough Line May Scare Away Bank Customers," *Financial Times,* 5 September 2000, 10.

20. Michael Peel and William Hall, "OECD Seeking Bank Openness to Beat Tax Evasion," *Financial Times,* 13 April 2000, 6.

21. Jo Johnson and William Hall, "French Accuse Swiss of Money-Laundering Sham," *Financial Times,* 22 February 2001, 3.

22. "Through the Wringer," *The Economist,* 14 April 2001, 64.

23. Michael M. Phillips, "U.S. Weighs Backing Away from Effort to Crack Down on Tax-Haven Countries," *Wall Street Journal,* 22 February 2001, A2.

24. Christopher Adams, Michael Peel, and Edward Alden, "Bush May Scupper Tax Haven Crackdown," *Financial Times,* 29 April 2001.

25. Hugh Williamson, "Köhler says IMF May Look Again at 'Tobin Tax,'" *Financial Times,* 11 September 2001, 4.

26. "In Search of a (Leading) Role," *The Economist,* 8 September 2001, 55.

27. International staff, "Tobin Tax Study Group Seen as a Sop for Protesters," *Financial Times,* 7 September 2001, 2.

28. United Nations Children's Fund, *The State of the World's Children 2001,* at www.unicef.org.

29. Christopher S. Wren, "U.N. Report Maps Hunger 'Hot Spots,'" *The New York Times,* 9 January 2001.

30. Vinod Thomas, "Why Quality Matters," *The Economist,* 7 October 2000, 92.

31. United Nations Development Program, *Human Development Report 2000,* 10.

32. Roger Cohen, "Growing Up and Getting Practical Since Seattle," *The New York Times,* 24 September 2000, sec. 4, p. 1.

33. Walden Bello, "From Melbourne to Prague: The Struggle for a Deglobalized World," September 2000, at http://www.lbbs.org/melbourne_to_prague.htm.

34. Oxfam International, "Education: Time for a Global Initiative," at http://www.caa.org.au/oxfam/advocacy/education/initiative.html.

35. Samuel Brittan, "Protest Against the Protesters," *Financial Times,* 28 September 2000, 19.

36. Editorial, "Protesters for Poverty," *Financial Times,* 28 September 2000, 18.

37. Noam Chomsky, *On Power and Ideology* (Boston: South End, 1987), 6–7.

38. Raymond Williams, *Keywords,* 94.

39. Ibid.